WIRED *for* GREATNESS

WIRED *for* GREATNESS

Spiritual Oxygen - Volume 2

PASTOR TREVOR R. WALLACE

urlink PRINT & MEDIA

Wired For Greatness

1603 Capitol Ave., Suite 310 Cheyenne, Wyoming USA 82001
1-888-980-6523 | admin@urlinkpublishing.com

URLink Print and Media is committed to excellence in the publishing industry.

Published in the United States of America

Library of Congress Control Number: 2023904622
ISBN 978-1-68486-391-4 (Paperback)
ISBN 978-1-68486-392-1 (Digital)

21.04.22

About The Author

Pastor Trevor R. Wallace is the Senior Pastor of Jesus Team Ministries in Lauderhill, Florida. A native of Jamaica, Pastor Trevor migrated to the United States in 1987. While serving in the United States Navy in August 1991 he started studying the Bible in boot camp. That same month he was given a choice to go to church or clean the barracks, so he chose to go to church. He started recording his first Gospel CD in 2001 entitled "Get With It" which was distributed by Universal Records. He has performed at many venues, preaching at some of them as well. He was ordained Pastor on June 11, 2006 and started Jesus Team Ministries in July 2006. He's since gone back into the studio and recorded his second Gospel CD "Jump For Jesus" which is distributed by Tate Music Group. Pastor Trevor lives with his wife, Loretta, son, Christian and two cats, Grace and Lionel, in Coral Springs, Florida.

About Wired For Greatness

For the past fourteen years, Pastor Trevor has taught a class called Wired For Greatness at a local outreach center on Mondays. We have seen over a thousand souls come to the Lord Jesus Christ and receive His salvation during this time. The book, on the other hand, took seven years to write. It is comprised of inspired writings from The Holy Spirit Himself! Each page has a topic that will satisfy the needs of various individuals. We believe that God made all people in His image and likeness, not for failure, lack and damnation but for victory, abundance and salvation! The words are alive and powerful. Allow them to minister to you like they have done for thousands of others. If you already know Jesus as Lord and Savior, then read and be encouraged! If you are not saved please read and then repent of your sins; this means turn from them. You can truly be great when you are connected to the great One. My prayer is that all who read this book will make it in the Kingdom of Heaven. Pay close attention: Enjoy the scriptures, the instructions, the corrections, the assurance, the guidance, the humor and all God will reveal to you in this book!

Be sure to bless your friends and loved ones with a copy!

Contents

The Good Shepherd Will Feed Not Mislead!

The blind leading the blind is very common these days. The unlearned pretends to know everything! The spiritually weak pretends to be super Apostles, Bishops and Pastors! All this for what? Money? Popularity? Fame? If this is where your mind is at, please consider the humility that Jesus exemplified. He is our Good Shepherd, and He will not mislead His people. In fact, this is what the Bible says in Isaiah Chapter 40, Verse 11: "He will feed his flock like a shepherd. He will carry the lambs in his arms, holding them close to his heart. He will gently lead the mother sheep with their young."

With that being said, Are you a sheep or a goat? Jesus rejects the stubborn goat mentality and leads the sheep who are willing to follow with humility. Be transformed by the renewing of your mind, my friend, and watch the Lord work miracles in your life! What other choice do we have? I think you know the answer; Satan. Make your choice today; turn to Jesus! Get fed spiritual and natural bread, or follow Satan and remain spiritually dead! There's no time to sugarcoat; too many are dying and going to Hell. The Good Shepherd is willing and able to change that! Follow Him!

God bless you!

Hey Church; What Spirit Are You Listening To?

I am convinced that the Enemy is sending mixed messages to the church. Words that sound good but are not the authentic Word of God. Maybe even spoken by the Pastor, but has no biblical proof.

Church; my brothers and my sisters – please listen to what the Holy Spirit is saying to the churches and do what He says! If you'll remember in Revelation Chapters 2 and 3 Jesus addressed seven churches, and the church of Philadelphia was found without fault. Jesus said something key in Revelation Chapter 3, Verse 22: "Anyone with ears to hear must listen to the Spirit and understand what he is saying to the churches."

I urge you to read Revelation Chapters 2 and 3 to see which church you are! Some pastors won't even read from Revelation; which is a sure sign of a church of Laodicea spirit, which you may or may not know is satanic. Study to show yourself approved so when you stand before Jesus he will say to you: "Well done, my good and faithful servant, enter into my rest." I can honestly tell you that the Holy Spirit inspired this writing, so the question is: Will you listen? I pray you do!

God bless you!

What Are You Committed To?

We commit ourselves to one thing or another on a daily basis. If we read our Bibles daily that's a commitment and if we refuse to read our Bibles, that is also a commitment. The problem is some commitments don't benefit as others do. This leads us to the million dollar question: What are you committed to?

I love the devotion of the early church. The Bible says this in Acts Chapter 2, Verse 42: "All the believers devoted themselves to the apostles' teaching, and to fellowship, and to sharing in meals (including the Lords Supper), and to prayer." These early Christians were on fire for God! They were seeking God with all they had. That's the commitment we should have towards the will of God! The wise individual will abstain from things that won't benefit and commit to things that will!

Are there desires you want fulfilled? Delight in the Lord and commit to His will! I guarantee your desires will become a reality in the Lord! He is able to do it for you, but why should He if you are not committed to Him? Take a self analysis, and commit to God; you will be glad you did!

God bless you!

Hard To Believe, But It's True.

One verse that's hard to digest when calamity strikes is Romans Chapter 8, Verse 28. It reads: "And in all things, all things work together for the good of those who love God and are called according to his purpose for them."

People will often ask, "Why does this have to happen to me, who loves God with my whole heart?" Sometimes the Holy Spirit leads me to tell them that without a test, there would be no testimony; or God is in total control, so we must continue to trust everything he does.

This leads me to a powerful verse in Psalm Chapter 33, Verse 4: "For the Word of the Lord holds true, and we can trust everything he does. It's hard to believe, but it's true! What I have seen over the years is God at work, supernaturally, in the worst of times!

Let me encourage you today to trust Him in all circumstances whether financial, health or relational. God will show up right on time for your breakthrough! You are next in line for the blessing, so stop stressing! Pray and believe by faith as you wait. Your God will open the right gate! Don't wallow in self pity; rebuke that spirit! I guarantee that the child of God will see much better days! Hard to believe, but it's true!

God bless you!

Stairway To Heaven.

Wouldn't it be great to have direct, physical access to God? To be able to walk right up to Him and praise Him in person? Well, this will be a reality for the Born Again Believers who live for Him! Genesis Chapter 28, Verse 12 says, "As he slept, he dreamed of a stairway that reached from the Earth up to Heaven. And he saw the angels of God going up and down the stairway." Jacob's dream would be an awesome reality right about now!

I can hardly wait for the day to be with the Lord and hang out with him, just to behold His glory! However, until then, let's keep climbing that spiritual stairway to Heaven! When the rapture happens, we will be at the top! Some may think what I'm saying is unreal. Do some research; try to prove me wrong, 'cause forever is a long time to feel!

Jesus Christ is the only one who can grant access to Heaven! Repent of your sins, and accept Him today! Revelation Chapter 3, Verse 20 says, 'let Jesus into your heart; welcome Him to dinner!'

Secure your place on the Stairway to Heaven!

God bless you!

The Last Shall Be First!

There is something special about winning a game or being in the lead to cross the finish line. Who doesn't want to finish a race in first place? Life is like a game that we all play; some play to win while others don't seem to care.

In Matthew Chapter 20 Jesus spoke about the vineyard workers. He says this in Verse 16: "So those who are last now will be first then, and those who are first will be last."

As we live and play this game of life, be sure to make time for Christ! It doesn't matter how old you are or the amount of knowledge you have. You may be saved but discouraged because your promotion is delayed. Don't worry; it's coming soon! Those who mean bad for you will be changed and do good for you!

How does "the last shall be first" apply to us today? If you're a new believer having little bible knowledge and the rapture happens in your beginner's stage, you will be caught up with the believers who've accepted Christ long ago! Don't worry about the rich and famous by this world's standard; keep doing what's right and when you meet Jesus you will know who is truly rich and famous – Jesus!
Strive to meet Him!

God bless you!

What Child Is This?

Babies are born every hour of every day. Some babies grow up and play very important roles in society – doctors, nurses, school teachers, pastors and others in leadership. In spite of all the babies born over the years, one baby stands out; He is the Baby Jesus whom we sing, "What Child Is This."

To explain further who He is, let's see what the Prophet Isaiah wrote in Isaiah Chapter 9, Verse 7: "His government and its peace will never end. He will rule with fairness and justice from the throne of his ancestor David for all eternity. The passionate commitment of the Lord of Heavens Armies will make this happen!"

There you have it; His peace will never end! To put it another way – He was the child of peace, and being God's son makes Him the Prince of Peace. During the Christmas season we love to reflect on this, but do we have the peace that surpasses all understanding year round? The only was to have real peace is to have Jesus, the Prince of Peace! I pray you'd repent of your sins today, and live for the One who died to take our sins away. Do it today, because tomorrow is promised to no one! Know Jesus, Know Peace. No Jesus, No Peace!

God bless you!

Holy Spirit Lead.

You may have heard a believer say, "The Holy Spirit led me to do… such and such…" Though one might have the very best intentions, sometimes the individual can be wrong! The best way to monitor the things we say and do is to ask ourselves, "Would Jesus say or do this?" It all comes down to that – the actions of Jesus!

Here is where it gets a little tricky. In order for the Holy Spirit to flow through an individual, he or she must be sold out to Jesus! The apostles goofed up a few times and didn't have faith, but seeing Jesus alive took them to another level! They believed and received the Holy Spirit!

Acts Chapter 2, Verses 32 and 33 say: "God raised Jesus from the dead, and we are all witnesses of this. Now he is exalted to the place of highest honor in heavens at God's right hand. And the Father, as he had promised, gave him the Holy Spirit to pour out upon us, just as you see and hear today.

Some thought the apostles were drunk because they spoke the word of God in different languages so that foreigners could be saved. When the Holy Spirit leads, we become other people centered and make spreading the gospel our first priority! Everything else is misleading! Christ gives the Holy Spirit so we can live like Christ!

God bless you!

Are You Covered With Guilt Or With Grace?

Some people live with overwhelming guilt! They never got a chance to clear the air regarding things they have done in the past. Sometimes the people they've wronged have died.

Here's some advice: Come to God; give Him your heart. He will remove the guilt and clear the air! David took his servant Uriah's wife and had Uriah murdered. I can only imagine the guilt associated with that! Look at what David wrote in Psalm Chapter 32, Verse 5: Finally, I confessed all my sins to you and stopped trying to hide my guilt. I said to myself, "I will confess my rebellion to the Lord." And you forgave me! All my guilt is gone.

If God did it for David, He will do it for you! He will give you the courage and strength needed to approach someone and offer a sincere apology. If that individual is unavailable, God will make a way to erase your guilt – just trust Him! Once the guilty stain is removed from your heart, you can truly enjoy the grace of God that saved you! We are all sinners. Some of us are covered with grace while others are covered with guilt and shame. Which one are you?

God bless you!

Prophecies Help Decide Our Destiny.

There are many prophecies in the Bible; yet they are often overlooked by Christians. Today I want to emphasize on the fact that Jesus will return soon! One might ask, "Did anyone prophesy about Jesus' coming the first time?" Yes, they did! Zechariah Chapter 9, Verse 9 says, "Rejoice, O people of Zion! Shout in triumph, O people of Jerusalem! Look, your king is coming to you. He is righteous and victorious, yet he is humble, riding on a donkey – riding on a donkey's colt." This prophecy was fulfilled in Matthew Chapter 21, Verses 1 through 11. In the book of Acts Chapter 1, Verse 11 you'll find another important prophecy. The angels asked the apostles this question: "Men of Galilee," they said, "why are you standing here staring into heaven? Jesus has been taken from you into Heaven, but someday he will return from Heaven in the same way you saw him go!" Pay close attention to this prophecy, my friends! Live for God and for the Lord, Jesus Christ! Once He returns, it will be too late to repent! Why repent? Only the repentant believer can make it into Heaven! Don't take this lightly! There are so many that ignore the word of God and end up in Hell. If you are on that path, allow the prophecies to change your destiny to Heaven! We cannot forcefully change someone's mind; this decision must be made in one's heart.

I have decided my destiny will be Heaven with Jesus! What's yours? Choose wisely!

God bless you!

You, Too, Can Be Cleansed!

We ALL sin… in thought, in deed – you name it. However, there are two classifications of sinners: the repentant and the unrepentant. Sin is like a leprosy that won't go away until the Holy Spirit comes in and helps rid us of it. Why are so many people wrapped up in sin? Quite simply; they don't want Jesus to come in!

My encouragement to you today is that you, too, can be cleansed from your sinful ways and make it to Heaven! The Bible says this in Luke Chapter 17, Verses 11 through 14: As Jesus continued on toward Jerusalem, he reached the border between Galilee and Samaria. As he entered a village there, ten lepers stood at a distance, crying out, "Jesus, Master, have mercy on us!" "Go show yourselves to the priests!" And as they went, they were cleansed of their leprosy.

The first thing we need to do is cry out to Jesus! "Jesus help me with my fornication, adultery, lying, cursing, gossip, anger, pornography – you fill in the blank! He is a loving father; He wants us to come to Him! Are you willing to cry out to Him and allow Him to wash you clean? Staying dirty is not cool – turn to Jesus; prove to yourself that you're not a fool! Get clean and stay clean, in Jesus name!

God bless you!

That's Right! There Is An Invisible Searchlight!

We all endure struggles in our lives. Maybe it's an anger problem or unforgiveness issues. Whatever your struggle, we can remember David's prayer, and that God has an invisible searchlight that points out all our flaws!

This is David's prayer in Psalm Chapter 139, Verses 23 and 24: "Search me, O God, and know my heart; test me and know my anxious thoughts. Point out anything in me that offends you, and lead me along the path of everlasting life."

Do we really want God to pinpoint our faults? Whether or not we do, that's what He does on a daily basis! We may as well try and live better, more Godly lives. If you love to speak curse words, keep in mind that you're pronouncing a curse over your life! If you love to steal, be advised that you are stealing your own blessings and leaving yourself with a curse! I could continue to list our shortcomings, but keep this in mind: God has an invisible searchlight in all of our hearts! Doctors cannot detect it; it's spiritual! That being said... what are we giving Him to look at in our hearts? Let's make it something, 'cause He sees everything!

God bless you!

Tell Me The Truth; How Are You Doing?

I can tell a whole lot about an individual by the way they respond to this simple question: "How are you doing?" Some responses are a straightforward, "I'm doing awful…" I then know how to pray for the individual in hopes that things will get better. Some respond, "I am ok…" which means barely making it; almost doing awful… Others respond by saying, "I'm fine…" which is good, but not yet great… while yet others may say, "I am blessed!" This response indicates a level of "connection."

You can't be "blessed" without the "BLESSOR" of life! Think about it. Here's one reason why Christians should always be joyful. David wrote in Psalm Chapter 34, Verses 4 and 5: I prayed to the Lord, and He answered me. He freed me from all my fears. Those who look to Him for help will be radiant with joy; no shadow of shame will darken their faces.

Are you radiant with joy or darkened by sorrow? Hurt due to the loss of a loved one is one thing but being down in the dumps on a regular basis should let you know that your life is incomplete; you are missing the key ingredient – Jesus! Get to know Him today! Don't delay! His arms are open wide! After that, ask yourself this question: "How am I doing?" You can respond, "I am truly blessed and highly favored" because your name is written in Heaven! Now that is something you can rejoice about!

God bless you!

Three In One Holy Trinity.

The trinity has been a cause of confusion to many people. I have heard some strange interpretations. One being, "Jesus is the Father, the Son and the Holy Spirit. Let's take a closer look. Jesus tells us in John Chapter 6, Verse 38 that He is here to accomplish the will of the Father, not his own! Therefore, He cannot be the Father and the Son together!

Now what may be a little more difficult to understand is the Holy Ghost or, the Holy Spirit. Jehovah's Witnesses believe He is a "cosmic force" while evangelical Christians know He is Jesus and the Father in Spirit. Jesus says this in John Chapter 14, Verse 11: "Just believe that I am in the Father and the Father is in me. Or at least believe because of the work you have seen me do." This proves that He and the Father are together. Jesus says in Matthew Chapter 28, Verse 20, "…I am with you always, even to the end of the age."

We can't physically see Jesus near us, but we feel His presence, we hear Him speak, He convicts our hearts and more! These are done in the spirit. There is one God with three parts. The more you seek Him, the more you'll discover His ways. Allow the Holy Spirit to lead your life, starting today! He will lead you all the way to Heaven!

God bless you!

Smile; And Give Your Face A Rest.

Did you know it takes more energy to frown than it does to smile? We sang this song in Jamaica: "Smile for a while and give your face a rest; raise your hands to the one you love best." We would point our hands up to Heaven to indicate that we love God the best.

That song got us all smiling, which reminds me of Proverbs Chapter 17, Verse 22: "A cheerful heart is good medicine, but a broken spirit saps a person's strength."

Some people have not yet experienced a close and personal relationship with Jesus Christ, so real joy is nowhere to be found! However, those of us whom are born again make sure to keep smiling even though our hearts may be aching. Our faith in God lets us know that He will fix whatever trials we're dealing with. It is imperative that we keep on shining our light for Christ, and it starts with a smile!

No one likes a sour puss! Change your attitude, and don't be rude! Smile!

God bless you!

Let's Treat Our Neighbors Better!

It makes me sad to hear someone say they were treated badly by a Christian. It's truly a bad witness and a lack of shining our light. If someone you know belittles another person, don't join in and help badger them! Your doing so makes you just as foolish as the individual talking badly!

The Bible says this in Proverbs Chapter 11, Verse 12: "It is foolish to belittle one's neighbor; a sensible person keeps quiet."

One might ask, "Who is my neighbor?" Everyone on this earth is your neighbor! Let's be followers of Christ! Treat your fellow motorists well; that person in the grocery store; that rude cashier at the gas station. I know some folks will try to get under your skin, but take note of this: The Holy Spirit within will thicken your skin! If anyone tries to alter your Godly character, flip the script and alter theirs with love and kindness!

Let's treat our neighbors better; what a way to share Jesus with them! It's easy to do wrong in a world where anything goes. Children of God should do better, because we know better! Jesus is watching!

God bless you!

Tell Me The Truth; How Is Your Fruit?

Whether you know it or not, we are judged each day by everyone we interact with. Some LOVE your hair! Others don't like your hair; some LOVE your outfit! Others don't like your outfit…

What about your attitude? If it's rude, you will be judged on it as well.

It goes a little deeper, though. We should observe our own actions and judge ourselves so that we don't come into judgment.

Jesus says this in Matthew Chapter 12, Verse 33: "A tree is identified by its fruit. If a tree is good, its fruit will be good. If a tree is bad, its fruit will be bad."

Our goal should be to produce good fruit! It all starts with the heart. Whatever we entertain or feed our spirit with will eventually come out! Let's plant and feed on good seeds so that we'll produce good fruit! Not only is mankind watching, but also remember that God is watching! He is the One who has the power to send a soul to hell!

My advice: Live life well. The world will inspect your fruit daily; make it good!

God bless you!

Are You A Faithful Foreigner?

Many people have left their place of birth and traveled to foreign countries. Some remain faithful to their birthplace and proclaim boldly that they are American, Barbados, British, Jamaican born, etc. There are always some who never tell where they originated from and never, ever plan on returning back to visit.

We who are in Christ Jesus have a place reserved for us in Heaven, so we are foreigners here on Earth! I love Abraham's story in Hebrews Chapter 11; Verses 8 and 9 say, "It was by faith that Abraham obeyed when God called him to leave home and go to another land that God would give him as his inheritance. He went without knowing where he was going. And even when he reached the land God promised him, he lived there by faith – for he was like a foreigner, living in tents. And so did Isaac and Jacob, who inherited the same promise."

Let's live as citizens of Heaven! Stop stressing the things of this world! Proclaim Jesus with confidence and boldness! He is all you need to succeed! Keep this fact in mind so that when we as Christians go to our home in Heaven, it won't be a visit!

Be faithful to God now as you reside as foreigners!

God bless you!

God Said It, So By Faith Receive It.

Imagine being in line at your local bank; it's your turn to see the teller. He or she invites you to come to the window, and you refuse to go. You then suggest that the teller toss you the money.

Sound ridiculous? Yet, this is how some Christians appear to God due to lack of faith. So… when will you step out on faith and accomplish the things God said you would accomplish? The Bible says this in Judges Chapter 2, Verse 1: The Angel of the Lord went up from Gilgal to Bokim and said to the Israelites, "I brought you out of Egypt into this land that I swore to give your ancestors, and I said I would never break my covenant with you." God said it and we can take Him at His word, so go and enjoy what he provides for you on Earth! However, always remember this promise in John Chapter 14, Verse 2: "There is more than enough room in my Father's home. If this were not so, would I have told you that I am going to prepare a place for you?" While enjoying life, don't take your eyes off heaven! Focusing too much on the pleasures of this world will cause you to miss Heaven! Not everyone will partake of this special, prepared place which requires faith in Jesus Christ! My question is: Will you partake of it? We can't save everyone, but we can save someone! Pass it on!

God bless you!

Who Do You Consult For The Best Result?

People consult a variety of avenues before making major decisions, business deals, starting relationships, etc. Some go to business consultants, others go to their psychic (which is insane), while others go to a best friend. I can relate to going to a "best friend," because I go to my best friend, Jesus, for the best result!

David was at war with the Philistines, and he needed some directives. The Bible says this in 2 Samuel Chapter 5, Verse 19: "So David asked the Lord, "Should I go out to fight the Philistines? Will you hand them over to me?" The Lord replied to David, "Yes, go ahead. I will certainly hand them over to you."

We all have our own battles to fight, but it's only when we consult Jesus that we get the victory! Our friends may hope the best for us, but they cannot facilitate! Don't get all wrapped up in the situation you are dealing with! Lay it at the foot of the cross, and Jesus will fix it! Consult Him today for the best results in your life! What's the alternative? Reject Him today, and the devil will insult your life! Choose Christ who died for you, and now awaits a right relationship with you!

God bless you!

You Have A Gift! Use It!

I often hear people respond after a complement on something they do well, "It's a gift." In most cases, that's true. We all have special gifts and talents that were given to us by God so we should say, "To God be the glory" after receiving a compliment.

The Bible says this in Ephesians Chapter 4, Verses 7 and 8: However, he has given us a gift through the generosity of Christ. That is why the scriptures say, "When he ascended to the heights, he led a crowd of captives and gave gifts to his people."

Some of us are multi gifted. Let's use our gifts for the glory of God first, and watch how everything else will fall into place for you! God didn't give you such a brilliant mind to just sit on your behind and do nothing! Get plugged in! Create your own ways to serve God in ministries near and far! Don't just use your gifts for selfish gain; be other people centered and you surely will gain! It's amazing how that works! Pray and ask God to reveal what he would have you do with your gifts! When He answers – and He will – begin using your gifts! Those who repent, accept Jesus as Lord and Savior and begin using their gifts end up receiving a gift! Eternal life with Christ Jesus!

God bless you!

Never Give Up The Fight For What's Right!

When I think about fighting for what's right, I can't help but remember one of the biggest battles in the Bible. Often overlooked, is the battle between Jesus and his human nature.

The Bible says this in Luke Chapter 22, Verse 42 through 44: "Father, if you are willing, please take this cup of suffering away from me. Yet I want your will to be done, not mine." Then an angel from Heaven appeared and strengthened him. He prayed more fervently, and he was in such agony of spirit that his sweat fell to the ground like great drops of blood.

Agony is putting it mildly! The devil pointed out all the trials Jesus had to endure. The beatings with lead tipped whips, being nailed on the cross and ultimately dying. However, Jesus knew that this was the only way to redeem mankind back to the Father. Jesus fought the flesh and won! Every day we will face an opportunity to sin or fight for what's right! Let's follow Jesus who did not sin although He was fully human! Remember this on your quest to Heaven: Quitters never win, and winners never quit!

Fight for righteousness, and you will stay blessed!

God bless you!

When You Think You Know It All Expect A Fall!

You know what it's like to meet people who think they know it all. They have all the answers, yet they fail to accept wise counsel.

True wisdom comes from God. I love what Jesus says in Matthew Chapter 11, Verse 25. At that time Jesus prayed this prayer: "O Father, Lord of heaven and earth, thank you for hiding these things from those who think themselves wise and clever, and for revealing them to the childlike."

We are never too old to learn! Don't assume you know it all! When we study the Word of God we gain wisdom, knowledge and understanding beyond measure! Satan tells us we are AOkay, we're good to go and we don't need anyone's help, while we fail spiritually, emotionally and morally.

Let's put a stop to our ego and repent of our sinful ways. Ask God for wisdom, and He will give it. When we have the wisdom of God, He will keep us from falling. The devil will come in like a floodgate, but God will lift up a standard against Him. Stay connected to God, and you will know all that you need to know! Humility will lead to a promotion, while pride comes before a fall.

God bless you!

Real Faith.

It's easy to have faith when everything is going well. Money in the bank, everyone is healthy, faith is great! However, it's more sight than faith when you can see your way through.

Let me share a few verses on the real faith of Esther. Esther just found out that her life, along with all the Jews, would come to an end on March 7. The king could not be approached unless he requested her. But, Esther felt she must do something! Esther Chapter 4, Verses 15 through 17 read: Then Esther sent this reply to Mordecai: "Go and gather together all the Jews of Susa and fast for me. Do not eat or drink for three days, night or day. My maids and I will do the same. And then, though it is against the law, I will go in to see the king. If I must die, I must die." So Mordecai went away and did everything Esther had ordered him.

If you are not familiar with this story, Esther's faith in God to deliver herself and her people paid off in the end! You might feel as if you are facing the worst scenario in your life. Keep the faith! Fast and pray for God's help. Repent of all your sin and turn to Jesus for help. Remember that Hebrews Chapter 11, Verse 6 says, "Without faith, it is impossible to please God! Let's please God to the best of our ability, and watch Him please us! Have real faith!

God bless you!

Driven By His Word.

Everyone has something that moves them. Status, popularity, fame, money... However, only a select few are moved by the Word of God spoken by a wise man or woman.

Let's see how the second wisest man to walk the face of the earth describes words of wisdom. Ecclesiastes Chapter 12, Verse 11 says, The words of the wise are like cattle prods – painful but helpful. Their collected sayings are like a nailstudded stick with which a shepherd drives the sheep.

Sometimes the word will sting, but the way I see it is this: It is better to be stung now than to be burned later, forever. Let the scriptures be the driving force in your life! The word of God never fails and will never disappoint you. Jesus said, Heaven and Earth will fade away but my words will remain forever. (Matthew 24:35) Let's not just hear His word, but live His word; and watch how God will reward you!

If you are driven by anything more than you are driven by the word of God, you need to rearrange your priorities! With God, there is no need for batteries; he's produced light for centuries without. When we are driven by His word, it flows through us and just like Christ, we'll shine a light!

God bless you!

Love Without Limits.

Highways have speed limits in most countries. They are posted for the protection of the motorists. On the contrary, our love should have no limits at all! Just like Christ Jesus, we should love not only with our speech but also with our actions.

The Bible says this in Matthew Chapter 14, Verse 14: Jesus saw the huge crowd as he stepped from the boat, and he had compassion on them and healed their sick.

We should also do as Jesus did to the large crowds we encounter on a daily basis! We should heal their spiritual sickness by showing unconditional love to them. Shine our light in such a way that it's impossible to go unnoticed! The world at large is hurting and we, the people of God, need to lead by an example of love. Don't just love those who love you back; love those who hate you as well!

Let's be forgiving, patient and kind with those whom are hard to love. Pray and ask God to fill you with agape love so you'll stop showing love with a gap in it! Being an instrument of love makes us look like Jesus! Whom would you like to resemble? You choose! Take the limits off your love and totally trust God; He will protect your heart!

God bless you!

It's Showtime!

Many people dream of being in the movies or on TV! Some accomplish the dream, but often times many will not. The reality is, every day of our lives "It's Showtime!" What do I mean by that? Job Chapter 34, Verse 21 says, "For God watches how people live; he sees everything they do."

We are all on the big screen! What type of movie are you starring in? The action movie – you're always on the go, doing one thing or another but you're transparent enough that others can see your nongenuine rituals towards all things God? The comedy – where everything is a joke, but not funny at all to God? A drama – where the boy or girl friend is a distraction and you can't even find time to read your Bible, pray or attend church? Or, the horror flick? A life filled with cursing, adultery, fornication, lying, anger, just to name a few?

Whatever you do, don't do the horror movie! A suggestion; star in a Christian movie, highlighting the good things in life like love, kindness, forgiveness and self control. When you do, "It's Showtime" to God and with great expectancy! He may even break out the popcorn!

You know God is watching – give Him something good to look at!

God bless you!

Avoid the Slippery Path!

The world is full of evil men and women who are constantly influencing people of God to walk in a wayward fashion. These tricksters infiltrate the churches and take advantage of unsuspecting souls.

It's embarrassing to talk about the corrupt leadership in churches, which leads to corrupted members! The robbery, adultery, fornication, lying, and unforgiveness, just to name a few! Please keep in mind that living those double standard lives lead to the slippery path!

The Bible says this in Jeremiah Chapter 23, Verses 11 and 12: "Even the priests and prophets are ungodly, wicked men. I have seen their despicable acts right here in my own Temple," says the Lord. "Therefore, the paths they take will become slippery. They will be chased through the dark and there they will fall. For I will bring disaster upon them at the time fixed for their punishment. I, the Lord, have spoken!"

Avoid the slippery path, my friends! Don't allow the devil to use his people to influence you negatively! You should, in turn, influence those people to turn and follow God! Walking on good, solid ground with God will get you to higher ground! However, walking the slippery path will cause you to experience God's wrath! Choose well!

God bless you!

The Great Observer.

It happens naturally for me; I meet someone and begin observing their conversation, body language, intelligence and so on. You may do the same; if not, you are encouraged to! Sadly enough… in the churches today, we must be extra careful with its leaders! Please observe even their characters!

Jesus had this to say in Matthew Chapter 7, Verses 15 and 16: "Beware of false prophets who come disguised as harmless sheep but are really vicious wolves. You can identify them by their fruit, that is, by the way they act. Can you pick grapes from thornbushes, or figs from thistles?"

Straight from the mouth of our Lord and Savior, Jesus Christ; observe those who serve, and you will see! There will be good, bad and in between. You will also observe those whom only observe others, do nothing for the Kingdom, yet complain. Don't get caught in a looking glass, seeing everything and doing nothing! My advice? Take a good, long look at yourself. What are your bad habits that need to be broken or good habits that should be enhanced? Be honest with yourself. Don't be afraid to ask God to take away the bad and promote the good! Jesus encourages us to observe, as he is observing our every move!

God Bless You!

God Can Solve Your Problems!

When problems get us down we sometimes turn to various means for assistance, often to no avail. The Israelites had problems too; much bigger than some of our problems. They were besieged by Babylon, taken from their homes and forced to learn new ways of living. So, I would say then had some pretty big problems... The good news is that they serve a pretty big God!

This is what He said to the Israelites through the prophet Isaiah. Isaiah Chapter 43, Verse 14 reads: This is what the Lord says – your Redeemer, the Holy One of Israel: "For your sakes I will send an army against Babylon, forcing the Babylonians to flee in those ships they are so proud of."

The God we serve is able to force our problems to flee! Whatever pains your heart can be fixed by the Great Physician; consult Him today! Stop trying to fix your own problems without going to God. If you don't consult Him, prepare to fail. I dislike problems so when they arise I lift up my eyes – not to the hills – but to my real help, Jesus! You can do the same! Allow Him to help today, don't delay! You can either treat your problems like waste and flush them in haste or like treasure and keep them forever. You decide!

God Bless You!

1777Need Him Make The Call!

Addictions, addictions, addictions… Where do I start? Okay, let's start by first recognizing the addiction. Most people who are addicted to drugs, alcohol, gambling, adultery, pornography, lying, stealing, hatred – just to name a few – don't recognize that they have a problem. It's easy to justify or rationalize why one should indulge in an addiction. Depression, boredom, loneliness, stress on the job are all popular excuses to indulge. Nonetheless, excuses will bring you more bruises!

Instead, we need to make the call to God for deliverance. 1777Need Him is a spiritual call; not one you make with a phone! The Bible says this in Proverbs Chapter 5, Verse 21: "For the Lord sees clearly what a man does, examining every path he takes."

God already know what mankind is doing; why not reason with Him about it? Some addictions I know are more critical and life threatening than others, but all negative addictions threaten one's eternal life. My advice: Make the call to God through our Lord Jesus Christ! Admit your addictions, confess of your sin and ask for His forgiveness. He will help you much faster than any other program known to man!

What are you waiting for? Make the call!

God Bless You!

May Your Will Be Done At All Times!

Many people set goals and work hard to attain them; which is a good thing! I strongly believe if we fail to plan, that means we plan to fail, so planning and setting goals is a really good practice!

In your goal setting and planning, don't ignore this very important prayer that Jesus taught in Matthew Chapter 6, Verses 9 and 10: "Our Father in Heaven, may your name be kept holy. May your Kingdom come soon. May your will be done on earth, as it is in Heaven."

This is so important to remember, my friends! We live in a world with drivethru theology, selfish behaviors, lack of care for those who don't have basic necessities and worst of all, where Jesus is crucified on a daily basis than on the cross at Calvary! Every time we sin and a nonbeliever says, "That's why I don't go to church…" we are pounding on the nail.

That's not God's will, friends. Let's remember who we are in Christ Jesus and let others see Jesus in us! That is God's will for us – to emulate Jesus! Make your plans, set your goals but always pray about them, and pray the Lord's will be done at all times! Maybe your life is a little sour but if you give Jesus the pilot seat, your life will be sweet!

God Bless You!

Godly Or Wicked? Not a Trick Question; The Proof Is In Our Actions!

Ask the average human being, "Are you Godly or wicked? They will tell you they are not wicked. They have never murdered anyone, robbed a bank or other things of that nature. Some may even say, "I am not the churchgoing type, but I believe in God."

Please keep in mind that anyone who fails to live for God and accomplish His will on a daily basis is considered wicked. David faced wicked enemies who didn't serve the God of Israel. This is what he said in Psalm Chapter 92, Verses 11 and 12: "My eyes have seen the downfall of my enemies; my ears have heard the defeat of my wicked opponents. But the Godly will flourish like palm trees and grow strong like the cedars of Lebanon."

God will punish the wicked who ignore Him, but He will reward the Godly who live for Him! Change allegiance, my friend! Stop fighting God and fight against the devil! Satan and his wicked followers will try and win you back but don't go back! Prove by the way you live that you are a child of God! The world is watching the actions of the Christian but more important, God is watching! Let's make Him proud! Be Godly and flourish!

God Bless You!

Don't Mess With My Son!

So many times I've heard people say, "God is good, and He understands my sin." While this is true, keep in mind that God never condones sin! Sin is sin, and it brings punishment.

People love to talk about the pleasant side of God; you know, God of grace and mercy, forgiveness, love… While He never ceases being these things, He has another side. A side that disciplines and severely punishes, even unto death! Many people ridicule Jesus and refuse to follow Him; that is the fastest way to experience God's other side. The Bible says this in Psalm Chapter 2, Verse 12: Submit to God's royal son, or He will become angry, and you will be destroyed in the midst of all your activities – for His anger flares up in an instant. But what joy for all who take refuge in Him!

The other side of God is to be kept in mind as we go about our daily activities. Honor God, the father, and Jesus Christ, His Son, to avoid the heavy hand of God. You may have your opinion in this matter with regard to whom you should worship or the lack thereof, but remember who made you! Due to the fact that God made us and we didn't make ourselves, He has a right to specify what kind of worship brings Him glory! That worship is a life spent living for God the father and the Lord, Jesus Christ! They are inseparable. Join the Trinity!

God Bless You!

What Are You Waiting For? Christmas?

When I was young I always thought I would live the wild life until I reached my forties, then get married and settle down with one wife. With regard to serving God, I imagined I would start in my sixties. I had no idea that God had other plans; or should I say better plans! There are many people with that same plan and to them I say, "Don't wait! Serve Jesus now!"

The apostle Paul thought He was serving God by persecuting Christians. However, he got knocked off his high horse and was forced to humble himself. Upon getting a word from God, here is what he was instructed to do in Acts Chapter 22, Verse 16: 'What are you waiting for? Get up and be baptized. Have your sins washed away by calling on the name of the Lord.' Salvation can only be attained when we're still living; there is no repentance in the grave! Don't wait until Christmas to start thinking of Jesus and the presents He brings! Seek Him now for His presence! Procrastination is the main ingredient for condemnation, so don't wait! God sends no one to Hell; people send themselves there by not keeping the Word. Heaven and Hell will pass away, but God's Word never changes! If you believe it, repent and enjoy your new relationship with God! Don't wait, just prepare to elevate!

God Bless You!

Love Your Enemies; Just Don't Trust Them.

Although many people have wronged you, forgiveness to all is still possible through faith in the Lord Jesus Christ. People often forget what Jesus says in reference to those who prove to us that they are enemies. It may surprise you but nonetheless this is what Jesus says in Matthew Chapter 5, Verses 4345: "You have heard the law that says, 'Love your neighbor' and hate your enemy. But I say, love your enemies! Pray for those who persecute you! In that way, you will be acting as true children of your Father in Heaven. For He gives His sunlight to both the evil and the good, and He sends rain on the just and unjust alike."

Nowhere in this area of scripture did Jesus say to trust your enemy. Some people don't mean you any good and maybe they never will, so watch your back! Don't allow yourself to be victimized; love some people from a distance! The worse enemies are ones whom subliminally try to get you to stray from the faith! They use various methods: parties, sex, liquor, drugs, money… Be wise and open your eyes; don't compromise! God sees your every action; we, too, should watch our enemies' actions towards us. They say love at first sight is alright; but trust at first sight may leave you with a bite!

God Bless You!

Please Stay Away From Them.

Most people see this topic and start assuming they should stay away from party folks who want us to engage in the same wild lifestyle. Maybe your thought was to stay away from drug users, drinkers, liars or thieves. While it is advised for us to avoid hanging out with these individuals, we should still pray for God to change them.

Nonetheless, take a look at whom the Bible encourages us to stay away from in 2 Thessalonians Chapter 3, Verse 6: "And now, dear brothers and sisters, we give you this command in the name of our Lord Jesus Christ: Stay away from all believers who live idle lives and don't follow the tradition they received from us."

This is where it gets dangerous, my friend: When people in the church that worship with you and claim to believe in Jesus are actually demons! They worship with their lips, but their hearts are far from God. Remember that by their fruit you will know them! It is our job to be fruit inspectors before getting too close to someone. If they are idle and not progressing spiritually, keep your distance! Stay away! Don't get in trouble and then cry, "Why me?" You have been warned! It's almost the last day so be sure to pray and stay away from the undercover enemy!

God Bless You!

They May Fall But The Godly Stand Tall.

When we hear the term, "fall" we assume it's sinful activity a Christian got involved with. While in some cases that may be true, there is one area of scripture that really gives me courage regarding a fall. Psalm Chapter 91, Verse 7 says: "Though a thousand fall at your side, though ten thousand are dying around you, these evils will not touch you.

David is referring to the literal falling to death. We often face persecution from the enemy, witness friends and family dying around us, but we remain unscathed. The true believer is surrounded by a force field of angels making him or her untouchable!

Although friends or enemies fall daily, keep your faith in Jesus Christ our Lord and stand tall! Don't take your eyes off Jesus as Peter did and start to sink! Jesus will see you through difficult times. He did it for David, He will do it for you! Be encouraged! Lift your head up! Everything will be alright! God has a plan, but we often won't see it until we've gone through the valley and across the desert. Stay with God, stand tall; He will see you through it all!

God Bless You!

Leaders, Beware; The Lord Is Aware!

Everyone receives an opportunity to lead in one capacity or another; from leading our children to leading ourselves. One thing we must always remember is that God is our ultimate leader! It is one thing to lead ourselves astray but please don't lead others astray because God will have something to say!

In Ezekiel Chapter 11, Verses 1 and 2 He says, "Then the Spirit lifted me and brought me to the east gateway of the Lord's Temple, where I saw twentyfive prominent men of the city. Among them were Jaazaniah son of Azzur and Pelatiah son of Benaiah, who were leaders among the people. The Spirit said to me, "Son of man, these are men who are planning evil and giving wicked counsel in this city."

It's sad when leaders mislead. Leaders, please beware; the Lord is aware! It's better to turn from sin now and receive the blessing, than to abstain from the blessing to enjoy sin. Don't pollute the truth for monetary gain because you just might gain something else: a curse!

Whether you lead a congregation, a business or merely yourself, God is watching so give him something good to look at. The eyes of the Lord are pleased with good behavior, especially in leadership, so lead well!

God Bless You!

Making A Difference In The World.

It's a crazy world with crazy people. Wrong is considered right, and right is frowned upon as being wrong. The Holy Spirit often reminds us Christians that we are just passing through this world – it is not our home! We are placed here "for such a time as this" to help many people find Christ. So we must remember what the Bible says in Romans Chapter 12, Verse 2: "Don't copy the behavior and customs of this world, but let God transform you into a new person by changing the way you think. Then you will learn to know God's will for you, which is good and pleasing and perfect."

The battlefield of the mind is fierce; the enemy, Satan, does not play fair, but we must fight him! Satan will tell us not to do more to reach people for God because we are too busy. This way he keeps us from receiving the bigger blessing from God! Let's rebuke that demon; take the time to get involved in making a difference in this world! Our spirit-led contributions of time, skills and/or resources will enhance the kingdom. Notice I said, spirit-led, not flesh-led. Pray and see what God would have you to do!

Start making a difference in the world today!

God Bless You!

Still Waiting On A Reason To Praise Him?

Some people don't feel that God has done anything spectacular for them, so they don't praise Him. Though the mature in Christ can produce more than a hundred thousand reasons daily (which is less than the number of heartbeats daily), there are many other reasons. We can praise Him because we were born and not stillborn and really praise Him because we are born again!

Back in Jesus' day on the earth, entering Jerusalem was one, big praise party! They blessed the Lord with praise on their lips, and Jesus enjoyed the praise! The Pharisees having no idea who Jesus was tried to stop the people's praise. This is what Jesus told the Pharisees in Luke Chapter 19, Verse 40: "He replied, "If they kept quiet, the stones along the road would burst into cheers!"

I won't be outdone by a rock or stones along the road! I pray you, too, will stop looking for something spectacular to happen before praising Him, and start praising Him, making it spectacular!

There are two kinds of people in this world: those who praise God for whom He is, and those who praise Him for His gifts! Be proactive with your praise! Jesus Christ sacrificed His all so we can make it to Heaven; if that is not worthy of praise, nothing is!

Let's praise Him for real! If it's real, God will feel!

God Bless You!

A Few Requirements for Heaven.

You've heard it said that we all go to Heaven when we die. Some actually believe that. However, it is not a true statement. In order to buy a mansion on Earth you must put the finances in place to make the purchase, but to acquire a mansion in Heaven has nothing to do with money! So if anyone tries to trick you into spending your resources to get in with God, don't buy into that.

Read for yourself and see what the Bible says in Psalm Chapter 15, Verses 1 and 2: "Who may worship in your sanctuary, Lord? Who may enter your presence on your holy hill? Those who lead blameless lives and do what is right, speaking the truth from sincere hearts."

So: If we know something is wrong yet we keep on doing it, we are not qualified for Heaven? The word of God said it, not me! I know we all sin in thought and in deed, nonetheless we shouldn't be comfortable in sin. True citizens of Heaven will feel a tug on the heart before entering into something sinful. Pay attention to God's tug on your heart, and depart from sin before it starts! Heaven should be on our minds at all times; if not you might be left behind!

God Bless You!

The Best Way To Get Back On Your Feet.

Sad, depressing stories; we hear them all the time. How friends or loved ones are doing bad due to lack of finances. They often say, "I'm just trying to get back on my feet." Well, that's a good ambition to have, and God wants you to get back on your feet, so... how do you do that?

The first thing I want to point out is that most people fall because they have strayed away from God who is able to keep us from falling (Jude Verse 24) or took their eyes off Jesus (Matthew Chapter 14, Verse 30)!

David did the same thing, and then he wrote something powerful in Psalm Chapter 119, Verses 59 and 60: "I pondered the direction of my life, and I turned to follow your laws. I will hurry, without delay, to obey your commands."

There you have it, my friend; hurry without delay to obey the commands of God. Often times when calamity strikes, people get wrapped up in self pity, doubt in God's ability to fix and depression. Turn to God's Word and His church for directions in righteousness! Your healing or answer to your problems may not come overnight, but at least you know it's coming! It will taste so sweet when you get back on your feet! God's way of getting our attention is sometimes painful, but not as painful as leaving Earth without Him!

God Bless You!

The Greatest Highlight Of Our Existence.

What a wonderful thing to be recognized as a local hero or for becoming Time Magazine's Man of the Year! Other highlights include getting married, having children and, yet even greater, accepting Jesus as Lord and Savior then getting water baptized!

While all these are exciting highlights of our existence, God has shown me what will be the greatest! Jesus says in Matthew Chapter 25, Verse 21: "The master was full of praise. 'Well done, my good and faithful servant. You have been faithful in handling this small amount, so now I will give you many more responsibilities. Let's celebrate together!' Jesus gives an idea of what we'll hear when we stand before Him on judgment day.

However, this highlight is reserved for the truly repentant, born again believer – not the lip service, Christian wannabes! Those who fake it will hear, "Depart from me, you, who break God's commands! For them that will be the worst day of their existence when they experience the Lake of Fire, which is far hotter than hell! I urge you to look into this further; be on par to experience God's grace, mercy, forgiveness, peace and eternal salvation! Hope to see you in Heaven!

God Bless You!

Tired Of Church? Same As Tired of Heaven.

Some people are very strange in the way they relay emotions. For instance a man once said to me, "I'm tired of church." That's a very unfortunate situation; which led me to believe that there is something or someone who caused his burnout. If a church is not preaching the uncompromised word of God, its people are suffering a great injustice! We should feel excited and encouraged after attending church and hearing God's word!

As a matter of fact, this is what Jesus says in John Chapter 8, Verse 47: "Anyone who belongs to God listens gladly to the words of God. But you don't listen because you don't belong to God."

Are you listening now? I sure hope so! Prayerfully your attitude will improve toward attending church and preparation for Heaven. Don't allow church folks to keep you from church! Go to church for instruction in God's word that you can apply and benefit greatly! Satan is good at getting on our nerves and using church people to do it! Please keep in mind that when people upset us, it's not the individual but the enemy influencing them. Let's be forgiving, loving and listen to God's word at home and in church. If you are gladly listening to God's word, chances are you are the church! Don't be tired of church; praise God until you are tired IN church and stay ready for Heaven!

God Bless You!

Heaven! The Best All Inclusive Resort!

Anyone who's cruised one of the major cruise lines or vacationed in an all inclusive resort knows how good it feels! Every kind of food, drink and activity are available for your enjoyment, and the biggest problem you have is figuring out what next to partake of! Amazing as this may be, can you imagine what Heaven will be like? For your information, Heaven is the best all inclusive resort! Did I mention it is the most beautiful too?!!

The Bible says this in Revelation Chapter 21, Verses 10 and 11: "So he took me in the spirit to a great high mountain, and he showed me the holy city, Jerusalem, descending out of heaven from God. It shone with the glory of God and sparkled like a precious stone – like jasper as clear as crystal."

Worldwide there are many beautiful, all inclusive resorts but none can compare to Heaven! The main reason is this: Heave will shine with the glory of God! The Glory of God is so awesome it cancels hunger, sickness, crying and pain. Let's face it – no other resort can guarantee that! Another reason: We're expected to pay in advance in order to enjoy the world's resorts, but a reservation for Heaven won't cost you any money!! All that's required is to repent of your sins and turn to Jesus! What are you waiting for?!! Make your reservation for Heaven right now, and I will join you at the greatest destination of all times!

God Bless You!

It Pays To Have Jesus As Your Defense When Prosecuted By God!

Lawsuits are no fun, especially if the outcome will cost you money or worse yet a conviction could land you time in jail. God also brings charges against people for breaking His law. Though most people don't mention it, the fact still remains that the spiritual court is now in session!

The Bible says this in Hosea Chapter 4, Verses 1 through 3: Hear the word of the Lord, O people of Israel! The Lord has brought charges against you, saying: "There is no faithfulness, no kindness, no knowledge of God in your land. You make vows and break them; you kill and steal and commit adultery. There is violence everywhere – one murder after another. That is why your land is in mourning, and everyone is wasting away."

What's your defense? The better question is: Who is your defense? His name is Jesus! We can repent of our sins, accept Jesus as Lord and Savior and be set free from the wrath of God! Many forget there is a serious side of God that won't stand for foolishness! How do you plead in life's spiritual courtroom? It pays to have Jesus as your defense when prosecuted by God! No other lawyer will suffice! Our trials ultimately lead to the supreme court, then to heaven or hell – choose well!

God Bless You!

Reach Out And Touch Him!

We touch others every day, whether in a positive or a negative way; from a handshake to holding hands in prayer. When we feel sick, we want to immediately reach out to grab hold of a doctor. While doctors are, indeed, a blessing, there are some issues that doctors are not equipped to handle!

In Luke Chapter 8, the Bible speaks about a woman with an issue of blood who exhausted all her money on doctors. When she heard Jesus was in town she knew if she could just touch Him, she would be healed. That's exactly what happened. Here's Jesus' response in Luke Chapter 8, Verses 46 and 48: But Jesus said, "Someone deliberately touched me, for I felt healing power go out from me." "Daughter," he said to her, "your faith has made you well. Go in peace."

What are you in need of today? Healing, restoration of relationships, financial blessings are all available when we reach out and touch Jesus! When we repent of our sinful ways, we place ourselves in line for blessings! The hand of God moves to and fro dispensing blessings; but if you don't reach out and touch Him you won't benefit! An encouraging touch to or from another is good, however touching God on a daily basis is the best! Your healing, your deliverance and your breakthrough are there for the taking! Touch Jesus Christ today! Start to pray!

God Bless You!

How Is Your Will Power?

To do or not to do certain things in life takes will power! Every day things like going to sleep, waking up and brushing your teeth don't take as much will power as abstaining from cursing a bad driver who just cut you off.

The reality is will power is attained when an individual exercises self control. So what does the Bible say about self control? Galations Chapter 5, Verse 22 says: But the Holy Spirit produces this kind of fruit in our lives: love, joy, peace, patience, kindness, goodness, faithfulness, gentleness and selfcontrol. There is no law against these things!

If you bear God's spirit you will exercise self control and have the will power to wait, proceed and persevere even if you bleed! That sounds like Jesus who, indeed, kept going until He accomplished the Father's will. Today, I know your will power to survive, run your business or household, or put someone down is strong – however, here's some food for thought: How is your will power to start and complete the assignment God gave you? Yes, we all have assignments from God! If you don't show up to work, you won't be a part of what needs to get done! You may not even hear about the assignment! Go to church so you'll hear what God wants you to do! Put will power to good use!

God Bless You!

Do Good Even When Facing Evil.

People will oppose our beliefs – that's to be expected – but their opposition should not change our position as a follower of Christ. Sometimes doing the right thing will make us an enemy to man. No worries, however; it makes us friends of God!

Jesus had a decision to make when faced with evil people who didn't understand what the Sabbath was all about. Mark Chapter 3, Verses 3 through 6 says: Jesus said to the man with the deformed hand, "Come and stand in front of everyone." Then he turned to his critics and asked, "Does the law permit good deeds on the Sabbath, or is it a day for doing evil? Is this a day to save life or to destroy it?" But they wouldn't answer him. He looked around at them angrily and was deeply saddened by their hard hearts. Then he said to the man, "Hold out your hand." So the man held out his hand, and it was restored! At once the Pharisees went away and met with the supporters of Herod to plot how to kill Jesus.

There will always be someone who disagrees with your doing good, but keep on doing good and pleasing God! Always remember that evil can only triumph when good people do nothing!

God Bless You!

I Thank You Lord With All My Heart.

When we are truly grateful to someone, most of us find a way to show it don't we? We might write a letter, buy and mail a card, send email, text messages or make a phone call. Funny enough, most of us don't make the same effort to thank God!

The one who created us and sustains us daily should be shown gratitude from the heart. David figured this out and wrote something powerful in Psalm Chapter 138, Verses 1 and 2: "I give you thanks, O Lord, with all my heart; I will sing your praises before the gods. I bow before your holy Temple as I worship. I praise your name for your unfailing love and faithfulness; for your promises are backed by all the honor of your name."

My advice to all is simply this: Give God thanks! Don't just thank Him for food; though many don't even do that! Thank Him for life! The greatest thank you one can offer God is a repentant heart that accepts Jesus Christ as Lord and Savior! One whom does the Father's Will be it painful or not! Analyze and see how thankful you are! Be honest with yourself and increase your giving of thanks! When God says, "You're welcome" that means your thanks and praises are well done!

God Bless You!

Finally I Can See Now.

"I can see clearly now, the rain is gone" is the title of a very popular song. However, I can't help but wonder how many people can really see; spiritually, that is. The natural man can only see so far with obstacles tripping left, right and center.

When salvation is received then the scales fall off the eyes, spiritually. The Bible tells us this in Psalm Chapter 146, Verse 8: "The Lord opens the eyes of the blind. The Lord lifts up those who are weighed down."

When I stopped just playing church and allowed God to truly save me my thoughts were this: "Wow! Finally, I can see!"

Has God opened your eyes yet? Walking in the dark will prevent you from hearing the bark; you will just feel the bite! Start a new trend, my friend! Allow God to open your eyes! Repent and be baptized! Then, you will rejoice when you receive the prize!

Reading glasses cannot help in spiritual darkness; you must accept Jesus who hands out Heaven passes!

God Bless You!

Let's Go Fishing.

Fishing is a favorite pastime for many individuals! Ice fishing, fly fishing, fishing for sport, fishing for food... How about fishing for people? You heard me right; fishing for people! In Matthew Chapter 4, Verse 19 when Jesus saw Simon and Andrew throwing their fishing nets, this is what He said to them: "Come, follow me, and I will show you how to fish for people!"

Peter had his moments of failure but once he stopped fearing for his life, he became a powerhouse! In fact, Acts Chapter 2, Verse 41 says three thousand people came to Christ after Peter preached! Not bad for an uneducated fisherman!

Let's stop with the excuses about what we can't do, and start fishing for people! The world around us swims above our nets; let's lift them up with the Word of God and our Godly lifestyles. If a fisherman in the natural refused to fish, his world would be in lack! If Christians refuse to fish, our world and the kingdom of Heaven will be incomplete.

Let's go fishing and catch future fisherman and women!

God Bless You!

It Will Only Make You Stronger.

People gravitate to natural ways of being made stronger like going to the gym and lifting weights. What about spiritual strength? Are you willing to go through challenges to get there? A question we often hear is, "Why me? I live for God; why the struggle?" Life has its share of struggles, full of ups and downs, but it's during those down times that we're often made stronger spiritually.

The Bible says this in James Chapter 1, Verses 2 through 4: "Dear brothers and sisters, when troubles of any kind come your way, consider it an opportunity for great joy. For you know that when your faith is tested, your endurance has a chance to grow. So let it grow, for when your endurance is fully developed, you will be perfect and complete, needing nothing.

Let's endure with the help of God, be encouraged and keep our eyes on Jesus! Learn from each challenge; ask God to show you solutions. Allow challenging times in health, business, relationships and marriage make you stronger in the Lord! Don't do what so many have regretted and allow challenges to derail their relationship with God. Get stronger in the Lord each day by talking to Jesus every day because soon you will see him face to face!

God Bless You!

Why Should I Give Up My Guilty Pleasures and Follow Jesus? What's the Benefit?

This world offers so many things one could indulge in, most of which contradict the Word of God; sexual activity, wild parties, drugs, alcohol, just to name a few. While some may find these exciting, nonetheless, they all have serious repercussions.

When a Christian witnesses to someone who is right in the middle of these lifestyles, they may ask this question: Why should I give up my guilty pleasures and follow Jesus? What's the Benefit? A good answer is found in Mark Chapter 10, Verses 28-30: Then Peter began to speak up. "We've given up everything to follow you," he said. "Yes," Jesus replied, "and I assure you that everyone who has given up house or brothers or sisters or mother or father or children or property, for my sake and for the Good News, will receive now in return a hundred times as many houses, brothers, sisters, mothers, children, and property – along with persecution. And in the world to come that person will have eternal life."

Getting more stuff is great, but eternal life with Jesus is the greatest benefit! I will take eternal life with Jesus any day over eternal pain and suffering with the devil! Isn't it time you place yourself in line to receive your benefit package? Repent today!

God Bless You!

No More Lies.

"No more lies." It's a serious statement. Some will say, "I am not a liar." Others will say, "I don't try to lie." While yet others will say, "It's just a little lie." First, let me say this: No liar will be going to heaven (Revelation Chapter 21, Verse 8). Lying to self is bad, lying to others is terrible, but lying to God is the absolute worse!

The Bible says this in Ecclesiastes Chapter 5, Verses 4 and 6: "When you make a promise to God, don't delay in following through, for God takes no pleasure in fools. Keep all the promises you make to him." "Don't let your mouth make you sin. And don't defend yourself by telling the Temple messenger that the promise you made was a mistake. That would make God angry, and he might wipe out everything you have achieved."

I have much respect for my brothers and sisters who do what they say, but even more so when they keep their promises to God! When we got saved we made a promise to have Jesus lead our lives. Let's be honest; is He leading your life or did you put him in the copilot seat? Let's keep our promises! If you know something is not possible, don't agree to it! If something should come up to change your plans, inform any individual you've promised immediately! Remember: a good name is better than great riches! A liar is a bad name. Speak the truth!

God Bless You!

Just Call Him.

We sometimes hide due to pride and not call a friend or loved one to say, "I'm sorry" or "Let's bury the hatchet." Many relationships are ruined, and the devil gets the glory. Let's change that from this day forward! Call and make amends with your family or friend! In order to do that, you sometimes need a supernatural intervention. If you have not done so before, call on Jesus!

The Bible tells us this in Romans Chapter 10, Verse 13: For "Everyone who calls on the name of the Lord will be saved." Salvation is the greatest accomplishment one can ever achieve, but we must call on Jesus! When the Holy Spirit is upon us we are able to forgive faster, love greater and bury all hate forever!

Who are you holding up in your heart; or should I say, Why keep the devil in your heart? Call on Jesus today! Repent of your sins, and go forth with power! We make phone calls every day, but not everyone calls on Jesus, although a telephone is not needed! Make the call today! He is waiting for your call! You will be pleasantly surprised when you hear Him say, all your filthy sins of the past are forgiven and forgotten! What a great deal! The only prerequisite is that you make the call! What are you waiting for? Call Him today, and keep the Devil away!

God Bless You!

Newsflash; Common Sense Is Not So Common!

As silly as it may sound, there was an individual who robbed a glue factory overnight, knocked over a barrel of glue and got stuck! He was discovered the next morning and after a good laugh, of course, the police were called. When we participate in illegal activities we lack common sense, even though one might think it is a foolproof plan. No plan is foolproof except for a true solution plan! The Bible says this in Proverbs Chapter 2, Verse 7: He grants a treasure of common sense to the honest. He is a shield to those who walk with integrity."

Those whom exercise common sense in thinking, "We can't defeat God, so we may as well join Him" have a special treasure! This prompts us to do things on the up and up. Let's not give Satan any glory in the way we live our day to day lives; let's give God the glory! For real common sense, seek the giver of common sense – Jesus! Staying neutral will give the same result as your car – you won't get far! Get in gear and go! Now that you see common sense in a whole new light, you realize why it's not so common; because most people refuse to live for God and the Lord Jesus Christ. Where are you today? It's a good day to repent and accept Jesus as Lord and Savior! Why delay when you can receive matchless wisdom today?! Common sense should not be a maybe; it should be a must!

God Bless You!

Made In God's Image, So Stop Looking Like The Devil!

Many products are labeled, "Made in America." For those born in America that statement also most likely applies! Way before we decide to become born again, the Bible says in Genesis Chapter 1, Verse 27 that God made us in his image. This is important to know because He did not create us in the image of Satan! The devil wants the affection of God's people so he lures them in traps that change the look of the individuals. They walk different and talk different; for instance, lie, curse steal and engage in all manner of lustful, sexual activity.

Now what about those whom, whether or not were born in America, decide to become born again? God has an encouraging word for you in 2 Corinthians Chapter 5, Verse 17: This means that anyone who belongs to Christ has become a new person. The old life is gone; a new life has begun! Many Christians have forgotten this, and go right back to their old life; old boyfriend, old girlfriend, old smoking and drinking habits…

Let's take our Christian walk serious; repent of your sins today, and stop looking like the devil! The eyes of the Lord are looking for people who look like Him to receive a blessing! Don't wear a Christian mask on church days and look like the devil on other days! Look like Jesus always by living a life of praise!

God Bless You!

As Good As It Gets!

People love good things; good food, good jobs, cars, houses, clothing – just to name a few; and there's nothing wrong with that! However one should never forget who gives these good things – God. The Bible says this in James Chapter 1, Verse 17: Whatever is good and perfect comes down to us from God our father, who created all the lights in the Heavens. He never changes or cast a shifting shadow."

The big picture – Since God is the giver of all good gifts, then any and all individuals who want good, should get with God! Living for God is as good as it gets! We will not only have joy and peace along with his many blessings here on earth, we still get heaven!

I don't know about you, but second best doesn't cut it for me! Nothing compares to life, eternally! I am not saying the good things on Earth are not worth enjoying, however, they shouldn't risk your eternity with God. A wise person won't become more excited over the gifts than they are over the giver! If you're smart, you'll know that there are more where that came from! Love God more than the good gifts He gives! Start with repentance because when you do, He forgives!

If your name is written in Heaven, that's as good as it gets!

God Bless You!

What's Impossible For Man Is Possible With God!

A student in my weight training class said, "This is just too heavy to lift; I could never lift this much weight." However with my hand on the 45 pound bar with 100 pounds on each side he had the courage to lift 245 pounds with no help from me.

What's keeping you from lifting your heavy "weight"? It's time to partner with God and watch your "impossible" become a reality!

The Bible says this in Mark Chapter 10, Verse 27: Jesus looked at them intently and said, "Humanly speaking, it is impossible. But not with God. Everything is possible with God." Jesus was responding to Peter's question about who could be saved if having a lot of money is a hindrance. Allowing money to become your God is bad; however, you can have billions and not worship it once you truly serve God.

Wherever you are today – in need of healing, relationship restoration or finances, God is able to do the impossible! Maybe you are afraid to venture into your ministry call; God is able to see you through it all! Don't rely on man – we are able to fail; but God never fails!
Expect the impossible with God!

God Bless You!

It's Alright To Fight With The Devil!

Some Christians are so nice, calm and peaceful that often times people take their kindness for weakness and try to abuse them. Just a word of advice: We are not the enemy's doormat! Satan and his disciples are good at manipulation, even using God's Word to have their way. We see this example in Matthew Chapter 4 when Satan tempts Jesus.

The same is true for us Christians today! We are being tempted by the devil to sin and be taken advantage of in other circles. We must fight back spiritually! What did Jesus do? Matthew Chapter 4, Verses 10 and 11 say: "Get out of here, Satan," Jesus told him. "For the Scriptures say, 'You must worship the Lord your God and serve only Him.'" Then the devil went away, and angels came and took care of Jesus.

Jesus fought with the power of God's word! We need to do the same! Stop getting beat up by the devil! Rebuke him, and he will flee from you! Remember: It's alright to fight with the devil! But failure to fight means you lose! Enjoy earth, but fight and be a winner who makes it to Heaven! Our spiritual fight will encourage others to join in and do the same! Praise His name!

God Bless You!

Do You Know How Strong You Are People of God!

How many times have you heard someone say they aren't strong enough to resist a temptation or accomplish a task? It's said on a daily basis, and most of the time those saying it are absolutely correct!

Here's a twist: Should a born again believer say that, they are absolutely incorrect! Once saved, you inherit a supernatural strength to overcome any and all circumstances! The Bible says this in Psalm Chapter 148, Verse 14: He has made his people strong, honoring his faithful ones – the people of Israel who are close to him.

Praise the Lord! Let's stay close to Jesus! Make him your best friend and your life won't end; you will live forever! In your partnership with the Lord Jesus Christ, you will experience spiritual strength to survive and not fail God in your activities! The devil won't leave you alone; believe me, you are not alone, but you must keep on resisting him! Just think: one day in the near future the rapture will occur and when we are with Jesus, there will be no more attacks from Satan! Be strong in the Lord and the power of his might and fight the enemy! (Ephesians 6:10). In Christ: We are strong! Outside of Christ: We are weak and will be defeated! Connect with Christ today! Show the devil how strong you are while giving God the glory!

God Bless You!

Let's Clean Up Our Thoughts!

The mind is a wonderful thing, so don't waste it! Notice I'm saying the Holy Spirit said, "wonderful," not, "wondering." When we sit around wondering why we don't have love, peace, joy, a spouse, a house, a car, a job… it turns into worry. What's the solution? Let's clean up our thoughts, and start thinking like God does!

In Isaiah Chapter 55, Verse 8, He says, "My thoughts are nothing like your thoughts," says the Lord. "And my ways are far beyond anything you could imagine." Impure thoughts keep us far from God, but He loves pure thoughts! Take every thought captive so you can analyze and correct before a continued focus on the negatives! Knowing that God is very much aware of what we're thinking should make us start thinking about NOT entertaining the devil! Reading the Bible helps us think more about the ways of God. The same is true for prayer and regular church attendance. Ask yourself this question: Are my thoughts pure, or am I just focused on getting more? Only you can answer that question!

Keep in mind that in all your getting, you should get wisdom. Wisdom only comes from God. Your thought process should be, "I will repent of my sin, accept Jesus as Lord and Savior, and I will get His wisdom. After that, everything else will fall into place! Change your thoughts today!

God Bless You!

Deception Leads to Disgrace.

There's a sickness going around called, "getting over on others." It is based on the demonic spirit of deception that drives people to be dishonest for self gain. The devil is a deceiver and all of his followers do the same. Praise God, we have the option to give our lives to God instead! This is what David wrote in Psalm Chapter 25, Verses 1 through 3: "O Lord, I give my life to you. I trust in you, my God! Do not let me be disgraced, or let my enemies rejoice in my defeat. No one who trusts in you will ever be disgraced, but disgrace comes to those who try to deceive others."

If you are sick with "getting over on others," your only antidote is Jesus! First, stop deceiving yourself in thinking, "I am ok; I don't need God, Jesus or church…" and repent today! Then, ask Jesus to come in; He will uproot that deepseated demon and throw him out of your heart. You will avoid disgrace with Jesus and win life's race! Now; about those individuals whose head is harder than average, whom decide to ignore a right relationship with Jesus? Well, expect your deception of self and others to increase! Expect your joy and peace to decrease, and plan on being disgraced in the future. Don't take it lightly! Take this encouraging word to heart, and repent today without delay!

God Bless You!

Did You Accept His Friend Request?

In social media it is common to receive a friend request. The request may come from someone in our past, present or someone you don't know. For the unsaved the same is true with regard to Christ Jesus; they don't know him personally, but He wants to be their friend! We all know of somebody, but we don't have a personal relationship with everybody; just ensure you get personal with Jesus! This is what the Bible says in Romans Chapter 5, Verse 11: So now we can rejoice in our wonderful new relationship with God – all because of what our Lord Jesus Christ has done for us in making us friends of God.

This rejoicing and confident assurance can only be achieved when we accept His friend request! You can accept friends all day long on social media but if you are not a friend of God, you are a friend of Satan! What are you waiting on to accept him? Let's be honest – do you really have joy or just temporary happiness? All of us who are saved have many guarantees from God, "to meet all our needs according to His riches in glory" is one of them. Stop trying to facilitate your needs on your own when a friend who will stick closer than a brother or mother is awaiting your acceptance! Don't delay; repent of your sins today and see where He takes you in life! It will be far better than you ever imagine with Heaven as the grand prize!

God Bless You!

Do You Appreciate The Good Shepherd?

Talk is cheap if it's not from the heart! We say thanks every day for the most part but do we really appreciate what the individual did, or are we just being polite?

Though we all go through the motions at times, we all have something that we really appreciate. For me; I really appreciate Jesus, the Good Shepherd! Jesus says this in John Chapter 10, Verse 11: "I am the good shepherd. The good shepherd sacrifices his life for the sheep."

Many religions out there require their subjects to sacrifice one thing or another; nonetheless, Jesus sacrificed himself! That sacrifice over two thousand years ago on Good Friday set the stage for our salvation!

The best way to show our appreciation is to repent of our sins and live for Him! Many say with their lips they appreciate, but their hearts couldn't care less! When we pray, God listens to our hearts. What are we saying? We're not against showing appreciation to others but make showing appreciation to Jesus, the Good Shepherd, your main priority!

God Bless You!

God says, "I love you." What's Your Reply?

Without a doubt we know God loves us, but do we reciprocate? Often times we open our mouths and give God a verbal, "I love you, Lord," that holds very little value if not backed by our actions.

Jesus says this in John Chapter 14 Verse 15: If you love me, obey my commandments." This is a very tall order to fill without the Holy Spirit helping us. Nonetheless because Jesus proved his love for us by leaving heaven, where He was worshipped, and died on the cross for all our sins, we can kill some bad habits and live for Him.

So? How motivated are you to live for Him? We should never lose focus on how much He loves us. Please redirect your love from perishable things to a perfect and imperishable God! The Commandments are simply this: "Love the Lord your God with all your heart, soul, mind and love your neighbor as yourself." You will never be able to love your annoying or peaceful neighbors as yourself unless you are led by the Holy Spirit! Today is a good day to repent of your sins and accept Jesus Christ as Lord and Savior! He will definitely help your behavior. Loving self and others is fine, but loving God is simply the best!

God Bless You!

Jesus said, Come Out!

We've all been there. Where, you might ask? We have all been in the tomb, clinging to spiritually dead people, places and things. Unfortunately, some people are still there! Some trying to find an exit, while others are quite comfy in there. How about you? Jesus says this in John Chapter 11 Verses 43 and 44: "Lazarus, come out!" And the dead man came out, his hands and feet bound in graveclothes, his face wrapped in a headcloth. Jesus told them, "Unwrap him and let him go!"

It doesn't matter how deep you are in the tomb today; Jesus is telling you to come out. If we fail to change our actions, we'll get the same results; don't complain! Many people want more out of life and Christ Jesus offers that, but you can't get your blessing in the tomb! Let's change some people that we hang out with.

You know – those who are spiritually dead. Stop going to those places that are controlled by Satan, and stop doing things that glorify the enemy! Come out of the tomb, today! Jesus is calling you! Answer today, and say hooray! This is the beginning of your best journey, all the way to eternity! If you send Jesus to voicemail, you will feel; answer Him, and come out!

God Bless You!

Love Is The Only Way To Glory!

"I love you, you love me…" should be more than just TV's "Barney" song. Love is the key that opens the gates of Heaven! Not having love for your fellow man results in having a key to Hell verses Heaven. Yes, I know our fellow man can be very annoying if we deal with them daily, but we too have our faults. With that in mind, let's focus on love so the world can see Jesus in us!

As a matter of fact, the Bible says this in 1 John Chapter 4, Verse 7: Dear friends, let us continue to love one another, for love comes from God. Anyone who loves is a child of God and knows God.

I have to agree with the Apostle John as the Holy Spirit led him to write that, and here is why: God is love; when we invite him in, automatically we should become love as well. Having hateful episodes toward one or more individuals will prove that God is not truly leading you. Repent today, and allow love to lead you all the way to Glory! If you truly love yourself you should love God who will give you the best life for all eternity, but it starts with loving your fellow man! So let's do it!

God Bless You!

Cockroach Christians!

We live in a very hurried pace society. Often times Christians don't get to attend Bible study or church on Sunday because of work and other obligations. Nonetheless, we must be careful to make the will of God a priority!

With that said, we must remember that we can be one of two things: the light of the world or cockroach Christians. What are some of the things a cockroach does? A cockroach looks for scraps to eat instead of feeding from the main course at the table; A cockroach walks around in the dark to avoid being seen; That is the caution we have today for the so-called Christians that hide their fate. A cockroach is just a bug to others when we see them as totally opposite from a butterfly.

Jesus says this in Matthew Chapter 5, Verse 15: No one lights a lamp and then puts it under a basket. Instead, a lamp is placed on a stand, where it gives light to everyone in the house.

Cancel the cockroach mentality, and shine your light as Jesus instructs us to! No need to eat scraps of the Word; feast daily in the Word of God! Do this my friend and you will be a delight in the eyes of people but more importantly, a delight in the eyes of God! Turn in your cockroach ID and be a butterfly!

God Bless You!

Is That The Best You Can Do?

People aim to look their very best on special occasions; weddings, graduations, birthdays, etc. You don't have to look at a bride in her gown and ask, "Is that the best you can do?" Ironically, during our everyday lives we tend to slack off on being our best spiritually. Let me explain. As Christians, we are the bride of Christ yet we commit spiritual adultery in our hearts and minds. Please be reminded of what happened to some slackers, also known as the five foolish virgins! In Matthew Chapter 25, Verses 8 through 10 it says: Then the five foolish ones asked the others, 'Please give us some of your oil because our lamps are going out.' But the others replied, 'We don't have enough for all of us. Go to a shop and buy some for yourselves.' But while they were gone to buy oil, the bridegroom came. Then those who were ready went in with him to the marriage feast, and the door was locked.

The five foolish virgins were locked out of heaven because they didn't do their best. What gets me is the fact that they had money to buy more oil, but chose not to. We have very busy schedules today, I know, but make sure enough Holy Spirit oil is in your lamp! When negotiating a price you ask, "Is that the best you can do?" Ask yourself that same question with regard to living for Christ Jesus! Be honest with your answer.

God Bless You!

More Than A Prayer; Reason With God.

The average woman speaks about 20,000 words per day while the average man speaks only 7,000 words per day! This research was previously conducted by the University of California. I can't help but wonder, how many of these words are spent talking to God? Or, how many of those words are spent talking about God?

God is upset with the Israelites, and He had Isaiah write this in Isaiah Chapter 1, Verses 18 through 20: "Come now, let's settle this," says the Lord. "Though your sins are like scarlet, I will make them as white as snow. Though they are red like crimson, I will make them as white as wool. If you will only obey me, you will have plenty to eat. But if you turn away and refuse to listen, you will be devoured by the sword of your enemies. I, the Lord, have spoken!"

How important is prayer and reasoning with God? It can save your life! The more we pray and get closer to God, the more we'll trust Him. The more we trust Him, it becomes easier to obey Him. When we obey Him, we can achieve our heart's desires. (Psalm Chapter 37, Verses 4 and 5). So you see, my friend, it's much more than a prayer. Your reasoning with God will open the right doors for you in this life and in the life to come! So put your back into your prayer life, and live for Christ!

God Bless You!

Only God Can Move The Right Pieces In Hand.

There are many pieces in the puzzle of life. Often times we're on a roll putting the pieces together, only to realize we missed a couple of steps. As frustrating as that might be, most people still don't learn. They refuse to seek help from God. In the puzzle of life, God is the only one who can move the right pieces in hand. Having all the right pieces will do us no good if we don't know how to put them together!

The Bible says this in Ephesians Chapter 3, Verse 20: Now all glory to God, who is able, through his mighty power at work within us, to accomplish infinitely more than we might ask or think.

My advice to you, my friend, is simply this: Stop trying to do it on your own! Turn to God for help while you are still breathing! Relationships may fail but God's love never will! He loves us so much and only wants the best for us! The faster we begin to trust in the Lord, the faster He will move the pieces in place so we can complete the puzzle! Don't make the same mistake so many others have made by procrastinating! Turn to God now! Though the pieces of your life are unattractive and scattered, God will put them together and make them attractive! Trust Him; He will do it!

God Bless You!

Are You Hyped About Jesus Or Just So So?

Imagine: You have been praying about your acceptance into the college of your choice, and you receive a letter saying, yes; you're accepted! That's a good time to get hyped! How about your boss calling you into his or her office to recognize your hard labor with a $25,000 a year raise of pay?! That's another reason to get hyped! Moving on… how about receiving a 7 bedroom, 7 bathroom mansion with movie theater totally paid for as a gift? That's reason to get hyped, right?!!

Well, that's exactly what Jesus did for us! Everyone who makes it to Heaven will receive a mansion! Number of bedrooms, undetermined! As a matter of fact, the Bible says this in John Chapter 14, Verses 1 and 2: "Don't let your hearts be troubled. Trust in God, and trust also in me. There is more than enough room in my Father's home. If this were not so, would I have told you that I am going to prepare a place for you?" Here's the thing: The rewards we receive in Heaven are good; but not as good as a love relationship with Jesus! Get to know Him; laugh with Him; share your deepest concerns with him! Jesus is more than a provider, a sustainer, a God. He proved that He is our best friend by sacrificing His life for ours! Why not sacrificed for Him? If you are breathing, you can get on the right track. Be honest; Are you hyped about Jesus, or just SoSo? Get hyped today!

God Bless You!

Let's NOT Go Crazy.

Contrary to The Artist Formerly Known As Prince's hit song, "Let's Go Crazy," we should NOT go crazy! We grew up listening to and singing many a song because we didn't know any better, but as Christians, we should dig a little deeper into lyrical content. Don't be hard-headed like the children of Israel in Jeremiah's day. Jeremiah had been prophesying for 23 years and they wouldn't listen, so God decided to send Israel into captivity for 70 years.

After He declared the punishment of captivity, God said this in Jeremiah Chapter 25, Verses 15 and 16: Then the Lord, the God of Israel, said to me, "Take from my hand this cup filled to the brim with my anger, and make all the nations to whom I send you drink it. When they drink from it, they will stagger, crazed by the warfare I will send against them."

Anyone who fails to live for God and the Lord Jesus Christ is crazy, why?! If you are not for Him then you are against Him, and that is one, crazy warfare that you cannot win! What's the solution? Let's NOT go crazy! Repent today and live for Jesus! Join His army and stay enlisted to serve Him! Stay sane!

God Bless You!

Don't Allow Your Feet To Lead You!

Every day some people go places they know they shouldn't be going! One guy says, "This is where my feet lead me, so here I am..." Let's check that and be a little more responsible by using our brains to lead and not just our feet. Your feet can get you into big trouble with both man and God! Jesus had this advice in Mark Chapter 9, Verse 45: If your foot causes you to sin, cut it off. It's better to enter eternal life with only one foot than to be thrown into hell with two feet.

You may or may not know this, but your feet can lead you to Hell; it's not cool. The moral of the story is this: Cut off the things that bring sin into your life and focus on righteousness. Don't just go with the flow; follow the Holy Spirit's lead! Your feet may tremble at the thought of going to church, but a visit or two should quiet that. Keep in mind that we will all have to bow before Jesus on the day of judgment; make sure your feet are very familiar with going to church and Godly activities before then.

Don't cut your foot off; cut the sin off. Start living! You can then lead your feet with the help of Jesus all the way through Heaven's gates!

God Bless You!

Quick To Loan And Forget Your Own?

It's really sad when men and women are so nice to everyone they meet on the street, on the job and at church but treat family like dirt. We may walk on dirt, but don't treat your family that way! Your spouse or your child asks you for ten dollars and although you have it, you say no. A friend calls you the same day, and you loan him twenty dollars! The word of God is clear on how we should treat family, relatives and those in our homes. This is what He says in 1 Timothy Chapter 5, Verse 8: "But those who won't care for their relatives, especially those in their own household, have denied the true faith. Such people are worse than unbelievers."

If there's a past, let the past stay in the past! Forgive, and move on! When it's all said and done, remember that blood is thicker than water! Even when you're angry, they are still your family! I'm not saying to ignore and not help a friend after prayer and God's leading but I am saying, help family when you can! Help isn't always monetary; you can lend a hand… or two, lend an ear and just be there when they need to share. When we're older and retired, the love we receive from family will be a reflection of the love we extended to family! Let's keep this in mind and be kind to family! Life can be a curse or a blessing; to have it taste good, use the right dressing!

God Bless You!

Waiting On The Right Call.

Phone calls – they can be happy, sad; they can make you breathe a sigh of relief, or make you mad. Nonetheless, there's a call that most people are unaware of due to lack of scripture reading. I like to call it, the right call! Jesus says in Matthew Chapter 28, Verses 19 and 20: "Therefore, go and make disciples of all nations, baptizing them in the name of the Father and the Son and the Holy Spirit. Teach these new disciples to obey all the commands I have given you. And be sure of this: I am with you always, even to the end of the age."

There you have it, my friends! Jesus calls us to be his hands and feet, leading people to Him and empowering them to do the same! The right call is staring you in the face! The question is, will you answer Him? Don't take this lightly; many have ignored the right call and suffered greatly! Some are suffering for an eternity. It's easy to write it off as unimportant right now thinking you have time to answer the call later, but later may never come! Stop what you're doing and listen! Jesus is calling! Answer Him!

God Bless You!

Family In The Spirit.

Anyone who is a born-again believer in our Lord and Savior, Jesus Christ, is a brother or sister to us Christians! We have brothers and sisters everywhere around the world! What makes us family is the Holy Spirit of God; not just church attendance. The Bible says this in 1st Corinthians Chapter 12, Verses 12 and 13: The human body has many parts, but the many parts make up one whole body. So it is with the body of Christ. Some of us are Jews, some are Gentiles, some are slaves, and some are free. But we have all been baptized into one body by one Spirit, and we all share the same Spirit.

Without the Holy Spirit living in us, we are not part of the body of Christ. How is your spiritual walk today? Do you consider yourself a friend or a foe to the Lord Jesus Christ? Here's some valuable news: You are either with Him or against Him; there's no middle ground! The wise person will choose him and receive His Holy Spirit. When you have Jesus you have Heaven but without the Holy Spirit, you have the devil and hell. What are you waiting for; Christmas? Repent today, receive the Holy Spirit… and new family!

God Bless You!

PMail.God.

Internet, social media, text messaging and email dominate our world today. .com, .org, .net are daily destinations for Americans and people worldwide. The Holy Spirit led me to pose a question: What about Pmail.God? If you haven't already figured it out, it's "Prayer Mail, dot God." In our busy lives, let's not neglect maintaining a healthy prayer life! Jesus, who is God in the flesh, needed to pray even with His hectic schedule! The Bible tells us in Mark Chapter 1, Verses 35 through 37: Before daybreak the next morning, Jesus got up and went out to an isolated place to pray. Later Simon and the others went out to find Him. When they found Him, they said, "Everyone is looking for you."

Jesus knew he was in high demand, but he also knew he needed time alone with God, the Father, to pray. During His prayer He received instruction, and in Mark Chapter 1, Verse 38 He replied, "We must go on to other towns as well, and I will preach to them, too. That is why I came."

People are quick to say they don't hear from God; let me offer a valuable piece of advice: turn off email and connect via pmail.God! Prayer is a two-way communication! Or it should be, if not perceived that way. Pray and then wait; the Lord will show up!

God Bless You!

He Is Worthy To Be Praised Is An Understatement.

As much as an individual may complain if he or she is honest with themselves, they can honestly say things usually get worked out. We have such a loving father who loves even those who don't reciprocate love back to Him. Whenever we have a need, He is ready to supply. We just need to ask Him. However, more important than making requests is praising Him! Yes, my friends; the key to victory days is in our praise! Why did David prosper in all his ways? He gave God praise! He wrote this in Psalm Chapter 22, Verses 23 to 24: "Praise the Lord, all you who fear Him! Honor Him, all you descendants of Jacob! Show Him reverence, all you descendants of Israel! For He has not ignored or belittled the suffering of the needy. He has not turned his back on them, but has listened to their cries for help."

I'm so glad we serve a God who hears and cares for us! He is worthy to be praised is an understatement, because without praise to God, my life would have no purpose! Begin to praise Him the right way; with our lifestyle and not just our lips! I don't know where you are with God right now, but if you desire to play in the majors spiritually, get your praise out of the minors! Step it up and always remember this truth: We need to send our praise more than God needs to receive them!

God Bless You!

Are You A Tasty Treat Or More Like Smelly Feet?

It is hard for everyone to like you, I know. That shouldn't stop you from trying though. Please keep in mind that people will judge you based on the way you look, but change their view by the things you say. After examining your fruit, so to speak, people will know if you are a tasty treat or more like smelly feet. We don't have to go around prejudging others, but we should be "fruit" inspectors. Jesus says this in Matthew Chapter 12, Verse 33: "A tree is identified by its fruit. If a tree is good, its fruit will be good. If a tree is bad, its fruit will be bad." We have sense enough to know right from wrong. Don't produce bad fruit! God is always watching and listening. Let's give Him a tasty treat by the way we live. Please God first in all you do, and everyone else will see you as a tasty treat! Don't cause people to retreat, because you have smelly feet! Wash them clean, so they won't smell mean! Let's leave a positive legacy through our Lord and Savior Jesus Christ for others to recognize, love and follow. Everything we think, say and do speaks volumes to God, first, and then to our fellow brothers and sisters! Invite Jesus into your heart, and tell Satan to depart! We cannot be the best without the best living in us!

God Bless You!

Don't Just Hear A Prayer, Say A Prayer.

"Please pray for me..." Certainly you have heard those words from family members, friends or even those you've just met. As Christians, we naturally desire to pray for others but often times we forget to remind them to pray for themselves as well. I've heard the stories before: "God wouldn't listen to someone like me..." or, "God is too busy to hear me..." Those are ever so wrong assumptions that keep people away from a healthy communicating relationship with God through prayer. Contrary to what you might have heard, this is what the Bible says in 1 Thessalonians Chapter 5, Verse 17: "Never stop praying." I must tell you; I have to pray all through the day even prayers as short as, "Help me, God!" When the pressures of life come down on us, whom do we have as our rescue? God is the answer! Don't neglect talking to Him when all is well with you! Pray in the calm and familiarize yourself with His voice so you can hear him plainly in the storm! Some say they can't hear from God. My response is, "You are not listening!" The more we talk with new friends on the phone, the easier it becomes to recognize their voices. Start talking to the King of Kings as a best friend; and often times, don't ask for anything. Just praise and thank Him! It's the best way to get close to Him!

God Bless You!

Don't Allow False Teaching To Prevent You From Reaching Him!

When we all get to heaven, what a day of rejoicing that will be! When we all see Jesus, we will sing and shout the victory!

Well, maybe… you see, not everyone is going to make it. False teaching, self-led theologies and ideas… I have personally witnessed so many fall off track with no desire to return and receive a good, convicting, Holy Ghost-filled teaching. Which is why Paul had this to say in Galatians Chapter 5, Verses 7 through 10: You were running the race so well. Who has held you back from following the truth? It certainly isn't God, for He is the one who called you to freedom. This false teaching is like a little yeast that spreads through the whole batch of dough! I am trusting the Lord to keep you from believing false teachings. God will judge that person, whoever he is, who has been confusing you.

Whether the false teacher is another or yourself, it's time to break free, repent of your sins and humbly follow Jesus! Rebellion is worse than witchcraft! Mark my words; if you follow the wrong lead, you will not succeed in making it to Heaven to see Jesus! Listen to the right teacher the Holy Spirit!

God Bless You!

Get Away From Me Satan!

If we knew certain people were out to harm us, we would try to avoid them. If after avoiding them they still show up in our face we ask them to get out of our face. Each day this is an issue with the deceiver, Satan. Every day he's in our face and tries to convince us to sin. The question is, "How do we handle it?" This is how Jesus handled it when the devil tried to steal God's worship. In Matthew Chapter 4, Verse 10 Jesus says, "Get out of here, Satan," Jesus told him. "For the scriptures say, 'You must worship the Lord your God and serve only him.'"

I love how Jesus used the Word to handle that demon! We should do the same! Don't smile with him or laugh at his ungodly jokes. Rebuke him! If you lie down with dirty dogs, you may catch fleas. Lying down with the devil will give you a disease! This spiritual disease will lead to physical and emotional handicaps. You've been warned! Someone trying to harm you? How will you respond? Again, my suggestion is for us to say, "Get away from me, Satan! The blood of Jesus is against you!" He'll eventually come back but resist him, chasing him away again!

God Bless You!

Be Well In Spirit & Body!

An initial diagnosis, hospital procedure and follow ups and can take a toll on us however our physical well being is important if we want to live a long, healthy life. Many people are on point with their physical well being but ignore the spiritual. I am overjoyed when friends and family members accept Christ and begin to prioritize spiritual things. It is truly a blessing for me to acknowledge someone as a man or woman of God because I know their walk. The Apostle John knew his friend Gaius' walk and greeted him this way in 3rd John Verse 2: "Dear Friend, I hope all is well with you and that you are as healthy in body as you are strong in spirit."

The Apostle Paul received a good report about his son in the Lord, and he was overjoyed! So, what about us? What can we do? First, repent of your sins and turn to God. Live for Him each day by obeying His word, the Bible. Then, be mindful of what you eat and stop eating when you are full. Gluttony will make you physically unhealthy! It's hard to be a witness for the Lord when we are too sick to even leave the yard! Let's be will in spirit first; then focus on the body! A great body will get you recognition on earth, but a right and Godly sprit is your ticket to heaven when you leave Earth!

God Bless You!

God Bless You Too!

When someone sneezes you may hear a person say "God bless you," which is normally followed by, "Thank you!" What we don't hear is, "No, thank you; I don't want God's blessing," or "God bless you, too!" First of all some people don't believe in God, secondly, some don't want others more blessed than they are!

Jacob went to his father, Isaac, and blessed him with his favorite dish. This is the blessing his father returned to him in Genesis Chapter 27, Verses 28 and 29: From the dew of Heaven and the richness of the Earth, may God always give you abundant harvests of grain and bountiful new wine. May many nations become your servants, and may they bow down to you. May you be master over your brothers, and may your mother's sons bow down to you. All who curse you will be cursed, and all who bless you will be blessed.

If you say, "God bless you" from a pure heart truly desiring for God to bless an individual, that blessing automatically returns to you! The same is true if you curse someone. Be quick to bless! Leave the curse out of your vocabulary and out of your heart and mind! If you bless someone and they fail to reciprocate the blessing, don't get mad! You will be blessed for pronouncing an authentic blessing! So for those of you out there who are quick on the "God bless you" draw, God bless you too!

Even If Life Gets Harder Seek The Father!

A long time friend says, “Life is hard.” “I know, my friend, but God is good.” While the thought that God has NOT been good to him goes on in his mind, the Holy Spirit used me to tell him to “Seek the Father.” Upon further conversation, I discovered what he had been thinking. So lovingly I point him to God the Father and the Lord Jesus Christ.

Even if life gets harder, my friend, Seek the Father! Remember: There is no repentance in the grave, so now is the time to seek the Father! As a matter of fact, this is what the Bible says in Isaiah Chapter 55, Verse 6: “Seek the Lord while you can find Him. Call on Him now while He is near.” What have you got to lose? You’re already stressed out, miserable, broke, not knowing if you are coming or going… Seek Him Now! People seek love, turn to another human being who fails them. They seek money, hit the casino, play the lottery only to realize that they, themselves, got played. To extend their lives they consult with a doctor, eat well and exercise and then die in a car accident.

So you see, my friends, the only real guarantee we have in this life and in the life to come is a right relationship with Jesus! He will open all the right doors and close the wrong ones! What are you waiting for? Seek Him today!

God bless you!

Never Too Busy For Salvation!

It's frustrating when you call a friend, loved one or a business regarding something really important to you and get a busy signal. It happened to me lately and the Holy Spirit spoke to me and said that He's never too busy for salvation! As a matter of fact He says in Romans Chapter 10, Verse 13: For "Everyone who calls on the name of the Lord will be saved."

One thing is certain when we call on the Lord Jesus Christ, we won't receive a busy signal! The repentant heart will receive salvation! Those bound will be set free! The demon possessed will be delivered! I have seen these miracles happen in my own life, so I know it to be true! How about you? Have you called on him? Maybe you just read posts about him on Facebook, Instagram, Twitter or What's App. That's awesome, but for salvation you have to invite Him into your heart, personally. Hanging out in the Christian community is, indeed, good but it won't benefit you eternally if you are not truly saved.

Let's get real with salvation, my friends! Call on Jesus now before your time to do so expires! There will never be a busy signal, so let that be your signal to call Jesus now! Secure your place in Heaven! I will see you there!

God bless you!

Don't Stay Burdened and Heavyladen!

Some people are prone to worry. They worry because it's nighttime, and they worry when it's sunny. They worry when they have little and worry when they have abundance. You get the picture. There are also some people carrying heavy burdens that wear them out. The good news is there is hope in Jesus Christ who says this in Matthew Chapter 11, Verse 28: Then Jesus said, "Come to me, all of you who are weary and carry heavy burdens, and I will give you rest." This supernatural rest in Christ is not your average rest that you get from sleeping; it goes way beyond that! A Hollywood celebrity may go to bed feeling at peace because they have an armed security guard looking out for them. How much greater should we as Christians feel when we have angels looking out for us?!

Whatever burdens we carry are not too heavy for Jesus to lift; he only needs to send one angel! My advice to you, my friend, is to come to Jesus with your heavy heart and surrender it all to Him! He will give you instruction in righteousness so you can work with the angels and resolve the issues in your life! Don't write this off before you at least give Jesus the opportunity to prove to you how awesome He really is! If you don't mind your burdens and pain then you don't need Jesus for that; but if you plan on going to heaven, call on Him now to be forgiven!

God bless you!

Are Your Days Filled With Praises To God, Or Complaints Because You Are Mad?

Let's face it. We can all generate a shopping list of complaints to God; regarding relationships, health issues, finances… you name it; but that won't solve anything. The fastest way to get results from God is through our praise. This needs to be implemented in our daily lives so God sees we are not faking it. David loved to praise and worship God, and for that God made him king of His people, Israel. Interestingly though, look at what David says with regard to praising God. In Psalm Chapter 106, Verses 1 and 2 he says: Praise the Lord! Give thanks to the Lord, for He is good! His faithful love endures forever. Who can list the glorious miracles of the Lord? Who can ever praise Him enough?" I love that fact, that we can never praise Him enough! Starting our conversations by saying, "Praise the Lord!" does a number of things! Number 1: It lets the other individual know who we are – someone who praises the Lord. 2. It makes someone think twice about using curse words or other negatives during the conversation. These are only two small parts of the blessing! The real blessing lies in the fact that God receives our praise and then blesses our days with what we need to proceed and succeed! So stop, put a "permanently closed" sign on your complaint department and an "always open" sign on your praise department! Don't be mad anymore; just praise God more!

God Bless You!

We Will Benefit From Good Work Ethics!

Work is a word that always brings on mixed emotions. Some of us work too much, others not enough, and yet others – not at all! However, everyone works hard at something; social media, playing games, talking on the phone, eating… but some "jobs" don't pay any money. That isn't always a bad thing; it just depends on what you are working on! Keep in mind that we will benefit from good work ethics! What are good work ethics, you might ask? Let's take a look at what the Bible says about work in Colossians Chapter 3, Verses 23 and 24: "Work willingly at whatever you do, as though you were working for the Lord rather than for people. Remember that the Lord will give you an inheritance as your reward, and that the Master you are serving is Christ."

So whether it's a 9 to 5 or missionary work oversees, do it as unto the Lord! You may be a banker or a homemaker, a pilot or a plumber; it doesn't matter the job title, do it as unto the Lord! We may not receive fair compensation or reward from man but the good news is, God will take care of us! Give God the glory in your work ethic! Show up on time with a smile! Work as if Jesus were in the building keeping an eye on you, because He is! Work to achieve God's benefits in store for you, and your ethics will influence others to do what you do! Let's get to work!

God Bless You!

Staying Quiet, Even In A Riot.

Everyday many circumstances cause people to freak out – from commuting to dining; from a distressing phone call to a fall. There may always be reasons to freak out, but we don't have to! David wrote this powerful Psalm while going through a wilderness season in his life. Psalm Chapter 62, Verses 5 and 6 say: "Let all that I am wait quietly before God, for my hope is in Him. He alone is my rock and my salvation, my fortress where I will not be shaken." My friends, we are able to stay quiet in life's riots once Jesus is leading our lives! Let's not focus on the problem more than on the problem solver! Jesus is the rock of our salvation! Hope in Him, knowing that He will not fail us as men do. Life is good at throwing curve balls; we should be good at sending kneemail (prayers) so that we don't fall! Stay calm, and call your best friend Jesus to defend! The world around us won't understand the reason for our trust, but we do! We have tasted, and we have seen that the Lord is truly good! Let's face it; anyone who has no hope in God and the Lord, Jesus Christ, is putting their hope in something else that will not satisfy! It's no wonder they freak out! How will you handle the riots in life today? I hope you pray. Then, stay quiet and wait on God to act!

God Bless You!

Don’t Give Up Without Knocking!

I was told a story about a man digging for gold a whole month in one spot. He got frustrated and gave up. Another gold miner came to the spot, dug for five minutes and guess what happened? He struck gold! Digging for gold reminds me of the many different goals we have. Yes, it gets frustrating when we meet roadblocks, setbacks and all manner of disappointments nonetheless we have to keep on digging or knocking on doors. Jesus had this to say in Matthew Chapter 7, Verses 7 and 8: “Keep on asking, and you will receive what you ask for. Keep on seeking and you will find. Keep on knocking, and the door will be opened to you. For everyone who asks receives. Everyone who seeks, finds. And to everyone who knocks, the door will be opened.”

That’s a bold statement Jesus made, so why are we afraid to test him in this? The problem is we cannot do it in the flesh, but in the spirit! Asking, seeking and knocking must be Holy Spirit led, which will in turn glorify God. We can ask for our needs as well, and God promises to supply. So keep this in mind: You are enroute to your victorious place, so keep on knocking! Be sure of this one thing when the door opens; give God all the glory and praise for opening it! Get ready; and knock!

God Bless You!

Meant To Die.

Most people in life will not give up their lives for another person. Maybe a Mother or Father for their child would consider it, but it's not the norm. So, the thought of someone dying for mankind is truly powerful! Please keep in mind that Christ Jesus left Heaven and came to Earth for that very reason. He meant to die; it is not by chance!

This is what Jesus said in John Chapter 12, Verse 27: "Now my soul is deeply troubled. Should I pray, 'Father, save me from this hour?' But this is the very reason I came!"

Jesus stuck to the mission so we can be saved from sin and enjoy life everlasting! Here's the thing, though: we must stick to His salvation plan. Don't be wishy-washy; since Christ willfully died for our sins, let us willfully die to sin and live for righteousness! Opportunities will arise to do wrong, but open up your eyes and heart and do right! If you really want to do something, sooner or later you can do it!

God Bless You!

Are You Passing Your Inspections?

When building a home or business from the ground up, it is customary to hire a contractor whom may also hire subcontractors for the project. Permits must be obtained, and a series of inspections will follow. Interestingly, you won't be permitted by the inspector to continue on to the next phase until you pass the preliminaries. After completing the work and passing the inspections, you receive a final inspection and a certificate of occupancy. Let's see how this relates to the Christian. We are inspected each day by God, and this is the standard that He uses. In Matthew Chapter 22, Verses 37 to 40 "Jesus replied, 'You must love the Lord your God with all your heart, all your soul, and all your mind.' This is the first and greatest commandment. A second is equally important: 'Love your neighbor as yourself.' The entire law and all the demands of the prophets are based on these two commandments."

Please make every effort to comply, because our inspector, Jesus, doesn't miss a thing! Any hidden hatred needs to be gotten rid of; unforgiveness, cursing, lying, fornicating, adultery, etc. Remember, our inspection is based on our loving God more than self. If you are trying to go to the next phase in life, start by passing your inspections on love for God and people. Once you are successful, your final inspection an certificate of occupancy will sound like this: Well done, my good and faithful servant; enter into my rest!

God Bless You!

Don't Lose Your Flavor!

Ever been to a rather pricey restaurant and ordered a dish that looks delicious on the menu? However to your dismay it tastes horrible, lacking the flavor it appeared to have. It's happened to us all; nonetheless food is not the most important when it comes to having flavor. We are! Let me explain a little more with what Jesus says in Mark Chapter 9, Verse 50: "Salt is good for seasoning. But if it loses its flavor, how do you make it salty again? You must have the qualities of salt among yourselves and live in peace with each other."

It is so easy for the world to pour so many diluting ingredients on us, causing us to lose our flavor. Let's be mindful of that, and stop it. Don't blend in the negative crowd; allow them to experience your flavor and crave it; then you can point them to Jesus! Be a peacemaker. Shine your light. Try your best to avoid a fight! Pray for flavor, and God will keep you salty!

When you leave someone's presence, are they sad you are gone or glad you are gone? Let's season this dark and seasonless world with the love of Christ Jesus! Don't lose your flavor! Flavor your world!

God Bless You!

Don't Just Eat Anything!

People all over the world are dying from food poisoning; so anyone who cares about themselves will try their best to ingest nonpoisonous food. There's a time and place for everything; a time to eat and a time to sleep. However, today, let's focus on eating, or the lack thereof. The Lord's Supper: so many are eating the bread and drinking the mock wine. The Bible says this in 1 Corinthians Chapter 11, Verses 29 and 30: "For if you eat the bread or drink the cup without honoring the body of Christ, you are eating and drinking God's judgment upon yourself. That is why many of you are weak and sick and some have even died."

Often times, individuals take communion and continue living their filthy lifestyles. This will bring a curse in your life – even unto death. It's important to not eat just anything, but even more important to not eat holy things while living reckless. Notice I didn't say sinless. Some people try not to sin and make an honest effort to live for God. That's fine. Others break every rule in the Bible and don't have any remorse about it. Save yourself from God's wrath. Allow God to save you, repent and accept the Lord Jesus Christ! Live for Him and partake of his holy table with confidence and peace.

God Bless You!

Who Is Your Guide?

I like to travel with the family to different cities and countries. One of our favorite things to do is hop the local bus tour that shares that city's history with us through a knowledgeable tour guide. Sightseeing is great, but what about our daily lives? Who is your guide?

For some, it's the Law of Moses; others rely on friends and family. What about Jesus through the power of the Holy Spirit? Jesus says this in Luke Chapter 16, Verse 16: "Until John the Baptist, the law of Moses and the messages of the prophets were your guides. But now the Good News of the Kingdom of God is preached, and everyone is eager to get in."

I'm not speaking negative about the law, I'm just simply stating that grace through the Gospel is a much easier way to make it into the Kingdom. Allowing the Holy Spirit to guide us each day is the way to go my friends!

Don't get left behind because your guide is blind! Turn to Jesus today, and don't delay! Keep in mind that the only way to the Father is through His Son, Jesus! He is my guide; how about you?

God Bless You!

Are You Coachable?

We all know a Mr. or Mrs. Know-It-All! As much as one may know, there is always room to grow! The truth is, no one knows everything about everything! God sent His son Jesus to coach us all the way to Heaven! Jesus appointed leaders of His church to teach His word to the masses but just like in Jesus' days on Earth in the flesh, people rejected instructions.

Jesus says this in Luke Chapter 11, Verse 31: "The queen of Sheba will stand up against this generation on judgment day and condemn it, for she came from a distant land to hear the wisdom of Solomon. Now someone greater than Solomon is here – but you refuse to listen."

So the question is: Are you coachable? Will you allow Jesus to minister to you through Hs Holy Spirit and His appointed teachers? Always test the spirit by the spirit before you digest it. Balaam was blinded by greed so God spoke to him through a donkey! Let's not be blinded by pride and end up wide! Stay on the straight and narrow and please, please, please pray about whom to follow! Feel free to follow me, AS I FOLLOW CHRIST! Let's do our best to look like Him, but it starts when we hear from Him! Listen and obey is the absolute best way!

God Bless You!

Keep His Name Holy.

A teacher asked her second grade class to put up their hands if they know the name of God. Talk about hysterical answers… nonetheless one child said, "His name is Hallowed" from Matthew Chapter 6, Verse 9 (KJV). Although it's not His given name, we are to hallow His name, or, keep it holy.

The Bible says this in Matthew Chapter 6, Verse 9 (NLT): "Pray like this: Our Father in heaven, may your name be kept holy." This is huge, my friends! So much, that the third commandment says, don't use His name in vain! Notice how Jesus prayed: He said, Heavenly Father, may your name be kept holy. He did not keep calling him "Father" or "God;" He knows He's already got God's attention! When we pray, let's keep this in mind so we don't sin while praying. For example; if I'm in a conversation with someone they wouldn't say, "Trevor, how are you? Trevor, isn't it a nice day? Trevor, what's the plan, Trevor?" Because I know my name is Trevor. The repetitious calling of one's name is annoying; I imagine how God must feel when people do this! I know people mean well when they pray and we encourage prayer; this is intended to enhance growth into a mature prayer life. Don't use His name in negative conversations and blasphemous connotations. Keep His name Holy, and give Him the glory!

God Bless You!

The God Who Keeps Us From Shame And Disgrace.

Life is fifty-fifty with a lot of things, from personal relationships, employment, business, you name it. There is one thing, however, that we should never leave to a fifty-fifty chance and that is a right relationship with God, the father and the Lord, Jesus Christ. When we prioritize a relationship with Satan, he leaves us in shame and disgrace. Let's turn our priorities around and prioritize a right relationship with God.

Here is a good reason to do that. In Psalm Chapter 25, Verse 3 David says, "No one who trusts in you will ever be disgraced, but disgrace comes to those who try to deceive others." Our God will always show up at the appointed time even if it's the eleventh hour and 59th minute! His ways are higher than ours so we really can't figure Him out, but we can rest assured, we who trust Him have the victory!

Playing a game of falling backwards expecting to be caught by a friend may not always end well; not so with God! He is able to keep us from falling. If we fall, He is faithful and just to forgive us of our sins and cleanse us from all unrighteousness. The world is watching to see us fall or fail, but we who trust God will always prevail! Don't worry about shame and disgrace; seek His face and enjoy the victory in this life's race!

God Bless You!

Let's Go Out With A Bang!

I love concerts! The headline artist usually does something spectacular at the end. Maybe sing their biggest hit song, complete with fireworks show. How about us in this life? What can we do that would create the same effect as pyrotechnics at a concert or 4th of July firework display? The answer may surprise you; nonetheless, here it is.

Leaving this world having gained true repentance and salvation sets off fireworks we can't even imagine! Can you fathom a party in heaven on your behalf? In Luke Chapter 15, Verse 10 Jesus says: In the same way, there is joy in the presence of God's angels when even one sinner repents."

My friend, what are you waiting for?! Let's go out with a bang! Here's the catch: No one knows the scheduled time to go! The smart individual would stay ready and not allow the fire deep down in their soul to stop blazing. Some choose to earn millions on Earth and end up poor for all eternity. Don't get trapped and leave earth like that! Repent! Go out with a bang, holding on to our Savior's hand! Don't look to be seen by men; as long as Jesus, our audience of one, approves our actions! Create fireworks in Heaven with your Godly lifestyle!

God Bless You!

Let's Put On Something New!

Most people tend to like new things: cars, houses, relationships... Dressing up in something new; shoes, clothing and jewelry will spark the attention and compliments of family and friends. Nothing wrong with that, but here is some food for thought: nothing looks or feels better than dressing up in Christ! Let's take off our old, sinful attire and dress to impress God! As a matter of fact, the Bible says this in Ephesians Chapter 4, Verses 22 through 24: "...throw off your old sinful nature and your former way of life, which is corrupted by lust and deception. Instead, let the Spirit renew your thoughts and attitudes. Put on your new nature, created to be like God – truly righteous and holy.

Let's put on something new and be righteous and holy, so God can get the glory! Clothes, shoes and jewelry won't have the same effect on God. To impress God, we must dress like him spiritually; physical attire is not of great significance. Get rid of the old, my friend, because in the end we win! Keeping your old, sinful ways is setting yourself up for defeat in the end! Think on these things and put on Christ so you can go forth with power! You know what to do: Show Jesus the new you!

God Bless You!

Words That Condemn; Don't Use Them!

It's easy to use hurtful words in retaliation or initiation. Words of condemnation are often prevalent in homes where parents deposit them into the hearts of youngsters. In turn, they grow and feed others the same filth they were fed.

With that being said, here is the reality of the matter: Words that condemn; we shouldn't use them. Here's what Jesus says in Matthew Chapter 5, Verses 21 and 22: "You have heard that our ancestors were told, 'You must not murder. If you commit murder, you are subject to judgment. But I say, if you are even angry with someone, you are subject to judgment! If you call someone an idiot, you are in danger of being brought before the court. And if you curse someone, you are in danger of the fires of hell." (NLT)

Words that condemn are not our friends, so don't use them! Use words that promote life, peace, joy and happiness; not negativity and death. Remember to choose your words carefully; the person you are speaking to will either benefit or hurt from them. Keep in mind that God is also listening to your words! Use only the good ones!

God Bless You!

Enjoy Your Bible; God Is Speaking!

Bible reading has declined tremendously over the past few years. We live in a high tech society where many don't even own a tangible copy of the Bible. There are many good reasons to keep a tangible Bible even if you have one downloaded on your phone or iPad: When you open your Bible to read, there's no mistaking it with social media, in or outside of church! This encourages others to read when they see us reading the Word! Another reason: Sometimes God will speak to us and say, "Open the Bible..." and at random we open to a powerful verse or chapter dealing with our current situation!

Remember John Chapter 1, Verse 1: In the beginning the Word already existed. The Word was with God, and the Word was God." Enjoy your Bible; God is speaking! I'm not saying your online Bible is bad; I'm just saying don't do away with your tangible Bible. You will miss a lot of what God is saying.

The Word is delightful even when He convicts us to change, because we have the ultimate victory! Satan is defeated when we live the Word; we are defeated if we don't! Be doers of the Word and obtain all God's blessings as you spend quality time with Him in His Word!

God Bless You!

When Will You Take A Break?

Let's face it; we could all use a break from one thing or another. For you, maybe it's a job that causes stress; for another, maybe it's cleaning the house, doing laundry, cooking… How about a break from paying bills? Monthly electric, water, cable and phone bills will always come, but God is able to cancel our bigger bills like mortgages and car payments!

When will you take a break from your stressing and ask God for your blessing? The Bible says this in Philippians Chapter 4, Verses 6 and 7: "Don't worry about anything; instead, pray about everything. Tell God what you need, and thank him for all he has done. Then you will experience God's peace, which exceeds anything we can understand. His peace will guard your hearts and minds as you live in Christ Jesus."

The choice is ours – We can choose to take a break from the worries of this world, or we can keep on stressing what we can't even fix on our own! My advice: Take a break, my friend! Even Jesus took a break from the crowds by himself and went and prayed to the Father (Mark Chapter 1, Verse 35). We should do the same! Don't allow your circumstances to break you; take a break and give them to Jesus to fix!

God Bless You!

What Are You Glad About?

It's crazy how people sit around and complain about all the things they are mad about. Why not change the way we think by focusing on the things we are glad about. Satan will always remind us of whom or what we don't have but let me tell you, Jesus is all you need to succeed! Instead of being mad, go to church and seek God. This is what David says in Psalm Chapter 122, Verse 1: I was glad when they said to me, "Let us go to the house of the Lord."

I know what David is saying; I look forward to going to church! How about you? Is going to church a burden or a task for you? Maybe you go because you are forced to go. If going to church is one reason you are mad, you need to talk to God. Establish a right relationship with Him, and He will lead you where you ought to be! We're often glad about food, fun, money or sun but our greatest joy should be our salvation! If you have salvation, you have accomplished the most important task in your human life!

We get glad about graduations and weddings but we should really be glad when our sins are forgiven! What are you waiting for? Be glad today, and leave the devil mad! Only the Lord can keep a smile on our faces!

God Bless You!

Don't Embrace Your Demons, Rebuke Them!

You may be the closest to Jesus among your peers, family members or church group, but you still have demons trying to get you to sin. That's their job and they do it, oh so well, for the most part.

So; what is our job? We are to be Christians, which means followers of Christ. So what did Christ do? In Matthew Chapter 4, the devil tempted Jesus to sin by turning stones into bread, commit suicide and worship of the devil but Jesus rebuked his proposition.

As a matter of fact in Matthew Chapter 4, Verse 10 when Satan crossed the line and tried to take God's worship from Jesus, this is how Jesus rebuked Satan: "Get out of here, Satan," Jesus told him. "For the scriptures say, 'You must worship the Lord your God and serve only him.'"

The devil has tricked so many people into false worship; try not to be one of them! Study the word of God, get close to Jesus and use his power to rebuke your demons. Satan won't quit, nor should we! Let's put on the whole armor of God and rebuke the demons! Don't embrace your demons, resist them, and they will flee! They will return, and we resist them again, giving God the praise! We all have a mission to resist Satan and his demons.

God Bless You!

What Are We Safeguarding?

There are many ways to safeguard money jewelry and expensive artifacts. We have choices of bank safety deposit boxes, home safes to armed security guards. Here's a twist to your safeguarding efforts – are you guarding your heart?

Yes, your heart! Here's what the second wisest man in history wrote in Proverbs Chapter 4, Verse 23: "Guard your heart above all else, for it determines the course of your life."

I can't help but wonder how many people are so focused on all the wrong things, yet they refuse to entertain change. Don't be so wrapped up in safeguarding your stuff, which is what you have, and ignore safeguarding your heart, which is based on WHO you have! Satan has an army of demons attacking us every day; don't allow any of his fiery darts to penetrate your heart! Put on the whole armor of God; stay safe and well protected! Don't let your guard down, or else, Satan will take you down!

God Bless You!

The Worse Kind of Failure Is Failure to Repent!

We have all failed in one area of life or another, be it a math test, a driving test or test of a marriage relationship. Don't be too hard on yourself; people fail every day. The thing we must do is learn from other's failures and don't repeat the same mistake! Though failing a test or trial is hard we can bounce back; but the worst kind of failure is failure to repent! The truth could be staring them in the face! Some people just won't believe and repent.

Jesus says this in Matthew Chapter 12, Verse 41: "The people of Nineveh will stand up against this generation on judgment day and condemn it, for they repented of their sins at the preaching of Jonah. Now someone greater than Jonah is here – but you refuse to repent."

The last thing you want to do is die without repenting of your sins! There is no repentance in the grave, so behave! Start right now! Many mistakes can be fixed or adjusted, but leaving this life without repenting and having Jesus as Lord and Savior will leave you truly busted.

God Bless You!

Have You Subscribed To Heaven?

Everything involves some form of sign up or subscription; social media, airline rewards to online shopping payment methods. Businesses encourage you to subscribe and offer benefits for your subscription. But what about the most important place you can subscribe to? You guessed it, Heaven! Yes, Heaven is the single most important place you should subscribe to! Jesus sent out His disciples to heal the sick and cast out demons. They came back rejoicing! Jesus said this to them in Luke Chapter 10, Verse 20: "But don't rejoice because evil spirits obey you; rejoice because your names are registered in heaven."

My question is this: Have you subscribed to Heaven? Was it a successful subscription complete with confirmation? You must be 100% sure that your name is registered as a citizen in Heaven. Social media may fail and other subscriptions may eventually fade away but Heaven and Hell will stand forever! Hell partners with the Lake of Fire, while Heaven partners with the New Jerusalem! Review your subscriptions carefully; be sure that you're subscribed to Heaven!

God Bless You!

No Withholdings.

During the hiring process employers give their new hires an IRS W-4 form to fill out. Taxable withholdings are entered on the appropriate lines as needed. The numbers add up to how much tax will be taken out for a greater or lesser return.

God is in the withholding business as well. For the many who refuse to live for Him, He withholds blessings, open doors, favor, you name it. However, let me reveal to you how to have No Withholdings and get all you desire from the Lord. Psalm Chapter 84, Verse 11 says this: For the Lord God is our sun and our shield. He gives us grace and glory. The Lord will withhold no good thing from those who do what is right.

So – are you doing what is right? That's the key to your victory – walking uprightly! Just so you know God looks forward to blessing us, His children but He cannot bless a mess so allow Him to clean you up. Repent of your sins and ask Jesus to come in. With all of your heart live for Him and where blessings are concerned, you will have No Withholdings!

God Bless You!

Don’t Allow Adultery To Register You For the Cemetery!

Adultery used to be bad; now it’s worse! The devil wants husbands and wives to fall, not just in the marriage but in a 6 foot deep hole! Proverbs Chapter 2, Verses 16 through 19 say: “Wisdom will save you from the immoral woman, from the seductive words of the promiscuous woman. She has abandoned her husband and ignores the covenant she made before God. Entering her house leads to death; it is the road to the grave. The man who visits her is doomed. He will never reach the paths of life.” This statement is also true for the woman who follows the adulterous man.

If you are married, please stay true to whom God gave you! It’s a decision married people need to make on a daily basis! Failure to do so may land you in the basement and then a 6-foot deep apartment. Death comes in many forms, but spiritual death is the worst because it separates you from God. Death of a relationship can be revived. If you feel you are on life support in your marriage, start praying! God will help! Don’t throw in the towel and sleep around. Give it to God, and see what He does! Remember: We are not responsible for our spouse’s actions, but we are responsible for ours! Stay true, and God will bring you through!

God Bless You!

A Few Rules For Christian Schools.

Where would this world be without rules and regulations? It would be in total chaos for starters! Can you imagine no stop lights in Manhattan, New York City? Rules are put in place to govern people and keep the proper order of things. The same is true on the spiritual side of things. We have the Bible which contains some dos and don'ts designed to help us.

The Bible says this in Luke Chapter 6, Verse 37: "Do not judge others, and you will not be judged. Do not condemn others, or it will all come back against you. Forgive others, and you will be forgiven."

Those are a few rules for Christian schools. Every Christian from 1 to 121 is enlisted in Christian school. Each day we are taught by the Holy Spirit himself! Without going to a church service we realize that new, positive thoughts and insights are coming our way! Let's pay attention to the rules He is giving us today for a better future! Stay on the straight and narrow and don't follow the enemy! We may not always like what God asks us to do, but in the end we win, so keep listening! Don't bend or break the rules and get expelled from Christian school!

God Bless You!

Let's Bring Back Harmony!

God loves it when people get along but sadly, we live in a world where harmony has been downplayed. We should read the scriptures daily because the word of God promotes harmony. Psalm Chapter 133, Verses 1 through 3 say:

"How wonderful and pleasant it is when brothers live together in harmony! For harmony is as precious as the anointing oil that was poured over Aaron's head, that ran down his beard and onto the border of his robe. Harmony is as refreshing as the dew from Mount Hermon that falls on the mountains of Zion. And there the Lord has pronounced his blessing, even life everlasting."

So – in a nutshell, with others we must live well! Our eternal destiny depends on our living in harmony first with Jesus and also mankind. If we claim to love God but not our fellow human being, then we are lying. Let's bring back harmony and forsake the enmity. God will bless us when we are harmonious, but a spirit of division or unforgiveness will prevent the blessing. Let's "bury the hatchet" so in the next life you will have no regrets!

God Bless You!

Have You Checked On Your Home Lately!

Upon arrival back home we often check on our homes making sure no one broke in or we didn't have a water leak, etc. especially if it's happened in the past. Some people have security cameras monitoring inside and outside of their homes. I'm not against keeping your home safe and secure, but don't neglect your heavenly home! Have you checked on your heavenly home lately? Are your eyes like surveillance, searching the scriptures to make sure the enemy, Satan, doesn't rob you?

The Bible says this in Hebrews Chapter 13, Verses 14 and 15: For this world is not our permanent home; we are looking forward to a home yet to come. Therefore, let us offer through Jesus a continual sacrifice of praise to God, proclaiming our allegiance to His name.

When we leave this earth, we go to our permanent home! I pray you choose Heaven. The other option is Hell, then the Lake of Fire. My advice to you, my wise friend, is to pay closer attention to your home in Heaven! If you don't have a home in Heaven as of yet, stop paying rent to the devil and own a home in heaven for free! Jesus already has your mansion waiting! The question is, will you accept it by first accepting Him? Don't allow your temporary home to ruin your eternal home! I refer you to my realtor, Jesus!

God Bless You!

Will You Let Me Know?

When asking a favor of a friend, we make our request and then ask, "Will you let me know?" This gives our friend the chance to check into things and to pray before saying, Yeah or Nay. Jesus did the same, only in reverse! "What do you mean," one might ask? Well, it's like this: Jesus died on the cross, raised from the dead and now offers salvation to whoever repents and accepts Him. That's a favor for free! However, He is a gentleman so He will not force us; instead His stand is, "Will you let me know?"

The Bible says this in Matthew Chapter 6, Verse 24: "No one can serve two masters. For you will hate one and love the other; you will be devoted to one and despise the other. You cannot serve both God and money." Jesus is waiting on the unsaved to let him know! I don't know how long He will wait on you, my friend, so choose life over death and good over evil; choose Jesus! If you live your entire life without Jesus, you are just letting Him know He is not a priority to you; your money and status is priority. Let's change that! Repent and accept His will so in the end you will be welcomed in Heaven! For those who refuse to let Jesus know something good, Jesus will let them know something bad. "Depart from me, I never knew you!" Let Jesus know something good today!

God Bless You!

Come Close To God and Be Clean.

When someone's taken a shower and put on clean clothes, they want to remain clean. When an individual who is clearly wearing dirty clothes approaches for a hug, there will be some hesitation or flat out rejection.

Praise God, who welcomes everyone to partake of eternal life! However, know this fact; while dirty clothes are not an offense to Him, a dirty heart is! Here's a verse that will help you to better understand: James Chapter 4, Verse 8 says, "Come close to God, and God will come close to you. Wash your hands, you sinners; purify your hearts, for your loyalty is divided between God and the world."

Most people will hang out with God in church on special days: Easter, Christmas, Mother's Day, Father's Day; but won't get close to God. They know that in getting close to God, He will expose them. Come close to God and be clean, my friends, before your dirt sends you below the dirt! Enough said!

God Bless You!

Have You Done A Friend Analysis Lately?

There's an age-old saying: "Show me your friend, and I will tell you who you are." This is not far from the truth, my friend! I can remember some old rolling mates doing some extreme things, and so did I. Years later after repenting of my sins and living for Jesus the desire to do those things are gone, and guess what? So are the friends.

As we get closer to God, we want friends who are close to God as well. Have you done a friend analysis lately? David did. This is what he wrote in Psalm Chapter 26, Verses 4 and 5: "I do not spend time with liars or go along with hypocrites. I hate the gatherings of those who do evil, and I refuse to join in with the wicked." I must say, this is some really powerful stuff! Even today as the Holy Spirit inspires me to write this encouragement, I am doing a friend analysis. We are not saying we're better than anyone else, but we choose where we eat physical food, so we should choose who will feed our mind and spirit. After analyzing the friend data, let's be honest with ourselves and cut loose those who don't produce Godly fruit.

We cannot change anyone; only God can, but we can change our affiliation with a demon. Don't allow a so-called "friend" to bring you to a spiritual or physical end! Listen to Jesus instead!

God Bless You!

All Our Needs Will Be Met.

Our "needs" often get confused with "wants." God never promised to give us everything we want; some things, He knows, are very bad for us! However, in Philippians Chapter 4, Verse 19 He promised to fulfill all our needs. So how does He accomplish this supplying of the Christian needs? He uses people like you and I to do it! In Romans Chapter 12, Verse 13 He says, "When God's children are in need, be the one to help them out. And get into the habit of inviting guests home for dinner or, if they need lodging, for the night." NLT

Pray about everything, family, and let's be the hands and feet of Jesus! I know there are some crazies out there, so stay in prayer! Don't ignore showing hospitality due to fear. God did not give us a spirit of fear (2 Timothy Chapter 1, Verse 7), so rebuke fear and start to share! We brought nothing into this world, and we will take nothing out, but whatever we do for others we will be rewarded in the next life! Let's be other people centered as Jesus is and sacrifice some of our daily activities and finances to help out others!

The best way to shine our light and look like Jesus is to love our brothers and sisters! Pray, and God will show you your family and expose the enemy! When we help supply the needs of others, all our needs will be met!

God Bless You!

Time Will Tell.

Children don't make a big deal about time. They aren't paying close attention to a clock or watch except perhaps while waiting to get out of class for recess. As we get older we're checking the time on our watches and telephones more often. As we invest time working for our employers, time will tell if we get a paycheck at the end of the week. As people get married with the highest of hopes, time will tell if the marriage will last.

What about the individuals who have not repented of their sins and accepted Jesus as Lord and Savior, yet they believe being a good person will get them to Heaven? Only time will tell who makes it to heaven and who gets landed in hell. It doesn't have to be that way. In 1 John Chapter 5, Verse 13 John writes: "I have written this to you who believe in the name of the Son of God, so that you may know you have eternal life." This is one of my favorite scriptures because I don't want to invest a lot of time and money and wing it saying time will tell when it comes to my eternity! Yes, everyone will live or exist forever; the two sections being smoking or non-smoking.

Make the right decision to live for God and the Lord Jesus Christ today! Don't wait, or time will tell you what you don't want to hear!

God Bless You!

Let's Fix Those Ugly Feet!

People often associate ugly feet with corns, bunions and weird looking toes. However, that is not what we are talking about today. The Bible says in Isaiah Chapter 52, Verse 7: "How beautiful on the mountains are the feet of the messenger who brings good news, the good news of peace and salvation, the news that the God of Israel reigns!"

When we proclaim the gospel, we have beautiful feet! What if we aren't proclaiming the gospel? Where does that leave us? You guessed it; with ugly feet! Let's fix those ugly feet! Tell someone about our Lord and Savior, Jesus Christ! In Romans Chapter 1, Verse 16, the Apostle, Paul, said, "For I am not ashamed of this Good News about Christ. It is the power of God at work, saving everyone who believes…"

Maybe you aren't ashamed; just a little scared of rejection. Keep in mind that they also rejected Christ. With so many people hell bound, it's inevitable for opposition to come our way. No matter how they come, we should still try and show them the way. Have you checked out your feet lately? God Is watching, and so are we!

God Bless You!

I Will Follow You Forever!

We make promises in life for various reasons, but some of the strongest promises are made to the people we love. For instance, a man promises his wifetobe that he will always provide for her and keep her safe, and a woman promises her husbandtobe that she will follow his lead forever.

Ruth made a promise to her mother-in-law whom she loved. She says this in Ruth Chapter 1, Verses 16 and 17: “Don’t ask me to leave you and turn back. Wherever you go, I will go; wherever you live, I will live. Your people will be my people, and your God will be my God. Wherever you die, I will die, and there I will be buried. May the Lord punish me severely if I allow anything but death to separate us!”

Ruth expressed her devotion to Naomi and willingness to follow her forever without knowing God for herself. She saw Godly qualities in Naomi that bought her to that decision. How about us today? We’ve read in the scriptures of all the sacrifices the Lord Jesus made for us, which were greater than Naomi’s! If Ruth can devote herself to Naomi, we can devote ourselves to the Lord Jesus Christ! If we follow Him He will get us to the right destination, safe and sound. We are led by the devil when we lead ourselves, so don’t be fooled! If you want your eternity to be better, follow Jesus forever!

God Bless You!

Don't Deny The Truth With Your Substitute!

In sports consisting of multiple players on the same team, we often see substitutions. Fresh legs are bought in to run, kick, you name it. This is business as usual in sports, and it's totally okay. However, what is not okay is when people substitute God's Word for their own traditions or belief system. Jesus explained these flaws to the Pharisees in Mark Chapter 7, Verse 8: "For you ignore God's law and substitute your own tradition." The Word of God is the truth so when we replace Him with our own ideas and beliefs we are substituting. That type of substitute is not cute – remember: sin is ugly! Seek first the Kingdom of God and all His righteousness then everything else will be added. Stop treating the Bible, God's Holy Word, like a buffet line, eating up only what is sweet to the taste. Go to a bakery for that!

The truth is absolute so He cannot change; His name is Jesus! Don't substitute Him with money, sex, drugs, hard liquor and things of that sort. You are the main athlete running this race, and there are no substitutes for you! Jesus is the only way to Heaven, and there are no substitutes for Him!

God Bless You!

God Will Provide For You!

We all have needs; some great, some small. For some, it's financial, emotional, physical, you name it! So who do we call? Not "Ghostbusters," but the Holy Ghost to provide for us! The mistake made by many is trying all other sources for help before trying God. Remember, our Father is a jealous God that won't accept the backseat to anyone or anything else! Please show Him the respect of a father and trust Him to provide all your needs!

Jesus says this in Matthew Chapter 7, Verse 11: "If you sinful people know how to give good gifts to your children, how much more will your heavenly Father give good gifts to those who ask Him." The key: Ask God! The problem is when someone stays away from church, doesn't read their Bible often, and prays only occasionally, they feel disconnected from God. Reverse that cycle, my friend; get close to God, the Father, and the Lord, Jesus Christ! Don't be like those that show up with a need then vanish when it's supplied!

Show up for God, and you will be entitled to His full benefits package! God will provide for you!

God Bless You!

Lord, I Thank You For My Land!

A farmer needs land to plant and harvest crops. Indeed, he or she could acquire the land and do nothing with it. The farmer could say, "I don't feel like preparing the soil, planting any seeds or watering them…" In this case, the farmer would have a very bad year for harvest. Spiritually, God has given us land to till, plant and harvest. The proper execution of these duties will lead to a great reward from the Lord! Some of the things He rewards us with are "physical land," for house, a business, you name it! David says this in Psalm Chapter 16, Verse 6: "The land you have given me is a pleasant land. What a wonderful inheritance."

Let us thank God for the land He has blessed us with thus far, and do His work so we can enjoy the land to come! Not just the temporary land but the eternal land in the New Jerusalem! Glory be to God, I am looking forward to that land when I can say to Jesus, "Lord I thank you for my land!" Are you excited about it today? If you are not, you need to refocus your mind on the eternal. Don't be so wrapped up emotionally with the physical land you have or are trying to acquire; instead repent of your sins and make plans for your land that's higher!

God Bless You!

There Is Nothing Like Going To Church!

"We are going to church." A very popular saying used in many homes throughout the years, I'm sure... Although "the church" is actually the people and NOT the building, we still love going into a cozy church building to worship God with church family.

David, my favorite worshiper of all times, wrote this in Psalm Chapter 22, Verse 25: "I will praise you in the great assembly. I will fulfill my vows in the presence of those who worship you." David knows that there is nothing like going to church! How about you, my friend? Are you super excited about going to church, or just going through the motions? If your church family is not very loving or family-oriented, you can make the difference by showing love! I often hear people say they don't like church folks; they are hypocrites. Remember: We, who are saved, and those whom just attend church are not perfect! However the key is to love people, in spite of!

Don't always go to church to look for Jesus; learn and grow so that when you show up to church, you bring Jesus with you! We are allowed to worship freely now; until the Rapture happens... after that, the antichrist will put an end to Christian churches! Let us go to church while we can and worship the One who holds the world in His hands!

God Bless You!

It's Misguided Hope If You Exclude The Lord!

I hope to see you soon! I hope I can get a raise of pay. I hope it doesn't rain today. I hope to meet a good wife. I hope to meet a faithful husband. I hope… I hope… I hope… For those of us whose hope is in the Lord, we add this to our hope: "God willing." You see, God's Will is supreme, and we want to include Him in all our hopes, dreams and aspirations.

The Bible says this in Psalm Chapter 33, Verses 20 through 22: We put our hope in the Lord. He is our help and our shield. In him our hearts rejoice, for we trust in His holy name. Let your unfailing love surround us, Lord, for our hope is in you alone.

My question is, are you hoping the Lord? Many put their hope in Man and get disappointed; or in money and are still not satisfied. The things of this world can never replace a right relationship with God! Here's my brotherly advice: Repent of your sins today, and invite Jesus into your heart as Lord and Savior! Next, put your hope in Him. Watch Him work miracles in your life! Jesus can open doors that lead to your fondest dreams, but you have to trust Him with your heart for Him to start! Peace and joy await you in God, the Father and the Lord, Jesus Christ, but excluding the Lord is misguided hope that will never become a reality. Let's hope in the Lord first, and everything else will be added!

God Bless You!

Standing On Holy Ground!

So; where is your holy ground? This may shock you, but I'll say it anyway. For those of us whom are truly saved and have the Holy Spirit living within us, everywhere we step is holy ground! Now, let me clarify some things. If a born again believer steps into a freaky night club or someplace where evil is dominant, the Holy Spirit will speak and instruct us not to stay there. However if that individual stays, then the Holy Spirit leaves.

Exodus Chapter 3, Verse 5 says, "Do not come any closer," the Lord warned. "Take off your sandals, for you are standing on holy ground." This reminds me of the Holy of Holies; the inner most chamber in the temple. When Jesus died, the curtain in thc temple ripped from top to bottom (Luke Chapter 23, Verse 45). So now the same is true for us who walk with the Holy Spirit; we don't have to be in church to stand on holy ground! Jesus opened the door for us so we can stay holy at work, at home, at play… everywhere! So, remember to conduct yourself accordingly; for you are standing on holy ground! For those of you whom are not saved, please do so as fast as you can! Unholy ground will lead to a hot place – Hell. Holy ground, here, will lead to holy ground in Heaven. See you there!

God Bless You!

Are You A Soul, Forgiven?

The story goes like this: A little boy goes into his neighbor's yard and picks a low hanging mango from a tree. The property owner shouts from the window, "Why are you stealing my mango?!!" The little boy replied, "It was not my intention to steal anything; I apologize." The little boy then offered the mango to the property owner. The property owner recognized the boy's sincerity and told him he could have the mango, but next time knock on the door and ask.

Let's learn a lesson from the little boy who sincerely apologized for his sin. We should do the same for our sin, and ask the King of Kings to live within! David wrote this in Psalm Chapter 32, Verse 2: "Yes, what joy for those whose record the Lord has cleared of guilt, whose lives are lived in complete honesty!"

When we are forgiven for all our sin, our soul can operate in peace. The Savior of the world is in the forgiving business, but not Mafia business; Jesus will not force us to do anything we don't want to do! A Soul Forgiven will do its best to accomplish the Father's Will. Let's enjoy the freedom we have in Christ Jesus and shine our light for all to see! Tell others about your joy, peace and true salvation, so you can help save someone! If you are a Soul Forgiven, talk about it!

God Bless You!

Better Make Sure It's Good Counsel.

"Trust me when I tell you..." "You can take that to the bank!" "I did it that way, and it worked for me..." People often speak these words, sometimes with the very best intentions. It's usually just before or after a loved one, friend or foe gives counsel. Let's be wise and pray about the counsel we receive; don't just act on impulse. It's always good to consult someone who loves and fears the Lord for counsel! As a matter of fact, the Bible tells us in Psalm Chapter 37, Verse 30: The godly offer good counsel; they teach right from wrong. That's the point – someone who is Heaven bound will try and get others on the same path; but keep in mind, the same is true for those who are Hell bound!

My wise caution: Better make sure it's good counsel! And since all good gifts come from God, without God, it can't be good! Someone may tell you to do something that will pacify your emotions temporarily, but what's the lasting effect? Seek first the kingdom of God and all His righteousness, then you will have all things added. (Matthew Chapter 6, Verse 33). Anyone who counsels you excluding God and godly principles is a threat to your eternal salvation! Please pray, pray and then pray; ask God to show you the way! Here's some really good counsel: Repent of your sins, allow God to lead, and then follow!

God bless you!

It's Because We Love.

God created us with love, sustains us through love, and saves us by love. So you see, we are designed by the Creator Himself to be walking, talking, love machines! Then why is it so hard for people to show love to their fellow man? The answer is clear: They are unlearned in the scriptures.

One Bible verse that convicts me when my flesh wants to be less loving is Ephesians Chapter 4, Verse 2: "Always be humble and gentle. Be patient with each other, making allowance for each other's faults because of your love." Gets me every time! I begin to remember the many times I sinned against God, and He forgave me when I repented.

We were created from love, so let's show love to all people! We were not created from hate; so why allow Satan to fill you up with hatred? It's because we love, we are able to smile the way we do and light up a room! Don't bring gloom to the room; light up the room with love! When people ask, "What's your secret?" Tell them with a smile that the love of God is in you, so you are sharing love with everyone! Hates may feel great, but love is greater! Choose to love, and live above!

God bless you!

Are You There Yet?

While on a road trip, we may often receive phone calls from concerned loved ones with this question: "Are you there yet?" Spiritually speaking we are all on a trip, but our journey has many stops. If you are on a journey to destruction, you can stop anywhere at any time and do anything. However if you are on a journey to Heaven, the first stop we make is at the foot of the cross to repent of our sins. The prophet, Isaiah, wrote this in Chapter 55, Verse 7: Let the wicked change their ways and banish the very thought of doing wrong. Let them turn to the Lord that He may have mercy on them. Yes, turn to our God, for He will forgive generously.

Are you there yet? Did you make the first stop at the foot of the cross, ask Jesus to come into your heart and forgive you of all your sins? Don't wait on this one, my friend; tomorrow has no guarantee! Recently I was told a tragic story about two young ladies, early twenties, who were invited to church. Out of respect to the one whom extended the invitation they did not oppose to going; but they went to a dance club that night. On their way back home, a head-on collision with another car claimed both their lives. Just remember: When we do anything, anytime, anywhere, the devil is there! Stay on the straight and narrow path; make it to Heaven where Jesus is!

God bless you!

What About You?

From the street to the workplace, we are always hearing of crimes and its victims. Then, popular questions I am often asked are, "Why me?" "What did I ever do to God?" In most cases God can ask these questions: "Why not you?" What have you done for me?

So – What about you, my friend? I love Psalm Chapter 75, Verse 9 which says, "But as for me, I will always proclaim what God has done; I will sing praises to the God of Jacob."

Are you doing your part in proclaiming the Good News about the Lord, Jesus Christ? Everyone can go to work and make a lot of money; but how many really go out there and win souls for the kingdom? It's a matter of priority; we each do what we deem important to us!

I pray this encouragement will spark the Holy Spirit Fire within you! When we get to Heaven, there's no one to minister to! Let's take the time and minister to others now! It's not only for the leaders of the church! All whom are a part of the family of Christ should be doing this! (Matthew 28:19) Once again; what about you?

God bless you!

God Said It, So He Will Do It!

People say things to us every day. Sometimes they even make promises that they are not able to keep. Not so with my God! He will fulfill all that He spoke to us through the prophets!

He says in Micah Chapter 5, Verse 2: "But you, O Bethlehem Ephrathah, are only a small village among all the people of Judah. Yet a ruler of Israel, whose origins are in the distant past, will come from you on my behalf." So said, so done! Jesus was born in Bethlehem of Judah. (Luke Chapter 2, Verses 4 through 7)

God gave you a vision, a mission or a promise that will be fulfilled; just believe Him and keep pressing! It is really dark in the valley of life but if we give up, we are stuck there; the only way out is to press on through! Trust God at His word, my friend! God said it, so He will do it! Don't lose hope and look to other gods that will not satisfy. Keep your eyes on Jesus, the one with the eternal master plan!

Though He may tarry, the God we serve will show up at the right time! Always remember our God works best in impossible situations, so there's no mistaken who gets the glory! He will do it for you!

God bless you!

Who Are You Serving?

Through the years my family and I have frequented many restaurants and have met many servers. Some are very pleasant and friendly, while some make you feel as if you're bothering them. As Christians we should never make someone feel that they are a bother, even if they are. We must pray for more patience, wisdom and discernment when dealing with human beings.

The art of serving others is beautiful when painted with serving God. Who are you serving? Jesus blew his disciples' minds with his statement in Mark Chapter 9, Verse 35: He sat down, called the twelve disciples over to him, and said, "Whoever wants to be first must take last place and be the servant of everyone else."

This should cause us to look at serving in a whole new light! Serving a wife, husband or child is routine, but what about a total stranger? How do we serve God by serving His people? The first thing we do is pray, and God will lead the way! A word of caution; Beware of the devil who will try to keep you super busy so you don't accomplish God's will! Let's put on the whole armor of God and serve others knowing that in the process, we are serving God.

God bless you!

The Secret of Success.

You may have heard the question asked: "What's the secret of your success?" There are many ways to address this question. One might say hard work and dedication. I agree with this statement but to be a little more specific, first we must define success. Does it mean being rich and miserable? Or, does it mean wealthy and peaceful?

For the secret to being wealthy, pay attention to Proverbs Chapter 11, Verses 24 through 25: Give freely and become more wealthy; be stingy and lose everything. The generous will prosper; those who refresh others will themselves be refreshed.

The secret: Be a giver! Keep in mind we can never out give God! Some will never give God a tithe of their income, so God will never entrust them with wealth. Some will see others in need, knowing they should assist as the Lord leads, but refuse to do so! The facts: These need to be addressed in order to enhance a life of success! Remember: If we do the same thing every day, we won't get a different result! God created us to enjoy great success in life! Dive into a life of Christ; give God glory with your generosity.

God bless you!

What Do You Live By?

Upon awakening, we start to think of all the things that need to be done for the day. I have to stop myself and say: "Hey; wait a minute – I need to pray and talk to God, in Jesus' name, first!" That's one of the things I live by. Everyone should examine themselves to see exactly what they live by, and make sure it lines up with the Word of God! The Bible tells us in Deuteronomy Chapter 8, Verse 3: "Yes, he humbled you by letting you go hungry and then feeding you with manna, a food previously unknown to you and your ancestors. He did it to teach you that people do not live by bread alone; rather, we live by every word that comes from the mouth of the Lord."

The ultimate lifestyle is following the Word of God! The Holy Spirit wrote the Bible, and He is the only one who knows the direction to Heaven! Let's live by His directions! I know you are smart, but not smart enough to make it to Heaven on your own! How much longer will it take for you to repent and start living by the Word of God? Hopefully, not much longer. Your business and fancy lifestyle I am not against; just make sure you put God first and everything else after. What we live by should be obvious to those around us!

God bless you!

Can You Truly Say, "I'm Golden"?

"I'm golden" is a term normally used when someone is doing way better than just "good" or "okay." However, the Holy Spirit wants us to look into "I'm golden" a bit deeper to see who is really "golden." Revelation Chapter 21, Verse 18 says, "The wall was made of jasper, and the city was pure gold, as clear as glass."

We who own a piece of heaven due to true salvation are the ones who are truly golden! Imagine... living in a city filled with gold! Until we get there, let's live that way now as children of God and citizens of Heaven! When you have plenty of money in your bank account to cover your bills, you are not stressed about it. The same is true for those of us who are living for Jesus! We have plenty of gold in our spiritual bank account, so we don't have to stress it!

You may not be as "golden" as you think you are. It all comes down to your relationship with the Lord, Jesus Christ. Some refuse to accept Him, and are fooled by the devil telling them, "God made you rich; you don't need Jesus!" My heart goes out to individuals who allow Satan to mold and fold them. I pray they would repent and be ready to walk on streets that are golden! Are you golden?

God bless you!

God's Love Should Bring You Back.

No one is perfect, I know that; but so many people have strayed away from the Lord and now find themselves in great misery! There is hope for the backslider, the lost, those who have missed their way; his name is Jesus! The children of Israel were the same way; rebellious backsliders, but God's love brought them back!

The Bible says this in Hosea Chapter 2, Verses 14 and 15: But then I will win her back once again. I will lead her into the desert and speak tenderly to her there. I will return her vineyards to her and transform the Valley of Trouble into a gateway of hope. She will give herself to me there, as she did long ago when she was young, when I freed her from her captivity in Egypt. (NLT)

Remember when you loved God with your whole heart? Now you just tolerate Him, but guess what? God's love never changed for you! Remember that today, and try not to sin against Him! Instead of running from Him, run to Him, the King of Kings! The world's love for us is conditional; let's choose the unconditional agape love of God. You are welcome back!

God bless you!

Thanks Again!

The best attitude is one of gratitude! When we show appreciation, it goes a long way! Most people are thankful when someone does or attempts to do something nice for them. When it's something really nice, we offer more thanks by way of a "thanks again!"

But how excited are we to give thanks when calamity strikes? When we lose a job or a loved one? It's a bit different now, I know, but it will definitely help with the healing process. The Bible says in 1 Thessalonians Chapter 5, Verse 18: Be thankful in all circumstances, for this is God's will for you who belong to Christ Jesus.

Not all circumstances are pleasant. I lost an aunt that was so dear to me. Glory be to God I can say, "Lord, thanks for blessing my life with her; the memories will never leave me. Thanks again, Lord, for her having known Jesus as Lord and Savior!"

In every tragic, painful circumstance, let us look for the opportunity to say, "Lord, thank you; and thanks again!

God bless you!

Let Us Be Demon Free!

So many people we come in contact with are loaded with demons! They range from lost demons to cursive demons; angry demons to lying demons. Using spiritual eyes and ears, you'll be able to spot them. Although born-again believers cannot be possessed by a demon, demons can still influence us if we allow them to. Here's one clue that we can use to prove that we are demon free. The Bible says this in John Chapter 8, Verses 48 and 49: The people retorted, "You Samaritan devil! Didn't we say all along that you were possessed by a demon?" "No," Jesus said, "I have no demon in me. For I honor my father – and you dishonor me…"

When we honor the Father, we cannot honor Satan at the same time. To honor Him means we obey His commands and be about His business! We've all heard the saying, "The devil finds work for idle hands." I have to agree with that statement. Let us be demon free by staying busy about the Lord's business! Put on the whole armor of God, and resist those demons when they try to penetrate! The devil will try, but don't give him a blithe; trust the Most High, who will take us to the sky!

Who the Son sets free, is free indeed!

God bless you!

Don't Let Your Thirst Be For The Worst!

Every day we thirst; some more than others but, nonetheless, we thirst. For water, juice, iced tea or for what I feel is the worst – soda! Soda is loaded with sugar, but many people don't care because it tastes so good!

That's the basis of thirst; we desire something that tastes good to quench it. Some people long for a marriage relationship or a child; and so they settle for someone ungodly to quench that thirst. Drinking salty water from the ocean won't quench your thirst; from what I hear, it only makes you thirst even more! The same is true when we expect someone or something to quench what only God can! Psalm Chapter 42, Verses 1 and 2 say, "As the deer longs for streams of water, so I long for you, O God. I thirst for God, the living God. When can I go and stand before Him?"

The writer of this Psalm is thirsty for the best! Anything or anyone else is the worse! It is quite alright to desire great things in life, but if you don't desire the greatest first, you won't quench your thirst! Distractions will come and go! Keep your eyes stayed on Jesus, your hearts pure and thirst only for Him! The best thirst quencher is the Almighty Father!

God bless you!

Keep On Asking God!

We sometimes sound like a scratched record when it comes to praying, but that's okay; it sure beats asking someone who is not able to help for assistance. Glory to God, we have a Heavenly Father whom never gets tired of us asking Him for things. Keep in mind that the things we pray for that glorify God get first priority!

Jesus encourages us in Luke Chapter 11, Verses 9 and 10 by saying: And so I tell you, keep on asking, and you will receive what you ask for. Keep on seeking, and you will find. Keep on knocking, and the door will be opened to you. For everyone who asks, receives. Everyone who seeks, finds. And to everyone who knocks, the door will be opened.

I truly believe God's Word with all my heart, especially after seeing so many miracles! Jesus encourages us in this area of scripture to pray without ceasing because every day we have needs. Some people don't pray due to guilt from sinful activity. My friend, that's when you need to pray! Don't allow the devil to convince you NOT to ask God for help! God is our hope, help, strength, peace and joy! Start asking Him! Or continue asking until you get your blessing! God hears our prayers and answers in His timing, so keep asking!

God bless you!

God's Special Favor Awaits Those Whom Are Ready!

Crystal Lewis has a song entitled, "People Get Ready, Jesus Is Coming." The song also contains the following verse: "Soon We Will Be Going Home!" I love that song but I would change "Get Ready" to "Be ready!"

Jesus says this in Luke Chapter 12, Verses 35 through 38: "Be dressed for service and well prepared, as though you were waiting for your master to return from the wedding feast. Then you will be ready to open the door and let him in the moment he arrives and knocks. There will be special favor for those who are ready and waiting for his return. I tell you, he himself will seat them, put on an apron, and serve them as they sit and eat! He may come in the middle of the night or just before dawn. But whenever he comes, there will be special favor for his servants who are ready!"

We often talk about staying ready for the rapture – to go and be with Jesus, so stay ready! This wonderful reminder is the most important of reminders, so keep it on your daily calendar! Being ready for sporting events and vacations may not always work out in our favor but when we see Jesus in a favorable manor, we will be in a glorious state! Don't hesitate or drag your feet in ths matter, get rid of sin and live for the King of kings!

God bless you!

I Won't Complain.

Complain. We've all done it in one form or another. "It's too hot out." "It's too cold out." From great issues, to smaller ones I am sure we can all look back and plead guilty to complaining. Here are some scriptures to help us when we feel the need to complain: Philippians Chapter 2, Verses 14 and 15 say, "Do everything without complaining and arguing, so that no one can criticize you." "Live clean, innocent lives as children of God, shining like bright lights in a world full of crooked and perverse people."

I told someone recently that I try to live my life seeking solutions rather than complaining about the problems. I have learned over the years that complaining destroys marriage relationships, friendships and even got people fired from places of employment! So you see, this complaining thing is something that needs to be addressed! I saw a sticker in an office that read, "The complaint department is closed!" Another one read, "Don't mention the problem without your suggestions to solve it."

Here's a task for us all; let's personalize this phrase "I won't complain!" Don't just say it like you mean it, LIVE IT! Congratulations, my friend! You have made the first step to a way better tomorrow! Shine your light, and others will follow your lead!

God bless you!

The Importance Of Prayer.

Prayer changes things. God hears our prayers. When we pray, demons go away. So why don't more people take this serious? The reasons are clear, so let me share. (1) Many people are ungrateful to God. They neglect to thank God for food, clothes, homes, cars or even waking them up in the morning. (2) People are selfish. They refuse to talk to God when they can waste time on social media. They read other books and ignore the Bible. They watch TV until the TV starts watching them sleep, and play video games until the wee hours of the morning.

So, what about prayer? Good, undistrubed quality time in prayer? The Bible says this in Colossians Chapter 4, Verse 2: "Devote yourselves to prayer with an alert mind and a thankful heart."

Just as we devote ourselves to all these other activities, please devote some daily time in prayer when awake and alert! Satan is good at creating distractions, but God can keep us focused if we are in constant prayer! Don't allow the enemy to feed and lead; devote yourself to prayer and spiritually succeed!

God bless you!

Not Accepted.

Everyone wants to be in good standing – physically, emotionally, financially… It's a good way to be! But it cannot be obtained with a bad attitude or the wrong attitude. There are formulas for things in life that must be implemented in order to activate success. For instance: Someone trying to pay with food stamps in a clothing store. That person would hear: "Not accepted." This does not line up with the formula or procedure to buy clothes.

There's also a formula to being blessed by God. Deuteronomy Chapter 28, Verse 13 says: "If you listen to these commands of the Lord your God that I am giving you today, and if you carefully obey them, the Lord will make you the head and not the tail, and you will always be on top and never at the bottom."

Please keep His word in your heart, soul and mind! With God, we win! We will have whatever we need to proceed! You can take Him at His word! However when we're not truly living for Him, we can expect to hear "not accepted" more frequently and in many areas of our lives and ultimately at the Great White Throne Judgment! Don't allow things that should not be accepted into your life cause you to be "Not Accepted" by Christ!

God bless you!

Well Done; Let's Save Some More!

Last year our evangelism team spoke to strangers in stores, banks, everywhere they could – and invited them to come and hear God's Word. Many of those individuals gave their lives to Jesus! To that I say, "Well done! Now, let's save some more!" Jesus encourages us to stay busy in the fields to bring God glory. Let's look at His response to a servant who invested five bags of silver and turned it into ten. Matthew Chapter 25, Verse 21 says, "The master was full of praise. 'Well done, my good and faithful servant. You have been faithful in handling this small amount, so now I will give you many more responsibilities. Let's celebrate together!'"

There's a celebration in Heaven when we direct a lost soul to the Kingdom of God! Yes, Heaven celebrates whenever we're victorious over attacks and tough circumstances, but not quite as much as when a lost soul is saved! True believers will hear Him say, "Well done!" when we see him face-to-face! However now is the time to have Him say, "Well done" in the spirit as we encourage others to get with it!

Don't wait to hear, "Well done" when you can hear it now! Then Jesus will add, "Well done, my good and faithful servant; enter into my rest!

God bless you!

Do We Pursue Godliness Or Just Tolerate It?

Godliness is not just a word, it's a lifestyle! For some, it's a part-time endeavor to quench a guilty conscience. For others, it's talked about but not pursued. But for a few, the pursuit of godliness is a daily thing. Why should we go out of our way to be Godly? For starters, the Bible tells us this in Proverbs Chapter 15, Verse 9: "The Lord detests the way of the wicked, but He loves those who pursue godliness."

In order for God to be pleased with our ways, we must pursue Godliness! Sure – we can ignore this, but keep in mind that God can't bless a mess! Many people just tolerate Godliness in church or from a husband, wife or child, but don't pursue for themselves! Everyone is responsible for their own actions, so don't blame anyone if you end up spending eternity separated from God!

If you plan to spend forever with the King of Kings and the Lord of Lords, then you must start now! Jesus did what God, the Father, requested of Him; we who are pursuing godliness will do the same! You cannot fake it 'til you make it spiritually, because you won't make it! Be real with God and pursue godliness; then you will be pleasing in His sight and be alright!

God bless you!

Whats In Your Mouth?

You may have heard the Capital One commercial that asks, "What's in your wallet?" It makes me think of a few more things which are of greater value to me: "What's in my heart?" And, "What's in my mouth?" As the spirit of God leads, let's take a look at Psalm Chapter 113, Verses 1 to 3: "Praise the Lord! Yes, give praise, O' servants of the Lord. Blessed be the name of the Lord, now and forever. Everywhere -- from East to West -- praise the name of the Lord."

What's in your mouth? Praises to God or curses for your fellow man? We choose each day what we do and say, so let's make good choices! The devil is busy trying to get us off track; he wants as many people who are willing to join him in Hell. The tongue is a flame of fire; watch what you say! The best way to not curse others and yourself in the process is to constantly praise God! When we praise God, it brings blessings forth for ourselves and others! We reap what we sow, and what we say will either bless us or curse us; choose wisely!

God bless you!

To Live And Not Die We Love And Not Die.

People are good at being bad. You know what I mean; they always find all the wrong things to do or say to make us upset. Some people take it a step further and become a known enemy to us. One of the worst things someone can say to us is, "I hate you." How do we handle that in a Christian manner? The answer is this: We love them! Don't write me off as being crazy before you see what Jesus says in Matthew Chapter 5, Verses 43 to 45: "You have heard the law that says, 'Love your neighbor' and hate your enemy. But I say, love your enemies! Pray for those who persecute you! In that way, you will be acting as true children of your Father in Heaven. For He gives His sunlight to both the evil and the good, and He sends rain on the just and the unjust alike.

Keep in mind that the goal is to live and not die, so when we love we will not die spiritually. If the Holy Spirit is not living in us we do not have the agape love, so without Jesus we don't stand a chance!

Reach deep down in your heart, search for love and start distributing to everyone, whether good or bad! When we live like children of Heaven on Earth, we will be welcomed to Heaven after Earth! Let's live in love forever and not die!

God bless you!

What Are You Looking Forward To?

We look forward to many things during the course of a year, month, week, day, even hour! There's nothing wrong with looking forward, once you are looking forward to the right things! What are the right things, one might ask?

The Bible tells us this in First Peter Chapter 1, Verse 13: So think clearly and exercise self-control. Look forward to the gracious salvation that will come to you when Jesus Christ is revealed to the world.

I can look forward to a vacation, but not more than my salvation in Christ Jesus! It all comes down to priorities. Are we making God a priority or not? Every day is an opportunity for great success through Christ Jesus! Let's capitalize on that by putting Him first! This world is full of distractions; don't get trapped by them! Keep your eyes on Jesus, and look forward to Heaven! This is the formula for winning daily! Your love and patience will increase! More God equals more joy, peace and prosperity! Now that is worth looking forward to, from now unto eternity!

God bless you!

I Can't Believe It; There Is No Charge!

Ever received a gift so spectacular, rare and expensive that you felt you should pay something for it? Then the giver says, "There's no charge; it's free!" The best gift I've received is the Holy Spirit living in me, guaranteeing that I make it to Heaven! For those who have Him, we know that we could never have afforded to buy Him; thankfully, Jesus paid it all! This gift is not a reward for following the law or performing any other organized religious activity. As a matter of fact, the Bible says this in Galatians Chapter 3, Verses 13 and 14: But Christ has rescued us from the curse pronounced by the law. When he was hung on the cross, He took upon himself the curse for our wrongdoing. For it is written in the Scriptures, "Cursed is everyone who is hung on a tree." Through Christ Jesus, God has blessed the Gentiles with the same blessing he promised to Abraham, so that we who are believers might receive the promised Holy Spirit through faith.

You can't pay $100 or $1,000; it's through faith, not by financial purchase! Those of us who are truly living with the Holy Spirit within are the most powerful people on the planet! I still can't believe it; there is no charge for that! What an awesome God we serve, who makes it easy for us to go to Heaven! You may or may not be able to afford a Super Bowl ticket, but a ticket to Heaven is absolutely free for you and me! Receive your free gift today!

God bless you!

Are You Excited About Heaven?

I remember during my "B.C." days (Before Christ), I looked forward to the weekends for the parties! Now, I look forward to going to church and being around my forever family! You heard right; forever family. If you don't enjoy being around your church family, how excited are you about heaven? Every time we go to church, we experience a little piece of Heaven! The psalmist wrote this in Psalm Chapter 84, Verses 1 and 2: How lovely is your dwelling place, O Lord of Heaven's Armies. I long, yes, I faint with longing to enter the courts of the Lord. With my whole being, body and soul, I will shout joyfully to the Living God.

Do you feel the same way about going to church? If you don't, then you definitely don't feel the same way about Heaven! Keep in mind that we, the true followers of Christ, are the church! If others are faking it, let us lovingly show them a better way to live! Let's shine our light so more people can become the church; the church is the future heaven! Get excited about Heaven by living a life on Earth that points people to Heaven! God will see you and reward you accordingly. Are you excited about Heaven yet? You should be!

God bless you!

Part Angel, Part Devil.

While walking in the mall I saw the back of a t-shirt that sparked my attention. It read part Angel part devil. If that wasn't bad enough, the person wearing the shirt was a little girl about 10 years old. Her father was standing next to her and I wanted to say something to him but the Lord said not to. None the less the I need to this statement is this, if someone is parked devil they are full devil. You can't be lukewarm, we are either hot for Jesus or not for Jesus. Jesus says this in Revelation chapter 3 verse 16 but since you are like lukewarm water neither hot nor cold I will spit you out of my mouth. So don't be part Angel part devil, that's in an eternal death sentence. Whatever devilish actions in your life that you can pinpoint and rectify, start today. Repent of your devilish ways and start being a full angel. I know we are not perfect but we keep striving for protect for perfection. Most people are not even trying, but we who know better to do better. So start being the angel you were created to be today, give Satan a pink slip, yes fire the devil. The devil is not going to heaven and everyone who follows his ways won't either. Follow Jesus and be an angel!

God bless you!

Stormy Life? Invite Christ!

The storms of life are raging, we can make a list. Maritial issues, health issues, financial issues you name it. For many who live without true salvation, it can get so scary that they even commit suicide. People living without God have no bedrock to stand on just slippery ground.

My Advice for those outside of salvation and facing a stormy life is this, invite Christ into your hearts today and don't delay. The disciples were on a boat with Jesus and it got stormy while Jesus was asleep, but they knew who to run to. In Matthew 8:25-26 He says "The disciples went and woke him up, shouting, Lord save us! We're going to drown!! Jesus responded, why are you afraid? You have so little faith! Then He got up and rebuked the wind and the waves and suddenly there was a great calm."

We who follow Jesus The Prince of Peace can live each day in peace. We know that God will heal, provide, fix our marriages, straighten out our children etc. Don't allow fear from Satan to remove your eyes from Jesus, stay focused on the Lord.

God bless you!

Looking For Help In All The Wrong Places!

It's a regular issue mankind is faced with; from the least to the greatest. The issue? Looking for help in all the wrong places! Here are a few examples: Calling an electrician to fix a leaky faucet; Visiting your dentist to fix the pain in your knee! Although both electricians and plumbers are trades personnel, they have specific skills. Although dentists are doctors, they don't specialize in repairing knees. Nonetheless, people are quick to call on family members or employers for help, ignoring the King of Kings!

I love what David says in Psalm Chapter 121, Verses 1 and 2: "I look up to the mountains - does my help come from there? My help comes from the Lord, who made Heaven and Earth!" It amazes me how many people ignore a right relationship with God and, yet, complain every day! Getting the right help starts with going to the right source! His name is Jesus! Now is the time to run to Him for help! Stop complaining, and start praising! You will get help and find rest for your soul! Don't beat up yourself for looking elsewhere first; now you know better, so do better! Seek first the Kingdom of God and all His righteousness, and everything else will be added! (Matthew Chapter 6, Verse 33). Ask yourself this question: Whom am I really looking to for help? If it is not God, make some changes! God is willing to help those who look to Him for help!

God bless you!

We Have Authority Over The Enemy

How many times have you heard this phrase, "the devil made me do it." Without a doubt the devil convinces people to sin against God, so be on your guard. Any individual without true salvation will be a puppet for the devil to play with. Listening to an interview with Nicholas Cruz the shooter of the Marjorie Stoneman Douglas High School in Parkland Florida was sad. One thing he said was the absolute truth, and I quote. "The devil told me how to do it." If this young man was brought up in church and have true salvation he would know that we have authority over the enemy Satan. Jesus says this in Luke 10:19 "Look I have given you authority over all the power of the enemy, and you can walk among snakes and scorpions and crush them. Nothing will injure you." Jesus didn't say He gives us authority over some of the enemy's power, no but over all the enemy's power! These are the things we need to remember when faced with the choice to sin against God or not. Stop blaming the devil, repent of your sins and get saved for real, then live for Jesus.Take authority over the evil thoughts and desires, rebuke them and God will take you higher. We will either take authority over the devil or give him authority over us, we choose.

God bless you!

It's Less Stressful To Just Believe The Word.

All these modern day religions and trying to prove God does not exist is taking the world in a downward spiral of darkness. The atheist groups are growing by the day. In some areas more rapid than believers in Christ Jesus! The problem is they spend a lot of energy to fill an inner peace position that only God can fill.

What's the solution to the matter, one might ask? It's less stressful to just believe the word. The Bible tells us in Genesis Chapter 1, Verse 1 that "In the beginning God created the Heavens and the Earth."

The wise person would build on that foundation, while the foolish person rejects it. The main reason why people fail to believe is because they don't want to play by the rules! However, we need to realize that everything in life has rules from driving on the roadways to going to school, work or play. Why not just accept what the word of God is saying? The only savior of our souls is the Lord Jesus Christ! Repent of your sins today after you believe, and ask the Holy Spirit to lead and guide you! Don't invite stressing – invite a blessing!

God bless you!

Are You A Member of the House?

The U.S. House of Representatives has 435 members. They are known as law makers. These representatives make decisions on health care, housing, transportation, agriculture – you name it! Once they approve a bill, it is the law. Christians whom are truly saved belong to a different kind of house. We are a representative of God's house!

The Bible says this in Colossians Chapter 3, Verse 17: And whatever you do or say, do it as a representative of the Lord Jesus, giving thanks through Him to God the Father.

Clearly, I am not talking about a specific church facility but the church of Jesus Christ! Are you a member of the House? You can answer that question by the way you live. Your actions, your speech and your thought process will let you know. I am not coming down on you for not being a member, but Jesus won't come down for you if you remain that way. What should you do? Repent of your sins! Live in peace, knowing that you are a member in God's House of Representatives! We may not be Congress, but Christians are the congregation of holiness!

God bless you!

Oh, That Day Is Coming!

We all have days we look forward to. For some it's Sundays and Thursdays in church. I don't particularly look forward to Monday mornings the same way.

Daily activities, however, should never take away who you are in Christ. Although we're living in Babylon, please remember that we belong to God! We need to stay unspotted from this world, because one day will be judgment day!

The Bible says this in Isaiah Chapter 13, Verse 19: "Babylon, the most glorious of kingdoms, the flower of Chaldean pride, will be devastated like Sodom and Gomorrah when God destroyed them."

If you didn't know this fact, you better believe that day is coming! Some folks care about what will happen but most people who read this information couldn't care less! Be among the wise – utilize this information by changing the way you think and act! Turn to Jesus as your Lord and Savior! In doing so, you will make friends with the judge of the universe! Now that's what I call smart! Oh that judgment day is coming! Will you be ready? Be ready and stay ready for that day!

God bless you!

More Desirable Than Gold.

Everyone has desires – that's a fact. If you've never left the state or country you were born in, you may desire to travel. If you're incarcerated, you may desire to be free and if you're lacking in finances, you desire money. All our desires are possible once we are in God's will! The remedy is to desire a right relationship with God first and fall in love with His Word.

The Bible says this in Psalm Chapter 19, Verses 9 and 10: Reverence for the Lord is pure, lasting forever. The laws of the Lord are true; each one is fair. They are more desirable than gold, even the finest gold. They are sweeter than honey, even honey dripping from the comb." Let's be honest with ourselves and recognize where our desire for God's word is and work on it. I say, "work on it" because everyone has room to go deeper in the Word. We all sing "I love you, Lord" but God is more impressed by our actions!

Trade some TV time for reading the Word! Trade some computer or phone time for reading the Word! Only by practice can we be made near perfect and then, like David, desire God's Word more than gold. Money and gold will come and go, but God's Word will stand forever! Choose well!

God bless you!

It's A Matter Of Perspective.

When faced with trials the Christian may ask, "Where are you, God?" Some believe hardships will never come your way once you are "walking with the Lord." Here is a little twist on things: Don't you think God allows hardships so He can (1) test our allegiance to Him; and (2) help someone who may be in the same difficult state that you are in to become saved? Let us learn a lesson from the Apostle Paul who wrote this in Philippians Chapter 1, Verses 12 through 14: And I want you to know, my dear brothers and sisters, that everything that has happened to me here has helped to spread the Good News. For everyone here, including the whole palace guard, knows that I am in chains because of Christ. And because of my imprisonment, most of the believers here have gained confidence and boldly speak God's message without fear.

So you see, it's a matter of perspective! Let us be content in whatever state we are in, knowing that our Heavenly Father allows us to be there for a season. Pray and ask Him to reveal to you the purpose for your being in a hardship state. Be it physical, emotional, monetary or otherwise, there is a reason behind it to give glory to God! Don't complain; change your perspective and praise His name! The God we serve on top of the mountain is the same God we should serve in the valley!

God bless you!

You Can't Save The Date.

Weddings and parties take a lot of planning and preparation. Party and wedding planners often times send out a "save the date" card which is followed by the invitation.

The spirit of God tells us that the Lord will come like a thief in the night, when people are not expecting so we can't save the date! What can we do to be ready? The Bible says this in Matthew Chapter 24, Verse 42: So you, too, must keep watch! For you don't know what day your Lord is coming.

There you have it. Keep watch! "Keep watch of what?" one might ask. Your every action! Everything we say and do is recorded in the books of Heaven, so be mindful and watch what you say and do. Don't be so relaxed that you miss the opportunity to repent of your sin. You can't "save the date" for the rapture nor can we save the date of someone's death. Let us "save the place" since we can't "save the date". Choose Heaven as the place by the way you live; your only other option is a place called hell. Keep watch, my friends. This is one area you don't want to slack off in! God sets the dates and the times; live for Him and don't worry about a thing!

God bless you!

Hater, Murderer, Same Thing...

The words "hate" and "hater" are thrown around rather loosely these days. This is sad. We are called to love – even our enemies, because love and hate cannot occupy the same heart.

So to all the so-called "haters" out there, this is what the Bible says in 1John Chapter3, Verse15: "Anyone who hates another brother or sister is really a murderer at heart. And you know that murderers don't have eternal life within them."

Stop the hate and murder! Show love. Eternal life is at stake here! No matter what your emotions tell you, the word of God is greater! So, because the word tells us to love, let us love and fire Satan by giving him a pink slip. He is the promoter of hate spreading like wildfire throughout today's younger generation.

Spread this Good News of Christ in order to change the way people look at things. If each of us does our part, there will be a lot less murderers among us! Don't hate and murder; elevate and nurture!

God bless you!

Stop The Curse By Not Cursing Back!

Some folks are quick on the draw with the tongue! They blaze and the recipient returns the favor. If you even appear to come at them, just in case they'll aim to get you first! We can all learn a lesson from David with regard to retaliation to cursing. 2 Samuel Chapter 16, Verses 5, 6, 11 and 12 read: "As King David came to Bahurim, a man came out of the village cursing them. It was Shimei son of Gera, from the same clan as Saul's family. He threw stones at the king and the king's officers and all the mighty warriors who surrounded him." "Then David said to Abishai and to all his servants, "My own son is trying to kill me. Doesn't this relative of Saul have even more reason to do so? Leave him alone and let him curse, for the Lord has told him to do it. And perhaps the Lord will see that I am being wronged and will bless me because of these curses today." It's hard to bridle your tongue when you are being cursed out. However keep in mind that in order to benefit from it, we need to bless those who curse us. David saved Shemei's life although he was cursing and throwing stones at the king. People may curse us because of our faith and throw stones at King Jesus, but keep on blessing them! If you harbor a few unholy choice words, ditch them and upgrade your vocabulary to one of holiness! You don't have to retaliate – show love and bless them, which will elevate!

God bless you!

Please Lord, Just One More Second!

Imagine with me: Someone dies an unnatural death – for example, gunshot wound or car accident. Then request to return to the natural life to repent...upon which they would hear, Request Denied." I guarantee – many have made that request and received the same answer.

The Bible tells us this in Isaiah Chapter 38, Verse 18: For the dead cannot praise you; they cannot raise their voices in praise. Those who go down to the grave can no longer hope in your faithfulness.

Just a friendly reminder: We're unable to say, "Please Lord, just one more second" after we die! The time to get it right is now! Not tomorrow or next week! That day may come after your exit! 176,000 died yesterday and will die today, so it is only by God's grace why we are still standing! Get connected to Jesus Christ, repent of your sins and live for Him! That is the only way to stay ready for the next life to come! Don't believe the comedians who'll tell you there is no afterlife. They're in for a rude awakening! They will be asking for just one more second to repent! Good advice: Take a second now to consider what I'm saying so you won't have to ask Jesus for a second later!

God bless you!

No Need To Fear, But Be Aware Of The Plagues That Are Near!

When we hear of an outbreak of plague, the first thing one does is try and figure out how to avoid it! We'd relocate to another country if possible, wouldn't we? So why is it that so many people underestimate, or should I say "take lightly," the plague of sin? The problem is this: most people don't know they are living with a plague, so they ignore their sinful ways! However when the Holy Spirit is upon us, we see sin for what it is and do our best to keep sin outside of our homes!

The Bible says this in Psalm Chapter 91, Verses 9 and 10: "If you make the Lord your refuge, if you make the Most High your shelter, no evil will conquer you; no plague will come near your home." Whether the plague is a physical or spiritual one, it cannot and will not penetrate a true man or woman of God! The wages of sin is death. Don't allow a plague to kill you! Repent of your sins today! Turn to God and follow His lead! When you receive salvation, fear caused by sin will leave you! Whom the Son sets free is free indeed, but whoever continues to sin is a slave to sin! Sin is a stain that messes with your brain, causes you pain, and then flushes you down the drain!

God bless you!

No American Idols.

Idol worshipping is in its full extreme in America today. "Gods" are created from just about anything – for instance our homes, cars, jobs, money and relationships. While these things are necessary, we should not idolize them! Some people have tiny Buddha dolls or little Hindu elephants they pray to. These things are very, very dangerous! Believe it or not, they will prevent you from the blessing of the Lord!

The Bible says this in 2 Chronicles Chapter 14, Verses 5 and 6: "Asa also removed the pagan shrines, as well as the incense altars from every one of Judah's towns. So Asa's kingdom enjoyed a period of peace. During those peaceful years, he was able to build up the fortified towns throughout Judah. No one tried to make war against him at this time, for the Lord was giving him rest from his enemies." When King Asa did what was pleasing in God's eyes and got rid of the idols in Judah, the country was exceedingly blessed and had peace! We, in America, should rid ourselves of idols as well. Let there be no American idols, or in other words, nothing that we worship other than God! Let's apply King Asa's principle and expect blessings! Live without idols; live in peace! Live with idols; live in pieces. You choose!

God bless you!

The Right Sermon.

We've heard it said many times: "Actions speak louder than words." This is a true statement dating back to Bible days. John the Baptist was baptizing people in the Jordan River after they repented of their sins, but then he got upset with some religious folks. Matthew Chapter 3, Verses 7 through 10 say: "But when he saw many Pharisees and Sadducees coming to watch him baptize, he denounced them. "You brood of snakes!" he exclaimed. "Who warned you to flee God's coming wrath? Prove by the way you live that you have repented of your sins and turned to God. Don't just say to each other 'We're safe, for we are descendents of Abraham.' That means nothing, for I tell you, God can create children of Abraham from these very stones. Even now the ax of God's judgment is poised, ready to sever the roots of the trees. Yes, every tree that does not produce good fruit will be chopped down and thrown into the fire.

Talk about a sermon! If repentance is not a part of the sermon you preach or the life you live, you are living and preaching the wrong things! Start living and preaching the right sermon, before one is conducted OVER YOU!

God bless you!

Don't Be The Spiritual Undertaker Or His Customer.

For centuries people always come up with excuses on why they can't serve the Lord: "I have studying to do..." "Sunday's the only day I have for sleep..." "I have to find my run away dog..." Lately, the Lord has been impressing on my heart that Christians need to do more! We are being outdone vocally, and it seems evil is winning more people everyday than good!

How do we fix it? Each Bible believing Christian should pray and ask the Lord what it is we should be doing instead of finding an excuse not to serve. Matthew Chapter 8, Verses 21 and 22 say: Another of his disciples said, "Lord, first let me return home and bury my father." But Jesus told him, "Follow me now. Let the spiritually dead bury their own dead."

My encouragement is this: Don't be the spiritual undertaker or his customer! If you are not saved, you are the customer – spiritually dead. As the undertaker you may or may not be saved, but Jesus wants us to retire that position and move on. Some people will drain the life out of you. Sometimes they are sent by the devil to distract us from our purpose. Let's get in gear and change the atmosphere by following Jesus who witnessed to those who are far and the ones who are near!

God bless you!

The Obvious Victory.

Many Christians I've spoken with are often times living a less than victorious life for one reason or another. It's easy to become discouraged when our will fails after repeatedly asking God to make it a success. Take heart and realize that those following Jesus automatically have the victory because Jesus overcame the challenges of this world!

The Bible says this in John Chapter 16, Verse 33: "I have told you all this so that you may have peace in me. Here on earth you will have many trials and sorrows. But take heart, because I have overcome the world."

Victory is ours because we are saved – period! When Jesus died on the cross for our sins and was raised from the dead on the third day, He showed the watching world who has the obvious victory!

So let's lift up our heads and remember who we are in Christ Jesus! We are the resurrected of the Lord! We died with Him and were raised to new life as He was! The next step – stay on the straight and narrow path which will lead us to Heaven, the last accomplishment in our mortal lives. Losing tiny battles may hurt, but remembering that we win the war confirms our overall victory!!

God bless you!

God Will Turn Us When We Are Ready.

Often times people say, "I can't stop..." doing this or that... They have an addiction that keeps getting the better of them, or an attitude that is negative or rude. The fact of the matter is this: We cannot change ourselves – only God can! We may quit for a season, but find ourselves back into the same addiction after a while. So; what's the issue? Why doesn't God turn us away from our addictions? The answer is this: God sees our hearts and won't help rid us our issues until we really want to! When we're sick and tired of being sick and tired, then pray and ask God for help; then He will help us!

The Bible says this in Psalm Chapter 80, Verse 3: "Turn us again to yourself, O God. Make your face shine down upon us. Only then will we be saved." The very first step in problem solving is to recognize the problem. Ask yourself, "What are the struggles in my life?" Adultery? Fornication? Anger issues? Crack cocaine? Alcohol? Pills? These are just a few of the issues God is able to turn us from! The only prerequisite is to call on Jesus, and ask Him for help! Do it with a sincere heart, and He will turn you toward Him and grant you true salvation! Turn today! Don't delay!

God bless you!

The Other Side of God.

It is very popular among people that God is Love. While this is a very true statement, often times we forget that there is another side of God. God is also a disciplinarian. Don't get it twisted; He will only put up with foolishness for a little while giving us a chance to repent. After that, it's hell to pay.

Here is a declaration from the Lord regarding his favorite people of Judah in Jerusalem. Isaiah Chapter 3, Verses 8 through 9 say: "For Jerusalem will stumble, and Judah will fall, because they speak out against the Lord and refuse to obey Him. They provoke Him to His face. The very look on their faces gives them away. They display their sin like the people of Sodom and don't even try to hide it. They are doomed! They have brought destruction upon themselves."

Lately, many are provoking God to His face. They lie, steal, talk bad about others and God. Some say they don't believe in The One who created them and keeps them alive. How much longer before you experience The Other Side of God? I encourage you – repent today! Turn to God while the turning is good! Tomorrow may be too late! Some people are warned many times, but many people only get one warning. Try never to experience The Other Side of God!

God bless you!

How Is Your Work Coming Along?

A very popular question in casual conversation is "how is work treating you?" Often times the reply is "not so good I am looking for another one." Spiritually speaking though, the question God asks is this "how well are you treating your work?" It is a matter of perspective based on what the Bible says in Luke 13:24 "Work hard to enter the narrow door to Gods Kingdom, for many will try to enter but will fail. When the master of the house has locked the door, it will be too late. You will stand outside knocking and pleading, Lord, open the door for us! But He will say, I don't know you or where you come from." Don't confuse working to enter through the narrow gate with obtaining salvation. To believe in your heart that Jesus is Lord and to confess with your mouth the same is what saves you. After salvation comes daily positive actions such as killing the flesh, forgiving others, stopping our cursing and lying just to name a few. When God see our improvement in these and other areas it proves to Him that we are on the straight and narrow road. Notice I didn't mention church cleaning and other volunteer work in the churches. These you get rewarded for in heaven providing you make it in, so stay on the straight and narrow. So in essence our work is more spiritual rather than physical. So now, how is your work coming? Don't allow physical work to drown out the spiritual. Work well!!

God bless you!

Is It Safe Now?

It's very interesting to watch those guys from the local power company work on live electrical wire. The fact that one mistake can cost someone their very life makes you pray for them. They use rubber shielding over the wires for safety. They wear helmets, rubber gloves and goggles. Their main goal is safety.

I can't help but look at my own spiritual walk and ask, "Is it safe now?" Many times believers stray from the faith even while hanging out at church! We must stay close to God, the Father, and the Lord Jesus Christ because He is the only one that can truly make us safe! The Bible says in Psalm Chapter 121, Verses 7 and 8: The Lord keeps you from all harm and watches over your life. The Lord keeps watch over you as you come and go, both now and forever."

Whether it's physical or spiritual safety, only God can truly ensure it! Don't trust your money, common sense, alliances, alarm system or bodyguard for safety – trust God! After surrendering to His will for your life you can truthfully say like this humble servant: "Yes; it is safe now!" Heaven awaits those who are safe in the presence of God! All are welcome! Are you safe?

God bless you!

Undercover Wicked.

Upon hearing that an individual is "wicked' one might automatically associate that person with violent or spiteful actions. While this may be true there is also a very large percentage of this world who are actually undercover wicked.

Allow me to explain. There are people who are kind to everyone, pleasant to be around, repay their debts on time, etc. However, they lack a right relationship with God because they don't seek Him! The Bible says this in Psalm Chapter10, Verses 4 and 5: "The wicked are too proud to seek God. They seem to think that God is dead. Yet they succeed in everything they do. They do not see your punishment awaiting them..."

The one who lives life separated from God is wicked! The only way to get to the Father is through the Son, Jesus Christ! Please consider your actions, conversations, and very important – whom you receive instructions from! My advice: Read the Word of God for yourself, study to show yourself approved and draw close to God! We were created to worship and serve the true God, but if we fail we automatically worship the God of this world, Satan! Those are the two choices we have. Don't be an Undercover Wicked! Get connected to God!

God bless you!

Go And Tell It Everywhere.

People love to talk, so why not talk about something worthwhile? Gossip is prevalent in churches when it shouldn't be. Let's find something other than gossip and negativity to discuss. How about the Word of God? There are many wonderful things to discuss that would be far more beneficial than useless chatter! The Bible encourages us in Psalm Chapter 34, Verse 3. It says, "Come, let us tell of the Lord's greatness; let us exalt his name together." (NLT)

I am sure if we looked back over our lives we could make a list of many great things God has done for us! How about sharing that list with others? Our testimony builds the faith of others, so start telling! The eyes of the Lord roam to and fro looking for obedient people to bless! Jesus instructs us to get this gospel out! Use your resources: Facebook, Ttwitter, text, email, a phone call or person to person! The faster we accept this mission, the greater the chances of our friends, loved ones and even strangers being saved!

This life is not about us! It's all about Jesus! Let Him have His way in speaking through you because believe me when I tell you: YOU have something good to say!

God bless you!

The Biblical Road Less Travelled.

Every once in a while we have to look forward in the word of God to see what we can expect. It's not really a major concern for the redeemed; more like a friendly reminder to stay on the straight and narrow path. For those whom refuse salvation, the future reads different.

This is what the Bible says about the unbeliever in Revelation Chapter 21, Verse 8: "But cowards, unbelievers, the corrupt, murderers, the immoral, those who practice witchcraft, idol worshipers, and all liars – their fate is in the fiery lake of burning sulfur. This is the second death."

This is the first time many have ever heard this verse. You see; this area of scripture is not used to prostitute the gospel for monetary gain – instead it will convict the evil heart to change so Heaven is its gain! That is why it is the Biblical Road Less Travelled. If you fall into any of the categories mentioned, REPENT before it's too late! Don't allow what the Holy Spirit is saying to you now enter into one ear and exit the other! Invest in your salvation today and confirm that yours is sure! Eternity is a long time to spend in regret for your earthly actions! Be encouraged! Choose Jesus Christ while you still can! God bless you!

Just Zip It!

Zippers are very important in clothing and handbags. With regard to clothing they allow quick and easy access putting on and taking off. As useful as the zipper may be on one's pants or skirt, it is quite embarrassing when it's left open! The same is true when our mouths are left open for a long time!

The Bible says this in Proverbs Chapter 18, Verses 6 and 7: Fools' words get them into constant quarrels… The mouths of fools are their ruin; they trap themselves with their lips.

Has someone ever said something so painful to you, that you wished they had slapped you instead? A useful reminder: If you have nothing good to say, just zip it! Think things through before opening your mouth and saying something that will ruin you! Once the words are spoken they cannot be taken back, so just zip it! Don't allow Satan to influence you to curse, lie, spout verbal anger or speak death and negativity!

Turn to Jesus! Allow the Holy Spirit to influence you in speaking blessings, truth, peace, life and positivity! Don't delay! Just zip it today and when you open again, be sure to give God glory!

God bless you!

A New Kind Of Addiction.

When we hear the word addiction, we automatically think something bad. Drugs, alcohol, pornography... While in most instances our assumptions are correct, we need to keep in mind the meaning of the word. The word "addiction" means "dependency." Let's place a positive spin on the matter: Are you addicted to the Word of God? Are you dependant upon Him? If you answered yes to these questions, God sees you as a person of integrity!

David wrote this in Psalm Chapter 119, Verses 1 through 3: "Joyful are people of integrity, who follow the instructions of the Lord. Joyful are those who obey His laws and search for Him with all their hearts. They do not compromise with evil, and they walk only in His paths."

Reading and living the Word is that serious?! You bet it is!! If you're not there yet, it's time for a new kind of addiction! Many fail to believe God's written Word for one reason or another; however for those who seek will find God in his Word! Start seeking; stop sleeping! God will bless you in your new found addiction!

God bless you!

You're Not A Monkey; Don't Just Hang Around.

Often times I am asked this question: "How do I find my calling?" Many are preoccupied desiring to be a part of something great, while overlooking the greatest call of all!

In Luke Chapter 10 Jesus sent out seventy two disciples, giving them instructions to witness. Interestingly, He told them to pray for more workers! Luke Chapter 10, Verse 2 reads: These were His instructions to them. "The harvest is great, but the workers are few. So pray to the Lord who is in charge of the harvest; ask Him to send more workers into His fields."

It doesn't get any clearer than that! If we consider ourselves His disciples, we should go everywhere with the Gospel of Jesus Christ!

You're not a monkey; don't just hang around doing nothing! Roll up your sleeves! Get involved so that more people will be saved! That is your calling as a Christian! Everything else is "in addition to" should the Lord lead! Jesus Christ, the Holy Spirit in you, should not be the best kept secret, but the most revealed Good News!

God bless you!

Do I Know You?

It happens from time to time, doesn't it? Some stranger calls you by name in public. "Do I know you?" or "Where do I know you from?" Next comes the embarrassing reply: "It's me! You don't remember me?" A very common scenario, while it may not prove fatal there will come a time when Jesus will say, 'I don't know you' to those who ignore righteous living!

The Bible tells us this in Matthew Chapter 7, Verses 22 and 23. "On judgment day many will say to me, 'Lord! Lord! We prophesied in your name and cast out demons in your name and performed many miracles in your name.' But I will reply, 'I never knew you. Get away from me, you who break God's laws.'

We can ignore Jesus now, but He will surely get our attention when He sits as judge of the entire world. You would be wise to get to know Him for yourself! You cannot enter into Heaven based on Mama or Papa's relationship with Him. Each person must know Him for themselves or prepare to spend eternity in pain and sorrow. My knowing you is not important; but you knowing Jesus is!

God bless you!

Do You Plan On Moving North?

Birds fly south for winter as a means to stay warm. Spiritually, it's quite the opposite for Christians; we plan on moving north in an effort to escape the fires of Hell. Anyone who lives the uncompromised Word of God is very wise! That individual plans on moving North to Heaven!

The Bible says this in 1 Thessalonians Chapter 4, Verses 16 and 17: "For the Lord himself will come down from Heaven with a commanding shout, with the voice of the archangel, and with the trumpet call of God. First, the Christians who have died will rise from their graves. Then, together with them, we who are still alive and remain on the earth will be caught up in the clouds to meet the Lord in the air. Then, we will be with the Lord forever."

I know we're all super busy but be sure to keep your eyes northbound to Heaven! Don't be so consumed with Earth that you have no heavenly worth! Start sending up building blocks now by exercising your faith! It is a sure way for you to know that you plan to migrate! We will all relocate, so why not choose your destination.

God bless you!

It's Going To Be Revealed.

Have you ever lied, stolen something or did something evil that no one knows about? In the moment we may think, "I got away with it." We've all been there. When Cain killed his brother Abel in Genesis Chapter 4, Verse 8, no human being was around to witness, but God saw it. You know the story. Read it if you don't. God confronted Cain. Cain lied to God, adding insult to injury, and God banished him from the land that he occupied all his life.

The Bible says in Proverbs Chapter 11, Verse 21: "Evil people will surely be punished, but the children of the godly will go free."

Don't be fooled! There is a punishment attached to whatever evil thought or deed we feed! Keep in mind that it's going to be revealed to God whether or not man knows about it. So walk uprightly. Follow the ways of our Lord Jesus Christ knowing that we will be rewarded for exercising self control and doing good. There is no secret hidden from God, so you may as well retire your 007 badge! Whatever we think, say or do – it's going to be revealed, so let's make it good!

God bless you!

Cash Is Not Good Enough.

Some folks have lots of cash under the mattress saved up for a rainy day, or maybe simply practicing inhouse banking. For now, they can pull out what they need and make their purchases, but soon all that will come to an end. After God's people who are ready for the rapture are taken out of here, the antichrist will put an end to all usage of cash. The Bible tells us this in Revelation Chapter 13, Verses 16 and 17: "He required everyone – small and great, rich and poor, free and slave – to be given a mark on the right hand or on the forehead. And no one could buy or sell anything without that mark, which was either the name of the beast or the number representing his name."

In these days people will worship the antichrist because he brings about a false peace and great riches. Don't give in to that system, my friends, because there is no going back once you have been marked. Since cash, credit cards, gold and other means of trade will not be good enough, you should make plans to leave on the first flight out – the rapture! Failure to accept the mark of the beast will cost you your head being chopped off. Although it sounds bad, it is the best option for those who will be left behind. Don't be confused; study your Bible and live for God!

God bless you!

The Mystery of Our Victory.

No one likes to lose. Victory is far greater than defeat. However, our actions sometimes welcome defeat. Please don't invite defeat; the enemy does a good job of creating obstacles in our daily lives! In spite of these obstacles we can rest assured that as God's children, we have the victory guaranteed for us! "Can I really believe that statement," one might ask?

Well, let's see what the Bible says in Romans Chapter 8, Verse 37: "No, despite all these things, overwhelming victory is ours through Christ, who loved us."

The mystery of our victory is revealed in God's written word, so start living in such a way! Don't accept defeat from Satan, your enemy, whom tells you that you are worth less than you are! Spiritual attacks come in many ways but to God by the glory, we have the victory! When a Formula One race car driver wins a race, he celebrates hard – so let the celebration begin, my friends! Laugh at the devil whom is under your feet and shout, "Thank you, Jesus, for the victory! For those whom are saved, victory is sure! For the unsaved – there are no guarantees! Get saved! Get the victory!

God bless you!

The Natural Man Just Can't Understand.

Sometimes we read a verse in the Bible that makes us pause for a second and ask God: "Are you really saying what I think you're saying?"

One verse can be found in 1 Corinthians Chapter 6, Verse 7. It reads: "Even to have such lawsuits with one another is a defeat for you. Why not just accept the injustice and leave it at that? Why not let yourselves be cheated?

Obviously if you are in the middle of a lawsuit, you don't want to hear this scripture. However, let me point out a few things that the natural man just can't understand: (1) The apostle Paul is talking about lawsuits with believers, church people; (2) The lawsuit is a defeat for you because Satan will use you to keep someone away from Jesus! (3) He encourages us to accept the injustice and leave it like that because he knows all things will work together for our good! To explain this to some believers is challenging enough; imagine to a nonbeliever – they can't understand! Matchless wisdom awaits those who allow Christ to enter their fate! Get Jesus! Get understanding!

God bless you!

A SheBear Don't Compare.

It is a known fact that SheBears are vicious if you mess with their cubs. A mother bear will fight until the end to defend. It proves one thing: she loves her cubs!

We are more valuable to God than bears! God loves us so much that He sent His only begotten son to die for us! Jesus loves us so much that He willingly laid down His life for YOU and I!

Guess what? A SheBear don't compare. The Bible says this in Romans Chapter 8, Verse 38: "And I am convinced that nothing can ever separate us from God's love. Neither death nor life, neither angels nor demons, neither our fears for today nor our worries about tomorrow – not even the powers of hell can separate us from God's love."

So there you have it, my friends: God's love is so deep that He still loves those who've gone on to Hell, however, He is a just God and He rewards people according to how they lived on Earth. No one can understand the depths of God's love but just know this fact: God proved His love for us; it's time we prove our love for Him!

God bless you!

You Can Compromise For Love, But Don't Compromise Your Love.

This topic is a bit tricky. One might think that doing ungodly things with a husband or wife, boyfriend or girlfriend in the name of love is cool. In fact, it's the exact opposite. In an effort to please our loved ones, we displease the one who loves us most – Jesus!

The Bible tells us this in Matthew Chapter 22, Verses 37 and 38: Jesus replied, "You must love the Lord your God with all your heart, all your soul, and all your mind. This is the first and greatest commandment."

In whatever we do please keep in mind that the one who loves us most wants to be a part of our daily lives! Jesus reminds us that we should love God with every heartbeat and with every thought within our inner most being! When we love that way, we can rest assured that our love is not compromised. Some compromise in relationships to keep the peace is fine. Beware of attacks on your relationship with God! Seek Him first in all you do! Prove your love to Him! After all, Jesus died on the cross to prove His Love to you! Love is an action word; it's your move! To God first, and then His people!

God bless you!

Don't Stray From The Message.

Church services have really changed over the years. Church boards are instructing pastors to preach less on repentance and more on finance. Often times you'll even find churches that are not addressing sin at all! That is dangerous.

My encouragement for you is simply this: Don't stray from the message! After Jesus completed His forty day fast and temptations from Satan, His ministry began. What was His message, one might ask? His message is found in Matthew Chapter 4, Verse 17: From then on Jesus began to preach, "Repent of your sins and turn to God, for the kingdom of Heaven is near."

I don't know all the needs in every church, but I know we need to keep repentance in our sermons! Watered down messages may entertain you, or make you feel good for now, but what about later in Hell? We who are truly saved need to keep this in mind and encourage our fellow brothers and sisters to get back to the real message! Encourage them to repent of wrongdoing and seek out righteousness. Let's do our part in changing the world with the message of repentance! Do this, and you will look like Jesus!

God bless you!

Attacking God Where It Hurts.

If you've ever had to relocate because you were kicked out of your home, you know how Satan felt to some degree. Fortunately for the believers, we have a better home awaiting us in glory! With regard to Satan's demise, the Bible says this in Revelation Chapter 12, Verses 8 and 9: "And the dragon lost the battle, and he and his angels were forced out of Heaven. This great dragon – the ancient serpent called the devil, or Satan, the one deceiving the whole world – was thrown down to the earth with all his angels."

So, what does Satan gain by deceiving the whole world? Nothing but a bunch of lost souls! Why are they so important to Him? It is the only way he can attack God where it hurts! Satan wants revenge on God, and the best way to hurt God is to have His creation hurt His feelings. Giving in to temptation causes us to sin against God, and it makes Satan glad! If you die in your sin you end up in hell, then the lake of fire where people are permanently separated from God. This really hurts God but being the righteous Judge that He is, everyone must be rewarded or punished according to their deeds. Let's repent of our sins and join Jesus' team! Stop being Satan's partner in attacking God where it hurts!

God bless you!

It's Time To Return The Call.

The active telecommunicator receives voicemail. We review the voicemail and return all calls in order of importance; not in the order in which they were received! Sometimes when returning a call to an individual or business, we in turn reach voicemail because that party is now unavailable. We call it playing "phone tag."

Spiritually speaking, God placed the first call to us when He sent Jesus to die on the cross so all could be saved! 1 Peter Chapter 3, Verse 9 says: "...He does not want anyone to be destroyed, but wants everyone to repent." It's just a matter of returning the call! Life has us all very busy, but being too busy to secure your eternity with God is just plain foolish! For those who fail to return the call or to call on Jesus for salvation, you will not be chosen to spend eternity with Him (Matthew Chapter 22, Verse 14).

You don't need a dial tone to phone home. A sincere prayer is your spiritual phone! It's time to return the call, before your life ends with a permanent fall! God will then be unavailable to take your call! Don't delay, call today!!

God bless you!

Not The High You Anticipated.

Every day individuals look to people, places or things to give them a high. We begin relationships by falling head over heels in love, get married and divorce all in one year. We buy cars outside of our budget, adding stress, only to have to get rid of it. Some drink liquor or do drugs only to "wake up" to a hangover or in handcuffs.

Not the high you anticipated...

The Bible says this in Ephesians Chapter 5, Verse 18: "Don't be drunk with wine, because that will ruin your life. Instead, be filled with the Holy Spirit..."

My encouragement to you, my friend: Make a trade; get rid of manmade highs in exchange for the spiritual high in Christ Jesus! Repent of your sins and turn to God before your bad habits turn you into a corpse! Satan uses all manner of evil to glamorize the false high. Don't fall for it! Seek a real high with a right relationship with the Savior of the world, our Lord Jesus Christ! No one will force you to choose your high! That's right; no one will force you to live or to die! You choose!

God bless you!

Do The Correct Maintenance.

As a former sailor in the United States Navy, I remember my job as an electrician. My main duty was to conduct preventative maintenance services or (PMS). This entailed checking equipment for proper operation and making sure they had the oil or grease needed to operate. This kept us safe out on the high seas; after all, it's not like we could call a tow truck to assist us!

This same principle applies to our spiritual journey. We need to do the correct maintenance so we can operate as the Christians we are called to be! The Bible says this in Psalm Chapter 139, Verses 23 and 24: Search me, O God, and know my heart; test me and know my anxious thoughts. Point out anything in me that offends you, and lead me along the path of everlasting life.

Anyone serious about everlasting life should pray that prayer so God can show you what is faulty in your walk. Don't slack off on spiritual maintenance, such as attending Sunday worship services and Bible study during the week! It also involves daily Bible reading to receive instructions in righteousness and conversations with God all day long, better known as prayer. Do the correct maintenance and your spirit man will be well oiled and go forth with power!

God bless you!

Where Is Your Hope? Where Is Your Confidence?

An incident I remember while serving in the U.S. Navy: My ship stopped in the Caribbean and the Captain allowed us a swim call. The only prerequisite was this: For confident swimmers only! These were shark infested waters, so there were "Gunners" keeping watch in case the sharks posed a threat. My friend, Thomas, and I declared "no swim call for us" because if a shark attacked, the Gunner may accidentally shoot one of us instead of the shark!

The moral of the story is this: I don't put my hope or confidence in mankind, because we fail from time to time. However, God never fails! The Bible says this in Jeremiah Chapter 17, Verses 7 and 8: "But blessed are those who trust in the Lord and have made the Lord their hope and confidence. They are like trees planted along a riverbank, with roots that reach deep into the water. Such trees are not bothered by the heat or worried by long months of drought. Their leaves stay green, and they never stop producing fruit."

Need I say more? Now my question is: Where is your hope? Where is your confidence? Make sure it is in the Lord! Live in truth and go forth and produce fruit!

God bless you!

Searching For Treasure.

The church of Laodicea is famous for being a lukewarm church. They had riches, but were not wealthy in God. They knew how to do many things, but lacked the wisdom to get to Heaven. The Apostle Paul pleaded with them to make a change toward love and a strong relationship with God. He wrote this in Colossians Chapter 2, Verses 1 through 3: I want you to know how much I have agonized for you and for the church at Laodicea, and for many other believers who have never met me personally. I want them to be encouraged and knit together by strong ties of love. I want them to have complete confidence that they understand God's mysterious plan, which is Christ himself. In Him lie hidden all the treasures of wisdom and knowledge.

Real treasure is found in a close relationship with Jesus! Don't waste your time storing up treasure on Earth and go bankrupt in Jesus! Begin your treasure hunt mission today! Repent daily of any and every sinful way! Ask Jesus, the Holy Spirit, to enter into your heart and lead and guide you. Once you've accomplished that, you've struck gold! You are heaven bound! The streets of Heaven are made with gold! Be encouraged! Focus on Jesus and Heaven daily! Keep your treasure!

God bless you!

Discipline Yourself And Finish Well.

One of the biggest fears, I'm sure, for many marathon runners is getting cramped in the legs and not being able to finish a race. It is important to finish a race, but to finish well requires discipline.

The Bible tells us this in 1 Corinthians Chapter 9, Verse 27:
"I discipline my body like an athlete, training it to do what it should. Otherwise, I fear that after preaching to others I myself might be disqualified."

Once saved, always saved? I think not! This journey is a daily walk, trying our best to be pleasing in God's eyes! To be a true disciple takes discipline and though we are not perfect, we should strive for perfection. The Apostle Paul feared not making it to Heaven, so he trained his body to submit to the Holy Spirit. When we do the same, I can guarantee you that we will finish well! On this spiritual journey it's not so much how we started, but it's all about how we finish!

Will you hear, "Well done, my good and faithful servant?" Or, perhaps you are not faithful to God at all... Now is the time to analyze, discipline ourselves and finish well! Jesus is calling! Answer Him!

God bless you!

So You Think You Are A Disciple, Huh?

On the regular I hear people say, "I am a disciple of Jesus Christ." I can't help but wonder if they really mean what they say, or if they are just saying what sounds good. Inquiring minds will ask: "What are the requirements to be a disciple?" Jesus gave a very serious, thought provoking description of a true disciple. This is what He says in Luke Chapter 14, Verse 26: "If you want to be my disciple, you must hate everyone else by comparison – your father and mother, wife and children, brothers and sisters – yes, even your own life. Otherwise, you cannot be my disciple."

My apologies, if this area of scripture stresses you out, but this information needs to be shared among believers! When Jesus said to "hate everyone else by comparison," he meant we should love Him way more than anyone or anything else! Our soul/thought process is wrapped up in whoever or whatever we love the most. You can answer the question for yourself: When you awake, do you think of Jesus first? Some think of work, money, food, the telephone, relationships… you name it! If the enemy tries to steal the first fruits of your thought process, rebuke him and focus on Jesus! Do morning devotions, praise and worship and start your day off right as a true disciple of Jesus Christ!

God bless you!

The Godly Are Empowered.

Often times I hear people say they feel weak in their spirit. Satan zaps or strength from time to time, doesn't he? Friends and loved ones say things to hurt our feelings, we endure physical challenges, monetary issues, you name it. For individuals that are not saved I cannot promise you that you will be empowered right now. I understand that God rains on the just and on the unjust, and He promises not to give us more than we can bear. However, what He says about empowering the Godly is on another level!

In Psalm Chapter 75, Verse 10, the Bible says this: For God says, "I will break the strength of the wicked, but I will increase the power of the godly." God empowers His people so that we can survive life's greatest challenges. After the valley He gives us a high place, followed by the highest place, Heaven! If for some reason you have never experienced a high place spiritually, emotionally, physically or financially be sure you ask God why. He always does what He says He will do for us, the Godly, and also to those who are unrepentant sinners. Who is wicked? Anyone whom fails to live for Jesus! The problem may very well be you for failing to plug into the right power source. The godly are empowered by God! Anyone not empowered need to check their status on being godly, and be honest with themselves. Don't lose your power! Be empowered!

God bless you!

Home At Last.

One of America's favorite pasttimes is baseball. There is lots of running involved, but the main goal is to obtain the homerun. We can compare that to our spiritual journey, can't we? Our race is not for the swift or the strong but for those who can endure till the end! What will our end look like when we finish the race well? Actually it will be the beginning of something spectacular! In Matthew Chapter 25, Verse 21 Jesus says, "Well done, my good and faithful servant! You have been faithful in handling this small amount, so now I will give you many responsibilities. Let's celebrate together." Jesus is well pleased with His servant whom He entrusted to work with the talents/money He saw fit to give him. When it's all said and done, the servant is celebrating at home with Jesus. Keep that in mind as we journey each day that soon and very soon we will be home at last. Either that or we will be in a home for the lost. (Hell) Run the race as one trying to win the race and expect a safe homerun, in Jesus Name! Keep your eyes on the prize and great will be your future home!

God bless you!

Who Is Building Your House?

General Contractors are trained and licensed to build houses. From experience, I know one of the most important parts of building a house is laying the foundation. When the foundation is solid, then you can build up from there. We also have a spiritual house that needs building and our general contractor is the Lord God Almighty. This is what the Bible says in Psalm Chapter 127, Verse 1: "Unless the Lord builds a house the work of the builders is wasted. Unless the lord protects a city, guarding it with sentries will do no good." So now the question is this: Who is building your house? Spiritually speaking we can either have God or Satan, it all depends on the building blocks we use. Don't confuse Satan with the right general contractor because he is wearing a hard hat. Check him out first and then see if he is qualified to feed your spirit. Don't let your physical or spiritual house be a house of horror. Let's work together with our God and accomplish great things! Many houses look good on the outside, but the inside is a mess! The walls are damaged, the flooring is not level, etc. People also look good on the outside, but many have a very ugly heart because they ignore the ways of God. So let us have God build our house by obeying His Word!

God bless you!

Run for Cover.

Praise the Lord, my friends! What a blessing it is to know that we have a safe place in the loving arms of Jesus Christ. The storms of this life are raging and yet many people decide to be rained on, blown away and destroyed by them. To me that is foolish when they can easily ask Jesus to forgive their sins and live for him. In doing so, they would have run for cover and now Jesus would protect them supernaturally.

This is awesome. The Bible says in Psalms 84, verses 1 and 3, "How lovely is your dwelling place, O Lord Almighty." "Even the sparrow finds a home there, and the swallow builds her nest and raises her young – at a place near your alter..."

So there you have it. If birds are smart enough to rely totally on God, we should do the same. Remember: the devil will always shoot his darts at us but when we run for cover in Jesus Christ, he will put his entire armor on us.

God bless you!

Who Am I?

Welcome, friends!!! That is exactly how we want you to feel in the house of God!

Have you ever wondered who you are? We can be identified by many things. Our name, social security number, finger prints, date of birth, photograph, etc. However, the most important form of identification is to be in Christ. II Corinthians Chapter 5, verse 17 says if anyone is in Christ, he is a new person. They are not the same anymore, for the old life is gone and a new life has begun.

Wow; That is powerful! So now we have new lives to live. We should be giving God the glory with our new lives. If you did not receive his forgiveness and experience this new life, PLEASE; I beg you. Don't miss out on your full potential in Jesus Christ. Receive him today. Don't delay!

God bless you all!

Consuming Fire.

Praise the Lord, my friends! I thank God for each and every one of you and for those who take the time to read these words of encouragement.

Today I want to share with you a thought that is so often overlooked. Everyone has a fire that ignites them each day. However, far too many people add fuel to the wrong fire. Now here is another thought; what happens when the fire that consumes all your time goes out? Now you are left empty inside your heart. It is wise to be consumed by the right fire. John the Baptist spoke about Jesus in Matthew chapter 3, verse 11 that He will baptize us with the Holy Spirit and with fire.

Let's start burning on eternal fuel! Let God consume us for His good. Choose wisely!
(Hebrews Chapter 12, Verses 28 and 29)
(Deuteronomy Chapter 4, Verse 24)

God bless you!

Time To Grow Up!!

One, two, three, four, five, six, seven. These numbers represent our early years. You know; when it was cool to eat dirt! Ha ha! Playing in the dirt was the highlight of many youngsters' day.

However, there comes a time in everyone's life when he or she must grow up. Here is the problem, though; some people grew up in body size but did not grow mentally or spiritually. This can present a serious problem for both the individual and his or her associates. Imagine with me a young man on a date with a prospective wife, and after dinner he stops at the park and rolls around in the sand. That might be the last date! 1 Corinthians chapter 13, verse 11 says, "When I was a child, I spoke and thought and reasoned as a child does. But when I grew up, I put away childish things."

It's time to stop playing with the dirty, sinful activities that are readily available. Turn to God. Grow more in Jesus by reading His word and praying to Him daily. Don't be a spiritual infant; become a spiritual giant! Grow up!

God bless you!

The Cost of Following Jesus.

Luke Chapter 14, verses 25 through 33: The Cost of Being a Disciple. Great crowds were following Jesus. He turned around and said to them, "If you want to be my follower you must love me more than your own father and mother, wife and children, brothers and sisters – yes, more than your own life. Otherwise, you cannot be my disciple. And you cannot be my disciple if you do not carry your own cross and follow me.

But don't begin until you count the cost. For who would begin construction of a building without first getting estimates and then checking to see if there is enough money to pay the bills? Otherwise, you might complete only the foundation before running out of funds. And then how everyone would laugh at you! They would say, "There's the person who started that building and ran out of money before it was finished!"

Or what king would ever dream of going to war without first sitting down with his counselors and discussing whether his army of ten thousand is strong enough to defeat the twenty thousand soldiers who are marching against him? If he is not able, then while the enemy is still far away, he will send a delegation to discuss terms of peace. So no one can become my disciple without giving up everything for me.

Please prayerfully consider the cost!

God bless you!

Joy Is On The Way!!

So many people look into many different ways to find joy, yet they come up empty handed. Obviously, they are looking in the wrong places. Some wives put their trust in a husband and believe he will treat her right all her life, only to find that he is abusive and inconsiderate, among other negative adjectives. The same is true for some husbands depending on their wives to bring them joy, but to no avail. So you might ask, what can be done about that?

I am glad you asked! You see, real joy comes from God; not from the world or anyone or anything in the world. The Bible promises in Psalm Chapter 30, Verse 5 that if we live for God, even though we weep throughout the night, joy will come in the morning! God can change our spouses so the joy we expect through them will be evident.

So no matter what – stay focused on Jesus and He will touch the hearts of spouses, children, bosses, friends and even enemies. The sky is the limit because He is God, and He gives joy! Get close to Him now and your joy will be on the way!

God bless you!

Sick and Tired.

Praise the Lord, everyone! Here is a popular phrase that we all have used at one time or another: I am sick and tired! I am sick and tired of this job! I am sick and tired of this car; house; apartment; bad children; bad spouse! You get the picture.

So many times people, places or things get beneath our skin, and we get sick and tired of it. We have a tendency to avoid things that we get sick and tired of, don't we? Yes, we do! It's the same thing with God. He gets sick and tired too. Not in physical strength, but emotionally. Proverbs Chapter 1, verses 25 through 29 reads, "You ignored my advice and rejected the correction I offered. So I will laugh when you are in trouble! I will mock you when disaster overtakes you – when calamity overcomes you like a storm, when you are engulfed by trouble, and when anguish and distress overwhelm you. I will not answer when they cry for help. Even though they anxiously search for me, they will not find me. For they hated knowledge and chose not to fear the Lord."

Don't let the Lord become sick and tired of you. Live for Him! And when you call, He will answer!

God bless you!

Spiritual Healing.

Have you ever been sick? I believe we all have at one point or another. However, what we overlook at times are the many people around us that seem fine but are not. You see, spiritual sickness is not obvious all the time. Of course we can see the bad attitudes, the cursing, lying, adultery, fornication, stealing – you get my drift. Those are evidence of spiritual sickness. What about the people who show all the good things? You would never think for a second that person is sick. Don't be fooled! If anyone does not have a personal relationship with Jesus Christ, then that person is spiritually sick and needs spiritual healing.

Now how does that work? I am glad you asked! The Bible teaches in **Isaiah Chapter 53, verse 5** that Jesus "was wounded and crushed for our sins. He was beaten that we might have peace. He was whipped, and we were healed!" Now that spiritual healing only applies when we walk in the spirit. Don't expect to be healed of your sin stained condition if you are not clinging to Jesus. So allow Jesus to heal you, then you can assist others in their healing.

God bless you!

You Can Do It.

"Oh, you make me sick!" says the angry Mom to her seven year old son. "You'll be nothing but a failure in life! You will never accomplish anything good!"

Ouch! Those are some very destructive words that people tell children on a daily basis. If anyone listens to this type of verbal abuse long enough, they start to believe it. If you or anyone you know speaks to an individual like this, please correct yourself or that person. The Bible clearly states in Matthew Chapter 19, Verse 26 that **with God all things are possible**! The Bible also tells us in Philippians 4:13 that **I can do everything with the help of Christ who gives me strength**!

So please stop tearing people down and start building them up with the word of God! Whether child or adult, once Jesus is leading your life, go for the goal that He has placed in your heart. You can do it! Don't ever be afraid! Keep an active, daily prayer life, and you will be fine! Encourage others to do the same in Jesus' name!

God bless you!

Living The Dream.

Do dreams really come true? So many people ask this question. The answer is "yes" in some cases and "no" in other cases. Let's face it. You don't want a bad dream or nightmare to ever come true. However, a good dream we would welcome! In Genesis Chapter 40, Pharaoh's chief cupbearer and chief baker both had dreams. They were in jail for having offended Pharaoh. Now, one dream was bad and the other was good. In this case, they both came to pass. The chief cupbearer returned to his position, but the chief baker died.

Now my question to you is – What is it that God may be telling you in your dreams? Is He showing you things you need to rectify in your life? Are you haunted by dreams or blessed by them?

You can make a difference, you know! If you develop a close relationship with Jesus Christ, He will order your dreams and show you the way, just like He did with the wise men in Matthew Chapter 2, verse 12. So stop fearing your dreams! Seek Jesus with your whole heart, mind, soul and strength and start living the dream!

God bless you!

Why Not Serve The Lord.

Praise the Lord, my Friends! So many people tend to say, "I serve the Lord with all my heart," yet, their actions don't reflect that statement. Let's analyze that point for a second. What does it mean to serve the Lord? Do you have to bring Him coffee or tea in the morning? Not exactly!

What it means is that we open our hearts, let Him inside and give Him permission to have His way! Having done that it means everywhere He leads, we follow; whatever He commands, we do it with enthusiasm. We make Jesus our most important priority. There are so many things out there that people serve. For example, relationships, food, work... You name it, people serve it and in doing so they neglect the most important service of all – service to Jesus Christ.

Our brother, Joshua, said in Joshua Chapter 24, Verse 15, "But as for me and my family, we will serve the Lord." Now that is something we should all adopt to our daily living. Jesus said, "The harvest is plentiful, but the workers are few." Let's strive to increase that few.

God bless you!

Do You Believe?

We have all heard the phrase, "God can make a way out of no way." The question is, however, do you believe? There is another phrase that I strongly dislike and it is, "Seeing is believing."

In God's order of events we believe by faith and then we will receive, God willing. Now what is faith, anyway? Hebrews Chapter 11, Verse 1 tells us that faith is the confident assurance that what we hope for is going to happen. It is the evidence of things not yet seen. In a nutshell, we should believe Jesus is who He said He is, and He will do what He said He will do. So many people have a problem with believing that, yet it is so easy to believe in the "evolution" theory – man coming from monkey foolishness! I wonder if these "theorists" really listen to what they are saying! Maybe that isn't your problem today. Maybe you need to believe God for a better job; a better relationship with your spouse or child; finances...

Stop worrying and start believing by faith that God's good and perfect Will be done, and it will be done to best satisfy your needs! Believe in Him; I know He believes in you!

God bless you!

Take A Bite!

"God is good," says the old lady standing in the doctor's office. Everyone is puzzled due to the fact that her recently diagnosed cancer is no longer there!

They said, "This is impossible," and she said, "With God all things are possible!" (Matthew Chapter 19, Verse 26). One nurse asked, "What's the meaning of this; why is she so convinced that God is real?" The old lady told her that she had been praying with the elders of the church for a miracle, and God answered her prayer. She continued, "If you make a step towards God you will taste and see that the Lord is good, and blessed is the man who trusts Him!" (Psalms Chapter 34, Verse 8). "You need to take a bite," the old lady said. "You will never be the same."

We all need to encourage others with these words: Bite into the goodness of God, and stop feeding yourself with the garbage the world offers. Oh the joy that will be granted to those who taste! Do it today! Don't delay! What miracle do you desire in your life? Take a bite, and God will make it right!

God bless you!

Favor.

Favor. I like the sound of that. Imagine a world where God's favor is always present. From simple things like getting all green lights while driving on the road to major doors opening for your business and social relationships. Is that what God wants us to partake of? I'm convinced that God wants us to partake of His favor. However, like everything else in life we must follow certain steps to obtain that favor. Leviticus Chapter 26, Verses 3, 9 and 10 say, "If you keep my laws and are careful obey my commands, I will look favorably upon you and multiply your people and fulfill my covenant with you. You will have such a surplus of crops that you will need to get rid of the leftovers from the previous year to make room for each new harvest."

That is powerful! Now if that does not motivate you to start living right and obey God's commands, then I don't know what would! Ask yourself this question: "What is keeping me from receiving God's favor?" When you figure it out, get "it" out of your life! You will be glad you did!

God's favor: Make the necessary steps to get it.

God bless you!

Lead Me, Lord.

So many people have a problem with being led. It is so prevalent that even blind people sometimes want to find their own way. What's ironic is that some of the people who refuse being led want to lead others! That is ridiculous! If we are not obedient to the word of God and follow His lead, how on Earth can we lead others? However, here is something profound…

Everyone is led around by someone, whether knowingly or not. We are led by the Lord or by Satan. If you are saying to yourself, "I make my own decisions; I don't follow God or Satan," you are deceived! The fact of the matter is, you are either with God or against Him! Don't walk around blindfolded. Jesus said in Matthew Chapter 15, verse 14 after addressing the Pharisees that, "…They are blind guides leading the blind, and if one blind person guides another, they will both fall into a ditch."

The choice is yours. Don't be a Mr. or Mrs. Know It All. Call upon Jesus and follow His lead! He is the only navigation system you need!

God bless you!

Stand Firm Together.

Wow; what a profound statement! So many people forget that we are in this Christian walk together! It is not a solo act. We need to stand with each other in prayer believing by faith that the hand of God will move! When we do, people will be saved, healed, delivered, set free, you name it!

Here is what the Apostle Paul said in Philippians Chapter 1, Verse 27: "But whatever happens to me, you must live in a manner worthy of the Good News about Christ, as citizens of heaven. Then, whether I come and see you again or only hear about you, I will know that you are standing side by side, fighting together for the Good News." So you see, my friends, we need to stand firm together if we seek to accomplish great things for God! What does God consider a "great thing"? The Good News being shared by us, His people, to the lost, unsaved and hurting world at large.

So get on board and get motivated about the "Gospel," the "Good News;" let's stand firm together, then share Christ!

God bless you!

Stay Close.

Praise the Lord, my friends!

Just a gentle reminder that we need to stay close to our Lord and Savior, Jesus Christ. Sin separates us from God. You might ask, "What does that mean?" Well, you see it's like this; when we engage in sinful activities such as lying, stealing, fornication, evil thinking and the like, it causes the spirit of God to withdraw himself from us. When Satan sees we are not close to God, at that very second he attacks us to break us down and keep us down.

In 2 Kings Chapter 11, Verse 8 the priest, Jehoiada, told the guards to stay close to King Joash at all times. Today, the Holy Spirit encourages us to stay close to King Jesus. He will keep us in line and free from worry, doubt and a whole host of other troublesome feelings.

Who or what is closest to your heart? If your answer is Jesus, then well done! If it is not Jesus, then please prayerfully consider a change for the better!

God bless you!

It's Not Your War.

To God be the glory, great things He has done! So love He the world that He gave us His son!

Do you know your father in Heaven is crazy about you? You may love your child, but the love God has for us is far greater than the love we have for our children! If you saw the enemy attacking your child, wouldn't you do everything in your power to defend him or her? Our heavenly father does the same for His children! He fights for us, because He loves us!

In 1 Samuel Chapter 17, Verse 47 it says, "...everyone will know that the Lord does not need weapons to rescue His people. It is his battle, not ours." So don't let the battles of this world bring you down! If you haven't received Jesus as Lord and Savior, you need to do it! If you have already received Him, cry out to Him for help and make sure you do all that He calls you to do. When you do His will, He will surely fight your battles for you! It's not your war!!

God bless you!

Are You Wired Right?

Praise the Lord, my friends! Here is a thought: Are you wired right?

Imagine with me an electrician wiring a house and deciding to put any wire any where. Equipment such as air conditioning unit, stove and dryer all receive the smallest gauge wires and other devices such as switches and outlets receive bigger wires. Does this make any sense? Of course not! It will definitely start a fire sooner than he thinks!

Here is the contrast: Many of us are not wired to Jesus Christ. You may be in the same church with many others, doing your own thing but if you are wired to the wrong things and never get wired to Jesus, you will end up in the fire! Don't go there. Avoid it at all cost. Get wired to Jesus! This will ensure the proper operation of your life. Jesus said in John Chapter 15, Verse 5, "...Those who remain in me, and I in them, will produce much fruit. For apart from me you can do nothing." So there you have it. Check and see where your wires lead to!

God bless you!

Yes Lord, I'll Go.

Praise the Lord, for He is worthy to be praised!

Sometimes we are quick to praise Him with our lips, but what about with our actions? Are we willing to go whenever and wherever He sends us? Many of us focus on the blessings from God, however, what about laboring for God? I love what the Prophet Isaiah said in Isaiah Chapter 6, Verse 8 when he heard the Lord asking, "Whom should I send as a messenger to my people? Who will go for us?" Isaiah said, "Lord, I'll go! Send me." That is powerful to me because that was a very tall order he volunteered to carry out. It would include correcting kings, hence, putting his life in danger.

What is the Lord asking you to do? Where is He asking you to go so that you might accomplish His will? Let me lovingly encourage you to say Yes Lord, I will go! Yes Lord, I will do what you ask of me! Self will is dangerous. There are great rewards in following the leadership of the Holy Spirit!

God bless you!

If You Know Jesus, Rejoice!

I will bless the Lord at all times. His praise will continually be in my mouth.

When I look around me and see the changes God has made in my life, I must rejoice! Maybe you can remember with me going to work on Friday and all day thinking of what you'd be doing in the club later on that night. Dirty dancing the night away, drinking or maybe smoking. We thought we were living the life, didn't we? We were only fooling ourselves! We didn't know Jesus personally, so we were missing out on real joy! Romans Chapter 5, Verse 11 says, "So now we can rejoice in our wonderful new relationship with God – all because of what our Lord Jesus Christ has done for us in making us friends with God."

I encourage you to discover this wonderful new relationship with Jesus if you have not yet done so. If you have, rejoice!! And tell others!!

God bless you!

Are You In His Shadow?

Praise the Lord, everyone!

Psalm 91, verse 1 says, *"Those who live in the shelter of the Most High will find rest in the shadow of the Almighty."*

Wow; that is powerful! Think about it this way. If you are in God's shadow, that means He is taking the heat for you! Life always throws curve balls and things happen that we wish wouldn't. However, if we stay close to Jesus Christ He will fix our situations! He will keep us cool in the middle of life's desert. Trust in Him and be encouraged by His word because he means just what he said! Don't leave from under the shadow or else you will be consumed by the heat of Satan and all his tricks. Share this word with friends and family members and get them under God's shelter!

God bless you!

Don't Stray From The Faith.

Praise the Lord, my friends!! Just a few words of encouragement to keep you in the faith.

Far too many people we know have turned their backs on God's Will and selfishly pursued their own will. The problem with that is God is a jealous God and if we wander from the faith, He will be upset and that can lead to severe discipline. As a matter of fact **Psalm 119:67** says, *"I used to wander off until you disciplined me; but now I closely follow Your word"*. So it's best to follow His word than be disciplined by Him.

Now what if someone doesn't have a personal relationship with Jesus Christ? They are not excluded from the disciplinary actions, and God implements the reasons is God's Word is the law of life whether or not people choose to obey it. The traffic law of the land says green light permits you to go and red light commands you to stop. Whether or not you obey, it's still the law. God's word is the same. Live by it. Avoid being disciplined by God.

God bless you!

What Is Your Desire?

Praise the Lord, everyone! Today's topic is, "What is your desire?" We can all make a list. Some people desire houses, some cars, a spouse, children... You name it, people desire it.

Now, let me run something by you. Who do you think will allow your desires to become a reality? The answer is God. That's right, God, and despite the popular comments people make in saying that we accomplish things on our own, the answer is still God. It's like this: One plus one equals two. If all your friends tell you that one plus one equals three, you won't buy that because you know the truth and the truth is absolute. **Psalm 73:25** says, *"Whom have I in heaven but you? I desire you more than anything on earth."*

Now let me ask you again. What is your desire? Please be honest with yourself and if you don't desire Jesus Christ above everything else, I appreciate your honesty. However, for a fulfilled life, He should be your greatest desire.

God bless you!

Give Thanks.

Praise the Lord, everyone!

If you are reading these words or being read to, then you have something to give thanks for. It amazes me how a person can spend hours, days, weeks, months and sometimes even years complaining about what he or she doesn't have and not thank God for what he or she does have. If you fall into that category, quit complaining and start your thanksgiving. One day is set aside for thanksgiving in the calendar year. However, people with wisdom should give thanks every day! **1 Thessalonians 5:18** says, *"No matter what, always be thankful, for this is God's will for you who belong to Christ Jesus."* Don't be fooled; people with an ungrateful spirit will always lack something or another. Learn from their mistakes. Give thanks to the Lord for his many blessings, and I guarantee you his heart will be touched by your sincerity which will result in many more blessings for you. And I know we all love blessings! So start giving thanks!

God bless you!

What Are You Waiting For??

Praise the Lord, Everyone!

When I see people waiting at a bus stop, I automatically assume they are waiting on a bus. In like manner, I see people waiting in the drivethru line at a burger joint so I assume they are waiting to purchase food.

However, one thing is still a mystery to me. I see people living defeated lives, always complaining, lacking peace, joy and contentment, yet they have a "knowledge of God". Note, I said a "knowledge" of God. Not a "relationship" with God. It amazes me that Jesus said in **Revelation 3:20**, *"Look! Here I stand at the door and knock. If you hear me calling and open the door, I will come in, and we will share a meal as friends."* Yet people turn their backs on him every day.

Remember this though; the longer you wait to open the door to your heart and let Jesus in, the longer you delay the many blessings he has for you. So accept him now, don't delay! You will live good now and even better in Heaven! So ask yourself; What on Earth Am I Waiting For?!!!

God bless you!

You Have The Power.

Praise the Lord, my friends!

One of the biggest and most desired thing for people is power. For some people, if they can control others, buy whatever they want or travel wherever they want their lives would be "complete". At least, so they think. Now let's look at the most powerful man who walked this Earth – Jesus Christ. He told us the most powerful thing is love. Yes my friend, if you love the Lord your God with all your heart, soul, mind and strength and then love your neighbor as yourself, you will be complete. (Mark 12:29-31). The Holy Spirit gives us power when we are in Christ, and he teaches us all things. (Acts 1:8). Earthly power cannot compete with Godly power.

If you don't have it, get it! It's free!

God bless you!

Now That Is What I Call New!

Praise the Lord, everyone and Happy New Year! So many people make new year resolutions which sometime turn into aggravation. However, let me encourage you this new year season to set your thoughts higher and not just on earthly rewards.

The Bible tells us in Revelation Chapter 21, Verse 1 and in Verse 5, "Then I saw a new heaven and a new earth, for the old heaven and the old earth had disappeared." "And the one sitting on the throne said, "Look, I am making all things new!"" Now that is what I call new! We have Heaven provided for us if we accept Jesus Christ as Lord and Savior and live for Him!

Whatever we plan to change in the new year, make sure you keep Heaven in mind. Heaven will be new like you have never seen before! Don't miss it! Going to the gym? Bring the King! Stop smoking? Start talking about the King! Stop drinking? Start praying more to the King! In everything, involve Jesus the King so you will be guaranteed a part in the "new".

God bless you!

Jesus To The Rescue!

Bless the Lord, O' my soul, and all that is within me, bless His holy name! The name that is above every other name is Jesus. We need to remember that fact. So many people are in trouble and yet they fail to call on Jesus for rescue. I don't know what you are up against; maybe someone wants to kill you; maybe your landlord or mortgage holder wants to evict you; maybe your relationship is in shambles – the list goes on and on.

Well, there is good news! Jesus Christ works best when man says it cannot be done! He will rescue you just to prove them wrong, if need be. The Bible says in Psalm Chapter 18, Verses 16 and 17, "He reached down from Heaven and rescued me; He drew me out of deep waters. He delivered me from my powerful enemies, from those who hated me and were too strong for me."

We all, at some point or another, feel as if we are in deep water. My friends, cling to Jesus! He is the life ring that will float you back to shore. He will rescue you! Don't be afraid to call His name and make your request known. Do what is right, and He will do right by you!

God bless you!

Journey Mercies.

The following is a true story. A girl in college was about to go on a road trip with four of her friends. Her mom said to her, "Go with the Lord, my daughter." Because the car was full, the girl jokingly replied, "The only place He can ride is in the trunk!" How sad is that!!? Really sad! During the trip the car ran off the road and crashed. All of the girls died. Ironically, nothing happened to the trunk of the car! To make an even greater statement, it was said that there was a tray of eggs in the trunk and not one of the eggs were broken! Obviously, God accepted her pitiful invitation and rode in the trunk.

Who do you depend on when traveling? Yourself? David says in Psalm Chapter 20, Verse 7, "Some trust in chariots and some in horses, but we will remember the Lord our God." You see, engines may fail; human instinct may fail; but God never fails! If you are traveling to work or to another country, always pray and ask Jesus to protect you and to give you journey mercies. It is not a joking matter. Please don't assume you will make it back home. Many people do not. Take time to pray before you get on your way and be sure to thank him when you return!

God bless you!

Love! Don't Hate.

May God be glorified with our lives as we go through various trials and tribulations. Jesus promised we would have those kind of days, when it is so easy to hate our fellow man. Then we turn around and say we love God.

Remember: we cannot hate any man and truly love God. Fresh and salt water cannot flow from the same spring. The book of I John, Chapter 4, Verses 7 and 8 read, "Dear Friends, let us continue to love one another, for love comes from God. Anyone who loves is born of God and knows God. But anyone who does not love, does not know God – for God is love." So you see, real love for mankind extinguishes hate. The two cannot share the same body/temple. If you find yourself overwhelmed with hatred, confess it to God and ask Him to take it away and then fill you with His perfect love. The closer your walk with God, the more love you will acquire to distribute amongst your fellow man. It was love that lead Jesus to a sacrificial death, and love should lead us to forsake negative emotions and forgive people as soon as they trespass against us. With practice you, too, can love!

God bless you!

God's Promises Are Pure.

Praise the Lord all His people! So often we hear the phrase, "I promise." The sad thing is many of those promises don't come to pass. The individual may say it with a pure heart, however, circumstances arise that prevent him or her from fulfilling the promise they made.

Thanks be to God, He does not have any circumstances that prevent Him from keeping His promises! However, we can forfeit His promises by our disobedient lifestyle. If we do as the word of God commands His pure, genuine promises will stand.

The Bible says in Psalm Chapter 12, Verse 6 that, "The Lord's promises are pure, like silver refined in a furnace, purified seven times over." So, we can cling to God's word. His promises – they are true! Please remember Jesus also promises to return soon; to meet some people as friends and others as a judge. Be sure you are ready to meet Him, and in the meantime enjoy his pure promises!

God bless you!

It's Not Over Until God Says It Is Over.

Let everything that has breath praise the Lord! No one has an excuse if he or she can breathe. God, who is the giver and whom sustains life, ordains a specific purpose for us all. Many of us are motivated in the beginning and attack our calling with great enthusiasm; for others, that same enthusiasm only lasts for a little while.

Why? Because when the going gets tough, most people quit. Thank God, Jesus didn't quit on us when the going got tough! My point? Hang in there! No matter the task God has called you to do – great or small – hang in there, and He will see you through. Philippians Chapter 1, Verse 6 says, "And I am sure that God, who began the good work within you, will continue His work until it is finally finished on that day when Christ Jesus comes back again."

Wow! To me, that is great encouragement! Knowing that my heavenly father determines when it is over keeps me motivated. Not mankind, not situations and definitely not emotions! We can all rest assured that God holds the key to start and finish. Don't stop driving; He will provide all your needs!

God bless you!

Cheerleader.

Praise the Lord at all times! Praise Him for His miracles! Praise Him for His goodness! Praise Him for His forgiveness! Praise Him for your being alive after all you have been through! Don't refrain from praising His name!

When Jesus arrived in Jerusalem, the Bible says in Luke Chapter 19, Verse 38 that the people shouted, "Bless the King who comes in the name of the Lord! Peace in heaven and glory in highest heaven!" When some Pharisees heard, they told Jesus to rebuke them but Jesus replied in Luke Chapter 19, Verse 40, "If they kept quiet, the stones along the road would burst into cheers."

Always remember who Jesus Christ is and live your life giving Him the "cheers" He deserves! Become a "cheerleader" and encourage others to "cheer" on our Lord and Savior Jesus Christ! Far too many people cheer on the enemy, Satan. Let's change that! The Holy Spirit is here – let's give him cheers!

God bless you!

A Gentle Answer.

Praise the Lord, all ye people! Only the joy of the Lord can keep us calm and gentle when people say things to aggravate us. So many times Satan uses people at work, at play or even in our homes to get on our last nerve! You know what I mean – already your day is not all you want it to be, and here comes the icing on the cake from your employer with a negative remark.

I keep this verse handy in my mind at all times. Proverbs Chapter 15, Verse 1 says, "A gentle answer deflects anger, but harsh words make tempers flare." If someone approaches us wanting "a fight," our first option should be to resolve it peacefully. A gentle answer will calm a person down in most cases. Let's start being the bigger man/woman. Let's make God proud by not talking too loud! We must first please our spirit man before satisfying the flesh, so keep your conversations holy and hold your raging tongue!

Let's get our point across without forsaking the cross!

God bless you!

Love In Motion.

You have heard it said many times before. "I love you." From a relative, or in romance. Yet, many people use the word "love" loosely. If we really knew what "love" means, we would all live a totally different lifestyle!

I Corinthians Chapter 13, Verses 4 and 5 say, "Love is patient and kind. Love is not jealous or boastful or proud or rude. Love does not demand its own way. Love is not irritable, and it keeps no record of when it has been wronged." You may say, "I cannot do all those things," and I assure you without a close relationship with the Lord Jesus Christ, it will be impossible! However once connected in the spirit with Christ, your love will truly be in motion! It will become easier to forgive and go on with your daily plans. God IS love, so we who are in God must show love.

Let's start a wave in our world by making true love a priority! That's what Jesus did, and it's what he's still doing today!

God bless you!

Letting Go.

It can be very hard to say goodbye to a family member, relative or close friend; someone you love, cherish and maybe even depend on from time to time. Sometimes we hold on to people or to things that God wants us to let go of. Love can reunite us with loved ones, and love can prevent us from continuing harmful behavior. Nevertheless, we must learn to let go.

One of the best stories Jesus told was about the prodigal son who in Luke Chapter 15, Verses 12 and 13 took his half of the inheritance and left town. Shortly thereafter in Verse 20 poverty reminded him that he could return to his father, so he did

Whatever it is the Holy Spirit is telling you to let go of, just let it go! If your child is about to go to college, just pray and let him or her go! If you have an addiction, just pray for God's help and let it go! Know this –if you live to honor the Lord Jesus Christ, He will impress on your heart the things you need to let go of. Begin listening to the prompting of the Holy Spirit; remember – what God has for you is for you!

God bless you!

Time To Rise.

How long have you been under oppression? How long have you been suffering? How long have you been struggling? Well, it's time to rise! You may say, "that sounds great but you don't know my oppression, my suffering or my struggle." No, I do not, but God knows! I believe that God can help us to rise from any situation – no matter how bad it may be – even from the dead!

In Luke Chapter 24, Verses 5 and 6, the angels asked the women who were looking for Jesus, "Why are you looking in a tomb for someone who is alive? He isn't here! He has risen from the dead!..."

If you can bite your finger and feel pain, that is a test to make sure you are alive... Once you have that part covered, the rest is quite simple. Trust the Lord Jesus Christ in all that you do. He promises to see you through! I know that many will embrace a compromise or two, but let me lovingly tell you this: compromise keeps you in the stone sealed tomb.

The third day has come and gone so it's time to rise!

God bless you!

God Rules.

God rules! Praise Him because He does! Some people believe they are in charge of their lives, and all that they accomplish is by human strength. It is quite foolish to believe such a thing as it was God who created us, and furthermore, it is God whom sustains us!

Many are caught in this game of self praise and self rule. Don't play that game; you will lose! King Nebuchadnezzar thought he was in charge of it all, saying 'Just look at Babylon! I, by my own might and power, have built this beautiful city as my royal residence…' but while he was yet still speaking God said in Daniel Chapter 4, Verses 31 and 32, 'O King Nebuchadnezzar, this message is for you! You are no longer ruler of this kingdom. You will be driven from human society. You will live in the fields with wild animals and eat grass like a cow."

I learn a lot from that area of scripture. God rules! We need to remember that and honor Him in all of our doings. Don't develop a swelled head or you may lose the position God allows you to occupy! He rules!

God bless you!

Open Your Gift.

Have you ever received a Christmas present a couple of days before Christmas? Did you put it under the Christmas tree, or did you open it before Christmas day? Many people can't wait to open a gift; they always jump the gun. Now; how about the people who receive so many presents that they overlook one? It "slipped through the cracks;" perhaps got thrown out with wrapping paper.

Do you know that more than half the people on the planet overlook the best gift ever to mankind? In John Chapter 4, Verse 10 when Jesus spoke to the Samaritan woman at the well He said, "If you only knew the gift God has for you and who I am, you would ask me, and I would give you living water."

So many people are not familiar with what Jesus Christ has to offer, because they refuse to open their gift. What gift is that, you might ask? Jesus Christ is the gift, but the key is when you open up your heart and let Him in to reveal all things to you!

The best gift ever is Jesus Christ. Open your heart, let Him in, and make use of your gift!

God bless you!

Definition of Love.

Oooh, baby! I think I love you from head to toe! Really? Love is more than just a pop song. This thing called love is very serious. Imagine this with me: God so loved that He gave His only begotten son. The Son so loved that He gave His life for us. How much do we love? Before we can answer that question we need to know the meaning of the word love. 1 Corinthians Chapter 13, Verses 4 through 7 tell us that, "Love is patient and kind. Love is not jealous or boastful or proud or rude. Love does not demand its own way. Love is not irritable, and it keeps no record of when it has been wronged. It is never glad about injustice but rejoices whenever the truth wins out. Love never gives up, never loses faith, is always hopeful, and endures through every circumstance.

Are you for real? Yes! All of the above define love. Which leads me to boldly say, if a man, woman, boy or girl is not in love with Jesus Christ, having the spirit of Christ lead them daily, it is **impossible** to truly love by God's standards! Only God can help us to love in that manner, and keep our sanity! Do you want to love'? Start by loving God with your life and not just with your mouth!

God bless you!

A Ram In The Bush.

If you are a believer in the Lord Jesus Christ, your faith will be tested at some point or another. That is a good thing! You are supposed to be triumphant if Christ is leading your life! He will make you stronger and teach you total dependence on Him.

Many times in my life I have experienced a testing of my faith, however, God has always shown up right on time! He provides me "a ram in the bush", so to speak. You know the story in Genesis Chapter 22, Verse 13: "Then Abraham looked up and saw a ram caught by its horns in a bush." Abraham was instructed by God to sacrifice his promised son, Isaac. Although his faith was tested, he obeyed God. He was stopped right on time, and God gave him a ram in the bush as a sacrifice.

Don't give up on God, no matter how low your valley may be. When in despair, call on Him and He will be there! Just do what He commands, and I guarantee you He will do as He promises! Like Abraham, your ram is in the bush!

God bless you!

Is That Your All?

All to Jesus I surrender, unto Him I freely give. I might give Him a Sunday morning, but not Sunday night, Monday morning, or any other night or morning! Is that your all? Some of us do the wrong thing even though we know it is a sin. We plan it through and do it with hopes that God will forgive us. Is that your all?

Let's examine ourselves and start giving our all to God! Praising God is a lifestyle. Attending church on a weekly basis is critical for your spiritual growth. Hebrews Chapter 10, Verse 25 says, "And let us not neglect our meeting together, as some people do, but encourage and warn each other, especially now that the day of His coming back again is drawing near."

My friends: if you are not giving your all to God, don't expect joy, peace and a good report in your life. Why is that you might ask? Well, God gave us His all when He sent Jesus Christ to die on the cross for us. Sometimes we forget that and in turn offer God scraps of our time and energy. Imagine if God treated us the way we treat Him. Let's get it right by giving our all to God. Nothing else in life is as important as that!

God bless you!

Example.

Praise the Lord, my friends!

What a powerful word, "Example." What does it mean? Well, it depends on how you receive it. It could mean we watch what someone else does and do it, or we can be an example for others. For the Christian, it should be both. Our brother, the apostle Paul got a good handle on example when he stated in 1 Corinthians Chapter 11, Verse 1, "And you should follow my example, just as I follow Christ's." There you see the pattern. He follows Christ, his students follow him and others follow his students.

Now this leads me to ask; what kind of Christlike examples are we setting? Far too many people set ungodly examples. As Christians, we need to break the trend. Let's start being kinder; smiling more; saying, "God bless you" more; helping others more; saying, "Praise the Lord" more; forgiving more; loving more.

God takes a picture of our lives and keeps the videotape of our example, good or bad. Let's remember to set good examples!

God bless you!

What's Your Motivation?

Praise the Lord, my friends! It's another day to get up and do what we have to do! Today's thought is motivation. What is it that motivates you to accomplish your plans; to seek success; to do what it is you do? Is it the number one response: money? Is it popularity? Fame? Lust? Status? Title? What is it that drives you?

A man once told me he was "money motivated". I told him that I am motivated by God. What does that mean, you might ask? Well, the answer is simple. Proverbs Chapter 16, Verse 3, tells us, "Commit your work to the Lord, and then your plans will succeed." Being motivated by God is making His work priority by connecting it to the regular jobs we do. We need to seek to do God's will daily by speaking His word and by living it. Say for instance while it is sadly not usually allowed to discuss religion on the job, then wait until you get a break to share God with a friend and thereafter always look for an opportunity!

Be motivated by the Spirit of God, not by the spirit of Satan.

God bless you!

Get Hot For Jesus.

Praise the Lord, everyone! It is a disturbing thing to speak to someone for minutes, hours, days or even weeks who says they are a Christian and not see Jesus Christ reflected in that person. I am sure many people feel the same way I do. Anyone who professes Jesus Christ and doesn't live the life, I encourage you to get hot for Jesus!

In Revelation Chapter 3, Verses 15 and 16 Jesus addresses the church in Laodicea saying, "I know all the things you do, that you are neither hot nor cold. I wish you were one or the other! But since you are like lukewarm water, I will spit you out of my mouth!" Remember, the word Christian means "Follower of Christ" or "Christlike".

So do what Christ did. What was that, you might ask? He went around telling people to repent because the kingdom of Heaven is at hand! Do this lovingly. Have integrity. Be kind, honest and trustworthy. For the least you do for God's creation, you also do unto Him.

God bless you!

Believer.

Praise the Lord, my friends! It amazes me when people explain their beliefs. There are so many good people in the world, however, when it comes to a relationship with Jesus Christ, they shy away from it.

You see, it's not just a matter of church attendance or title; it's all about knowing Jesus personally! Many people may argue that point which is okay if it leads to deep research in-to the truth. However, if the argument results in just a bunch of hot air, then it is quite sad. God with His matchless love for us has made it so easy to be saved. In Acts Chapter 2, Verse 21 it says, "And anyone who calls on the name of the Lord will be saved."

What is it going to take to make you a believer? First believe God for salvation and believe Him for sustaining mercies which are new every morning. It is challenging enough to live as a believer; to live without Christ must be exceptionally hard. Cast your cares on Jesus! Don't just take my words for it; seek Him for yourself! You won't be disappointed! Believe in Him!

God bless you!

Your Heart's Desire.

Praise the Lord, my friends!

Desire is something we all have. It may be to eat from a particular restaurant or to relocate into another city or country. Some people desire to be left alone and not bother with the rest of the world. I hope that is not your desire; we need to communicate with others in order to witness!

Now let's analyze this desire thing...What are the steps to take in life in order to achieve your heart's desire? Well, the Bible tells us in Psalm Chapter 37, Verses 4 and 5, "Take delight in the Lord, and he will give you your heart's desires. Commit everything you do to the Lord. Trust him, and he will help you."

Wow. So it's that simple? Yes it is. However, it takes discipline to delight in the Lord and to commit everything you do to the Lord. Pray first for self discipline, and start the engine for your glorious ride with your heart's desire! With Jesus Christ you will make it!

God bless you!

What If You Are Wrong?

Praise the Lord, my friends!

Recently I had a conversation with a young man, who in his own eyes, believes he is wise. He was lecturing me about Evolution, the beginning of mankind and the like. This young man even went as far as telling me that the Bible has me brainwashed, and there is no Heaven or Hell; he says when you die, that's just it; you die.

You may be wondering why I sat there and listened to this stuff? Well, the answer is simple. If we want a chance to share the gospel, we must be willing to hear the heart of the other person. When the young man finished lecturing, I asked him two questions. One: What if you are wrong? Two: Are you willing to risk an eternity in a lake of fire? I told him Proverbs Chapter 14, Verse 12 says, "There is a path before each person that seems right, but it ends in death". I also lovingly told him that he should study all the facts before ruling out the Bible and Jesus Christ.

Let's all lovingly share with the lost!

God bless you!

Do What Is Right.

Praise the Lord, my friends!

It is such a blessing to be in right standing with God! We should all make it a priority to live that lifestyle. Doing what is right is very rewarding! Don't underestimate God by ignoring what is right and clinging to what is wrong just to please your selfish desires. God is so awesome that He can make a way out of no way. He can open doors no one else can open and close doors that would not be beneficial for us.

The Bible tells us in Psalm Chapter 84, Verse 11, "No good thing will the Lord withhold from those who do what is right." So let's do what is right! God says to serve Him; serve Him! Stop serving the flesh which leads to death. Serve God which leads to true life! Jesus died for our sins. We now have power over sin if we partner with Jesus! That is the first step in doing right. Then, live for Him daily. You will be glad you did!

God bless you!

Receive God's Promises.

Praise the Lord, everyone!

Doesn't it make you mad when someone promises to do something for you and at the very last minute, they don't do it? Let's say, for instance, you need a ride to the airport at three p.m. A friend says, "Sure, no problem; I promise I'll pick you up at three o'clock sharp!" At two thirty you get a call. It's your friend saying, "Guess what? I can't make it. I am SO sorry." Now you have to catch a cab or make other arrangements. Some people in that scenario would start to curse and entertain sinful thoughts. People are born into sin, and part of that sin is breaking promises.

Let me remind you that God's promises can never be broken! However, the only way to receive them is through Christ Jesus. The Bible tells us in Galations Chapter 3, Verse 22 that, "...the only way to receive God's promises is to believe in Jesus Christ." Mankind will break promises, but get a hold of Jesus and all His promises will be yours!

God bless you!

Who Is Driving?

Praise the Lord, my friends!

Have you ever seen the bumper sticker, "God Is My CoPilot"? I don't like that bumper sticker. The reason is, that tells me the person behind the steering wheel is the pilot and not the Holy Spirit. If I were in the bumper sticker business I would make one that states, "God is the only pilot I trust!"

We shouldn't trust ourselves to "drive" our lives; we make way too many mistakes! Matthew Chapter 7, Verses 13 and 14 say, "You can enter God's Kingdom only through the narrow gate. The highway to hell is broad, and its gate is wide for the many who choose the easy way. But the gateway to life is small, and the road is narrow, and only a few ever find it."

My friends, let me remind you that every day is a "driving" day in your life, regardless if you leave your home! Make sure Jesus is in the driver's seat or else you will slip off the narrow road and end up on the destructive path. Get closer to Him today!

God bless you!

Call Upon His Name With Purpose.

Praise the Lord, everyone! Why should we praise Him? Because He is worthy to be praised!

So many people are unaware of that fact, or, maybe they know and don't care. Some people even use the name of the Lord in a cursive manner. How sad is that?!! The Lord Jesus Christ allows us to use His name in a worthy manner; for giving Him praise or to fight demon spirits that cause us to sin. In Luke Chapter 9, Verses 49 and 50 John tried to stop a man who was using Jesus' name to cast out demons. Jesus told Him, "Do not stop him." So, you see, we need to use His name with a purpose and with reverence.

The third commandment tells us not to use His name in vain; you will be punished if you do. When you pray, avoid calling His name five, ten, fifteen and twenty times. You wouldn't do that in conversation with a friend. He is in your presence when you pray. In Matthew Chapter 6, Verses 9 through 13 Jesus gave us an example of how to pray; He said, "Our Father" one time. Let's imitate Christ in all we do.

God bless you!

Trust in the Lord.

Some people will praise God all day long and thank Him for His goodness. "I trust the Lord," they say, however, the first time something happens that is contrary to that person's idea of what should happen, they have a trust issue with God.

For instance, someone loses a job. Some people lean more on their own understanding rather than completely trusting the Lord. Let me remind you what the Bible says in Proverbs Chapter 3, Verses 5 and 6: "Trust in the Lord with all your heart; do not depend on your own understanding. Seek His will in all you do, and He will direct your paths."

You see; it all starts with trust. Trust works hand in hand with faith, so let's start truly trusting the Lord! So what if you don't get paid what you want. Trust the Lord! So what if your marriage needs a lot of work. Trust the Lord! How about your health? Trust the Lord! Do you get the picture? By trusting the Lord and doing His will, all will be well. Keep Him first in your heart, and everything else will fall into place!

God bless you!

Don't Be A Paper Weight.

Praise the Lord, my friends! Some people are rooted in the word, to the glory of God, while others are still testing out the water. They may attend church regularly, however, they still dabble with sin. Please, I implore you; don't be that way! Stop worshipping all the wrong gods during your short life on Earth, and start worshipping the true and living God! You may say, "I don't worship idols." However, you are more focused on yourself than you are on the Lord! You, yourself, become an idol. I know; you didn't see it that way before. Now you have a chance to change your ways. Remember what God said in Isaiah Chapter 57, Verse 13: "Let's see if your idols can do anything for you when you cry to them for help. They are so helpless that a breath of wind can knock them down! But whoever trusts in me will possess the land and inherit my holy mountain."

So don't be a paper weight in God. Get serious and stand firm in the faith, then you will inherit the land promised to you filled with peace and joy! Always keep Jesus as main priority in your life.

God bless you!

Start Living.

Praise the Lord, everyone! We know that He is worthy to be praised, don't we? Then we should praise Him with our lives as well as with our lips! Let's allow our actions to sing praises to Him! Sometimes we glorify the enemy with our actions without even knowing it!

Let me encourage you today to start living in such a way that shines the light of Jesus Christ in all that you do. Don't illuminate on Sunday and then have a bad bulb on Monday! Each day God has a purpose for us to rightly represent Him. Don't participate in the sinful things that the crowds (at work, play or school) do; most of them are walking deads! Romans Chapter 6, Verse 11 says, "So you should consider yourselves dead to sin and able to live for the glory of God through Christ Jesus."

Start living the way you know you should. You always have a heavenly audience whether you are alone or with a group of people. Why not put your best foot forward and make God proud. Do this, and watch your quality of life improve daily!

God bless you!

In His Service.

Praise the Lord, my friends!

Have you ever felt like a fish out of water? Flapping around losing the hope of survival? It is a horrible feeling. I have been there before. Even when you are doing what God tells you to do, the pressures of life weigh us down. In times of despair, turmoil, sorrow, disappointment – you name it – I encourage you; call on Jesus for a revival of your spirit! David said in Psalm Chapter 25, Verses 1 and 2, "To you, O Lord, I lift up my soul. I trust in you, my God! Do not let me be disgraced, or let my enemies rejoice in my defeat."

There is a perfect opportunity to trust God even more during our times of dismay. We can rest safely in His loving arms. If you need to cry, then cry. However, rest assured that God has your best interest at heart! The fastest way to see change in your life is to live with a mind set on serving Him, doing what He wants you to do!

Be in His service; don't just attend service!

God bless you!

During Your Day, Please Stop And Wait.

Praise the Lord, my friends! There is none like Him. His promises are true, and He is faithful and just.

Have you ever experienced trials during your day which just put burdens on your shoulders? I believe we have all experienced such days. It doesn't matter – rich, poor, saved or unsaved – we all feel the pressures of this life. After all, this is Earth; not Heaven! However, there is hope for the person who believes in the Lord Jesus Christ and lives for Him! The Bible tells us in Isaiah Chapter 40, Verse 31 that "Those who wait on the Lord will find new strength. They will fly high on wings like eagles. They will run and now grow weary. They will walk and not faint." All these promises are guaranteed for he or she who stops during the day and waits for the Lord!

Don't let life's pressures cause you to lose faith. Stop and wait for peace. Stop and wait for spiritual direction. Stop and wait for patience. Stop and wait for forgiveness. Before speaking or "freaking out," stop and wait for God. He will show up, and you will fly high on wings like Eagles.

God bless you!

Mountain Mover.

Praise the Lord, my friends! He is worthy to be praised! He has given us so much authority on this Earth.

I am sure that everyone reading these words of encouragement has at least one mountain in their life. It could be a problem on the job, marital issues, physical or mental illness, financial illness… Ha! Ha! Ha!… Whatever the case may be – let me encourage you today to call upon the Lord and apply His word to your situation.

Jesus said in Matthew Chapter 17, Verse 20, "I assure you, even if you had faith as small as a mustard seed you could say to this mountain, 'Move from here to there,' and it would move. Nothing would be impossible."

I love that! This gives me authority to remove the mountains in my life by my own faith! So, to be a mountain mover we need to have faith. Faith comes by hearing the word of God, so read it, hear it and gain faith to be a mountain mover! You'd better believe I'll do the same; it's the only way we can make it.

God bless you!

Are You Blessed?

Praise the Lord our Savior!

Some people fail to praise Him because they don't realize how blessed they are. If you live in America, have a place to sleep and a dollar in your piggy bank, that makes you in the 25% of wealthiest people in the world! However, the thing that is most fascinating to me is not so much the material blessings here on Earth, it is my home in Heaven awaiting me because of my faith in Jesus Christ! As a matter of fact, Jesus says in Matthew Chapter 5, Verse 3, "God blesses those who realize their need for Him, for the Kingdom of Heaven is given to them." That puts a big smile on my face and enables me to declare to the world that, "I am truly blessed and highly favored by God!"

I don't know what your issues are in life. But I do know this; Jesus Christ wants to bless you like never before! You need to do your part though. Get involved wherever you can. Don't make lame excuses. If Jesus had made excuses, where would we be today? So get blessed by the Lord and stay blessed by being other people centered!

God bless you!

Family Matters.

To God be the glory, great things He has done! So loved He the world that He gave us His Son!

What a powerful phrase, my friends! Unfortunately, some people don't share that type of concern for others. Not even for a family member. There are so many people in the world today that are living under bridges, in shelters, on the streets… However, strangely enough they have well to do family and relatives. Let's not be the type of people who ignore our families needs. As a matter of fact, the Bible says in 1 Timothy Chapter 5, Verse 8 that "those who won't care for their own relatives, especially those living in the same household, have denied what we believe (as Christians). Such people are worse than unbelievers."

So you see, God is pleased when we get involved and lend a hand! That is exactly what He did for us by sending Jesus to die on the cross for you and me. So, represent God in your family. That is what really matters.

God bless you!

Safe In His Arms.

Praise the Lord, my friends! Have you heard the hymn, "Leaning on the everlasting arms; safe and secure from all alarms?"

That is the way we should all live. Unfortunately, fear has been creeping into the lives of so many Christians. We sometimes fall prey to this, forgetting who we are at times. We are children of the most high God! He is our refuge and strength, a present help in the time of trouble. Please remember this! The Bible tells us in Deuteronomy Chapter 33, Verse 27 that, "The eternal God is your refuge, and His everlasting arms are under you. He thrusts out the enemy before you; it is He who cries, 'Destroy them!'"

Wow! Did you see that? God is fighting our enemies for us – so why should we fear? Let me remind you that God never loses a battle or a war! There is no need to fear! If you received Jesus as Lord and try your best to please Him daily, He promises that His everlasting arms will always be there. We are safe in His arms because He promises to destroy our enemies. So stay in His arms!

God bless you!

Don't Quit.

Praise the name of our Lord, Jesus Christ, because He is worthy to be praised!

Have you ever felt like giving up on something? Maybe you are pursuing your dreams, and things get a little tough. Oh well, that's life… Don't quit! If you are led by the Holy Spirit to pursue your dreams, go for it! Far too many people quit when they are so close to greatness. Keep in mind that people who are in Christ are already victorious, so all we need to do is endure with patience. Hebrews Chapter 10,Verse 36 says, "Patient endurance is what you need now, so you will continue to do God's will. Then you will receive all that he has promised."

So, don't quit your dreams; don't quit your spouse. Don't quit your children. Don't quit your forgiving mindset and most important of all, don't quit your faith in Jesus Christ! Endure, and God will see you through! Yes; I said, God will see you through. You are never alone! He is with you!

God bless you!

Right On Time!

Praise the Lord, my friends!

Don't you just hate it when you are late? Some people get really bothered by that. I especially hate when I have to be at church at a certain time and things keep popping up that cause me to run late. That really bothers me!

We, as humans, get by being late occasionally. However; can you imagine God being late? Just the thought of it is nerve wracking! Everything positive would crash! The negative would triumph. That's how important our Lord and Savior is! So please don't be stressed out because what you feel should happen in your life is not happening fast enough! II Corinthians Chapter 6, Verse 2 tells us that, "At just the right time, I heard you. On the day of salvation, I helped you." Keep in mind that God knows all about everything so when He prepares the way, it is well prepared! He will take you to your destination – right on time! He will grant you that job – right on time! He will help your relationships – right on time, and ultimately Jesus will return – right on time!

God bless you!

Put Up Resistance.

Praise the Lord, everyone!

Most of us at some point or another have stretched a rubber/elastic band. No matter how far we stretch the rubber band, it always goes back to its original form.

Some of us are being stretched right now by many different factors. This often causes stress, and if we are not careful we may take our eyes off Jesus Christ. Let's not let this be an option! When the devil tempts us and uses his disciples to try and break us we MUST put up resistance and go back to our "rightful place" as the rubber band does! As a matter of fact, the Bible tells us in James Chapter 4, Verse 7 that we should, "Submit to God. Resist the Devil, and he will flee from you." Notice the words, "submit" and "resist." We need to do our part! Putting up resistance to sin will help us grow closer to God for a much better lifestyle. God is watching how well we resist!

God bless you!

Render Your Heart.

Glory be to God most high because He is worthy! It is truly amazing how some people hear a verse of scripture and without reading the text, misinterpret what it is saying. One example is, "render your heart, not your garment." Some people use that phrase with regard to their clothing. I can understand how they arrive at that, however it undermines what the text is truly saying. Joel Chapter 2, Verses 11 through 13 say, "the day of the Lord is an awesome, terrible thing. Who can endure it? That is why the Lord says, "Turn to me now, while there is time! Give me your hearts. Come with fasting, weeping, and mourning. Don't tear (render) your clothing in your grief; instead, tear (render) your hearts." Return to the Lord your God, for He is gracious and merciful. He is not easily angered. He is filled with kindness and is eager not to punish you.

It was customary for the Jews to tear their clothes and cry out to God when they had an urgent need for Him to do something for them. God lovingly reminded them that they need to "tear" or "change" their "hearts" toward Him. We need to do the same and render our hearts!

God bless you!

Get Off The Fence.

Blessed be the name of the Lord!

As the Holy Spirit encourages us, the enemy tries to lead toward depressing failure and to everything that contradicts greatness. We need to fight with all our might to stay right. Our responsibility is to make sure we choose Jesus and stay with him! Let's not fellowship with the devil on Saturday and then partner with Jesus on Sunday!

In other words, stop straddling the fence! How fast can you run with your right foot on one side of the fence and your left foot on the other? Jesus said in Revelation Chapter 3, Verses 15 and 16, "I know all the things you do, that you are neither hot nor cold. I wish you were one or the other! But since you are like lukewarm water, I will spit you out of my mouth!"

So please get off the fence! You don't want to taste bad to Jesus! Join the winning team! Get off the fence, and start running the Christian race full speed ahead with Jesus!

God bless you!

Be Of Good Cheer!

What a mighty God we serve! The songwriter says, Angels bow before Him, Heaven and Earth adore Him! God lifts the spirit. He revives people and puts their minds at peace. That is why I praise Him! He takes away the heavy load of this life and makes me cheerful. That same cheerful spirit – not the phony one – the real cheerful spirit is available to all who trust in the Lord Jesus Christ!

Psalm Chapter 94, Verse 19 says, "When doubts filled my mind, your comfort game me renewed hope and cheer." I love that. Doubt is no longer dictating my life. Fear is no longer dictating my life. All Christians who are living the Christlike lifestyle, be of good cheer! God is near, and He won't give you more than you can bear!

A cheerful attitude tells the devil that you are not paying any attention to Him. So start smiling!

God bless you!

Leave Your Comfort Zone.

Praise the Lord, everyone! It is so wonderful to just sit and relax at home in the recliner, drinking some juice and watching your favorite program on TV. Then, of course, your spouse comes along and asks you to get something from the garage! There goes your comfort zone! That is a mild scenario, however.

What if God is asking you to tell more people about Him? What if He is asking you to have an early devotional time in the morning, reading scriptures, praying and singing songs?

Let me encourage you to please leave your comfort zones and respond to the Holy Spirit leading. That's what Jesus did. The Bible tells us in 1 Timothy Chapter 1, Verse 15 that "Christ Jesus came into the world to save sinners…" We are followers of Christ, so if Christ can leave the comforts of Heaven to save our souls, we can leave our comfort zones, increase our studies to show ourselves approved and get active in leading people to Him. Pray about your involvement.

God bless you!

Make A Highway.

Praise the Lord, everyone! Human beings are so precious, yet so many people feel they have no worth. We are all placed here on Earth for a specific purpose. For instance, to become a doctor, nurse, teacher, fireman, etc. Now, those are excellent choices whether you are saved or not. However, as Christians we have an even higher calling. We should make a highway.

Before you tell me I am crazy, let me explain. Isaiah Chapter 40, Verse 3 says, "Make a highway for the Lord through the wilderness. Make a straight, smooth road through the desert for our God." If you are more confused now than before, let me elaborate further. John the Baptist was the best example of highway makers. He told people to repent because Jesus is coming. There are many ways for us to lovingly do the same.

Remember that Jesus is coming back! Let's start making highways for Jesus by pruning others with the word of God so they, too, can see his glory! You never know how large a highway you can make until you get started! It's not only a job for John the Baptist, but for Christians everywhere!

God bless you!

Restoration.

In these last and evil days, the people of God are under tremendous attack. These attacks may vary from emotional, physical, financial, to the greatest challenge of all – spiritual. During our suffering we hope and pray for a breakthrough of some sort but God in His matchless wisdom knows the perfect time to grant our requests. We can confidently endure the hard times knowing that God promises to restore His people. The Bible tells us in Psalm Chapter 119, Verse 107, "I have suffered much, O Lord; restore my life again as you promised."(NLT)

God's promises are true, so He will restore us at the right time. The battle will always be active in the spiritual realm so don't take off your armor! Putting our faith in Jesus Christ is the best thing we could ever do, but it also makes us an enemy to Satan. Satan will forever try to steal our joy, kill our dreams and destroy our relationship with Jesus, but don't allow him to! Satan afflicted Jesus with more pain than we ever felt, but God the Father restored His Son. He will also restore us who suffer for righteousness sake so be encouraged!

God bless you!

Victory Lane.

Every year for many years now I treat myself to an Indy car race. It is fascinating to see the professional drivers exceed two hundred miles per hour with ease. The winner, along with the second and third place drivers, get a chance to go to Victory Lane. We who are saved and living for Jesus Christ will someday experience the real Victory Lane!

John says in Revelation Chapter 15, Verse 2, "I saw before me what seemed to be a glass sea mixed with fire. And on it stood all the people who had been victorious over the beast and his statue and the number representing his name. They were all holding harps that God had given them."(NLT) We are now on the race track. Let's run well so that we will be a part of the rapture which for us will be Victory Lane! A second Victory Lane will be available for those left behind and who refuse to worship the antichrist, his statue and refuse to take his mark of 666. The latter of which should be "the road less traveled" since it will be a more severe battle. Decide today to make Jesus the way! Our Victory Lane is guaranteed and eternal, unlike the Indy races where you win some you lose some.

God bless you!

Get Ready to Laugh!

Some people find it harder to laugh than cry. Situations in life dictate their attitudes, countenance and actions. That should not be, because God is bigger than your situations! Even in the tough times we should laugh when trials come. We should laugh and take the issue to God. He is able to do the impossible for you, just as He did for Abraham and Sarah many years ago. Genesis Chapter 21, Verses 6 and 7 say, And Sarah declared, "God has brought me laughter. All who hear about this will laugh with me. Who would have said to Abraham that Sarah would nurse a baby? Yet I have given Abraham a son in his old age!" Indeed when I read this story I laughed, and I'm still laughing today! Imagine: a ninety year old woman giving birth and nursing a baby. Only a miracle working God with a sense of humor could pull off something like that!

So what is ailing you today? Turn it over to God, and then laugh about it. Don't try and fix problems on your own; there is no joy in that. Jesus came so we can have life more abundantly; allow Him to give it to you! Replace your sorrows with laughter – place Jesus at the center of your life!

God bless you!

The All Seeing Eye.

Many people believe what's done in the dark will never be revealed. Humanly speaking that may be true, but supernaturally speaking it isn't so. We have a God that sees all the good we do and all the evil we do. He knows the intention of our hearts, so there is no hiding from Him. In 2 Chronicles Chapter 16 King Asa forgot all the victories in war that God gave to him and placed his trust in the king of Aram. That was a huge mistake. God saw King Asa's heart turn away from Him. As a result, Hanani, a seer tells King Asa in Verse 9, "The eyes of the Lord search the whole earth in order to strengthen those whose hearts are fully committed to Him. What a fool you have been! From now on you will be at war." Be fully committed to God; give Him your whole heart. The Lord Jesus Christ wants to be involved in everything we do, why not allow Him? He is available to all who would only ask Him to come inside their heart. If you are not fully committed to God, you are committed to the devil. The all seeing eye is watching. Live for Him and obtain the victory, or turn from Him and accept defeat. God loves every person in the world. The question is – Do you love Him?

God bless you!

You Are Rescued!

In the Bible we see many times where God rescues the children of Israel from disaster. It is very comforting to know that we are safe in the loving arms of Jesus. Whatever problem we are faced with, just know that our Lord will not give us more than we can handle. One thing is for sure – if we live a life that honors God, our greatest enemy Satan, or his followers, will never triumph over us!

David says in Psalm Chapter 30, Verse 1, "I will exalt you, Lord, for you rescued me. You refused to let my enemies triumph over me."(NLT) So you see, the Lord is protecting us in all circumstances. We may not fully understand His ways, but keep the faith!

Bill collectors wearing you down? "You are rescued!" Do you feel that sin is winning the battle in your life? "You are rescued!" Feel as if you're on a sinking ship? "You are rescued!" Shout Hallelujah to the Lord, you are rescued! The greatest lifeguard is always on duty!

God bless you!

Are You Calling Him?

Telephone ring tones are fancy these days. You can personalize your tone to ring as a song you like, or just some other sound – for example, a rooster crowing. This is all well and good but there is one very special ring tone known to God alone when an individual calls on Him, and He is attentive to our plea. The Bible says in Deuteronomy Chapter 4, Verse 7, "For what great nation has a god as near to them as the Lord our God is near to us whenever we call on Him?"(NLT)

So the important question is, Are you calling Him? Don't miss the awesome experience of calling on God each day! He wants direct communication with you, in Jesus' name. Many people only hear from God through a Pastor or another believer. Let's change that; call on God for yourself. He knows your specific ring tone, and He will be exceedingly glad to hear from you! Turn off your earthly telephone for a while each day and pick up your heavenly telephone in prayer. God is waiting on the other end, and you will never get a busy signal!

God bless you!

Temple Benefits.

Going to church should never feel like an obligation. We should get excited to hear the word, fellowship with other believers and to make our requests known to God. I know; "the body is the temple where the spirit of God dwells", and, "we can pray anywhere at anytime". However, there is something special about getting together and praying with other believers in a temple that has been dedicated to the Lord! We encounter a corporate anointing that is great than praying solo at home! 2 Chronicles Chapter 7, Verses 15 and 16 say, "My eyes will be open and my ears attentive to every prayer made in this place. For I have chosen this Temple and set it apart to be holy – a place where my name will be honored forever." Wow! So you know for sure that God is paying attention to your request in church.

Many people pray with so many distractions at home – TV, radio, conversations... It is also beneficial to get to church early; find a spot and just reason with God in Jesus' name. Your job may have benefits but they don't compare with going to the temple and speaking with your savior there!

God bless you!

Just Have Faith.

There is a serious lesson to be learned about faith. We need to always remember that God created this universe from nothing, so we should stop relying on things we see and just have faith. The Bible says in Hebrews Chapter 11, Verse 3, "By faith we understand that the entire universe was formed at God's command, that what we now see did not come from anything that can be seen."

We are all guilty of having doubted God at some point in our lives. It is time to stop doubting and start having faith! First, we need to repent of our doubt, ask God for His forgiveness, and then start exercising true faith. The things that God has placed in your hearts will come to pass for His glory! Don't worry about the way things appear to be – just remember how big our God is!

Read in your Bible through the entire faith chapter (Hebrews 11) to see how our predecessors accomplished greatness by faith. We can do the same. Let's make God proud by showing Him our faith in Him! Just have faith!

God bless you!

Jesus Loves You!

Jesus loves me, this I know! For the Bible tells me so! Christians need to remember that fact when going through tough times. It is easy to smile and say, "Jesus loves me" when everything is going well, but often times we lose focus when a trying situation arises.

Let's change that! Jesus loves you through the good times and during the bad times! You can rest assured that He will take care of His chosen people! The Bible says in 1 John Chapter 3, Verse 16, "We know what real love is because Jesus gave up His life for us."(NLT) Are we giving up our lives for Him? If we are, it proves that we love Him. If we are not, then maybe we don't love Him like we ought to! His love toward us will never end, no matter what, but I must say this – a father disciplines his children when they do wrong.

If you feel a bit separated from Jesus, confess your sins and rekindle the Holy Spirit fire within. The love of Jesus is a spark able to ignite any spirit who is willing!

God bless you!

He Will Make A Way!

We may encourage someone or receive encouragement that God will make a way. Often times we still doubt in our hearts and miss a blessing that should have come our way. I feel that everyone who has a relationship with Jesus Christ should just believe Him for big things in life which will glorify Him. The ultimate example of the Lord making a way is found in Exodus Chapter 14, Verses 21 and 22. "Then Moses raised his hand over the sea, and the Lord opened up a path through the water with a strong east wind. The wind blew all that night, turning the seabed into dry land. So the people of Israel walked through the middle of the sea on dry ground, with walls of water on each side!"(NLT) I don't know where you are in life right now; maybe the bills or family matters are weighing you down; problems on the job; loss of a loved one – whatever it may be, God can make a way. There is no problem or situation too big for our God! He conquered death and the grave, so keep in mind that He can conquer your situation! He will make a way if we allow Him to lead the way! Put Jesus in the driver seat of your life and I guarantee you that if you don't doubt Him, you will be amazed at the places He will take you!

God bless you!

The Keys of Heaven.

Keys are essential in everyday living. We use them to open doors, start cars, lock up valuables, etc. However, the most important set of keys we need are the keys of Heaven. In Matthew Chapter 16, Verse 19 Jesus says, "And I will give you the keys of the Kingdom of Heaven. Whatever you forbid on earth will be forbidden in Heaven, and whatever you permit on earth will be permitted in Heaven." Interestingly, Jesus said, "I will give you…" not, I have given you. You see, the Holy Spirit was not yet given to Peter, so he didn't have the power to defeat Satan. You know the story – in the same chapter, verse 23, Jesus calls Peter, Satan. However, the same Peter in Acts Chapter 2, Verse 41 caused three thousand people to be baptized in one day! Jesus gave Peter the keys of Heaven in the form of the Holy Spirit, and Peter used it to get others into Heaven.

Do you utilize the power of the Holy Spirit within you to set the captives free and get them into Heaven? If you are truly born again, you have the keys for everyone else! The keys are available for you to take hold of. Don't arrive at Heaven's gate without your keys!

God bless you!

Avoid Stumbling.

Many people stumble in their walk with the Lord. Some even fall away and reestablish a working relationship with the devil. That, my friend, is a very dangerous place to be. Wouldn't it be nice to be in tune with God to the point where you will not stumble, you will not be moved even when facing the toughest times in your life? The mistake many people who fall away make is focusing on the problem, instead of trusting the problem solver! King David says this in Psalm Chapter 21, Verse 7: "For the king trusts in the Lord. The unfailing love of the Most High will keep him from stumbling."

So we see that the awesome power of God Most High will keep us from stumbling. Don't stumble, and you won't fall. Read the word of God daily and believe it! Everyone can make excuses why they stumble, why they fall, but God knows the heart of man and those who really try their best to please Him! Let us not be lazy in pressing forward in righteousness. Don't make excuses and give the devil power over you. Partner with our Lord Jesus Christ, and He will show you the stumbling blocks in plain sight so you can avoid them!

God bless you!

Roll Up Your Sleeves.

People, in general, love to be served. When at a nice restaurant and the server is attentive, polite and quick, we enjoy the good service. It may even prompt us to leave a bigger tip!

It is easy to have an, "I am to be served" mindset rather than one of, "I should serve others." Fortunately for the follower of Jesus Christ, we know the truths – that it is better to give than to receive; that it is better to serve others than to be served. Jesus said it best in Matthew Chapter 20, Verse 28, "For even the Son of Man came not to be served but to serve others and to give his life as a ransom for many."(NLT)

Some people won't leave the comfort of their homes to go out and help someone in need. Keep in mind that Jesus left his home in Heaven! Jesus came to show us the way we should live which will in turn glorify our Heavenly Father. Let's begin by rolling up our sleeves and getting involved with the service opportunities that God places in our path. Let's listen to the tugging on our hearts and obey; that is the Christian way!

God bless you!

Prophet or Prophet of God?

As much as it pains my heart to say this: There are many false prophets around. They have been around for a very long time, beginning with Lucifer, himself! We need to make sure that our connection to God is fully intact so we won't be easily deceived. Whatever actions we take, we must first get an approval from God. Sometimes God will use a prophet to guide our way. However, we must also know God for ourselves or foolish counsel will sound wise. 1 Kings Chapter 22, Verses 6 through 8 say, "So the king of Israel summoned the prophets, about 400 of them, and asked them, 'Should I go to war against Ramothgilead, or should I hold back?'" Then Jehoshaphat asked, "Is there not also a prophet of the Lord here?" The king of Israel replied to Jehoshaphat, "There is one more man who could consult the Lord for us, but I hate him. He never prophesies anything but trouble for me!"(NLT)

Don't get caught up in the tickling of your ears! Listen to sound doctrine from the prophets of the Lord! King Ahab dies in that same chapter after listening to the wrong prophets. Let's learn a thing or two from the dead. God's prophets may very well keep you alive!

God bless you!

Winner's Circle.

Most people take delight in winning, don't they? The reality of losing a football game or even a board game is not a good feeling.

How about losing the life race? The life race is quite unique, in the sense that everyone who finishes with Jesus Christ as their lord and savior will be a winner. Philippians Chapter 3, Verse 14 says, "I press on to reach the end of the race and receive the heavenly prize for which God, through Christ Jesus, is calling us." Anyone who ignores the will of God in their daily lives can boldly say, "I am part of the loser's circle in God's eyes." Don't make the will of man or of self supersede the will of God in your life. So many have died unexpectedly and have joined the loser's circle in hell. Be a winner. Shine the light of Christ in everything you do. So what if it takes a sacrifice. Jesus sacrificed His life, so stop making excuses! Jesus won by defeating death and hell. Let Him lead your life, and you will be a winner too!

God bless you!

He Is Watching.

When you're being watched by the boss you put your best foot forward, don't you?

I remember back in high school my first performance for the entire school in the auditorium. I hoped that I wouldn't mess up. Why is that? Because everyone was watching me; I wanted to do right. I now know that I've always had an audience even greater than the entire school also watching me, and still watching me today! His name is Jesus Christ; the author and finisher of our faith!

The Bible declares in Psalm Chapter 34, Verse 15 that, "The eyes of the Lord watch over those who do right; his ears are open to their cries for help." This area of scripture truly inspires me to do right. We should remember that the all seeing eye of God has twenty/twenty vision even in the dark! Don't go thinking you are invisible when you turn the lights out! Honor God in all that you do; He is watching you!

God bless you!

Honor Your Parents.

A woman once told me that she hated her mother. I was shocked! I asked her why, and she stated that her mom treated her badly as a little girl.

God knows the heart of all people and yet in His word in Ephesians Chapter 6, Verse 3 He says, "And this is the promise: If you honor your father and mother, "you will live a long life, full of blessing."" Take notice God did not say, "Honor your parents only if they treat you right." Whether or not our parents treat us right, we should honor them. That would be pleasing to God.

I hope that the love of God in you will cause you to extend forgiveness to parents who have done you wrong. You may say, "Pastor, you have no idea what they did to me!" You are right, however, I know what Jesus did for us and how much forgiveness he extended to this world! So in light of that fact, let's be Christians (followers of Christ), and extend love to the parents we have because when they are gone, they are gone. Honor them while you still can!

God bless you!

Promises, Promises.

"A promise is a comfort to a fool!" That is a saying that you may or may not have heard before. You can't help but wonder; is it true? I believe it depends on who is making the promise. While in high school I trusted a friend with a secret, and he promised me he wouldn't tell anyone. Yeah, right… That lasted a whole few minutes. He told his girlfriend the secret, not knowing that she would be a perfect candidate for employment with CNN news network.

Everyone won't break their promises, but you don't know who will! Here is what we DO know; God always keeps His promises! Solomon declared in 1 Kings Chapter 8, Verse 56, "Praise the Lord who has given rest to His people Israel, just as He promised. Not one word has failed of all the wonderful promises He gave through His servant Moses."

God promises salvation through His son, Jesus Christ, to all who believe in Him and live for Him. His benefit package is out of this world! Start enjoying God's promises! They are true.

God bless you!

Are You Safe?

Safety has always been important to everyone. As children, Mom and Dad watched out for us so wc wouldn't touch the hot stove, drown in the bathtub or get run over by a car. Those are very basic although important precautions, but what about now when we're all grown up with mature agendas? Are you safe?

Safe from what, you might ask. Safe from the wrath of God! Unfortunately your burglar alarm system, gated community or armed security guard cannot protect you from God's wrath. Let me lovingly say that the only protection that will guarantee your safety one hundred percent is a right relationship with Jesus Christ! Proverbs Chapter 18, Verses 10 and 11 say, "The name of the Lord is a strong fortress; the godly run to Him and are safe. The rich think of their wealth as an impregnable defense; they imagine it is a high wall of safety." God laughs at mankind. We sometimes think we have it all figured out. Well, we don't...

Run to God; not to the things created by God for your safety. My desire is that all who read these encouraging words receive Jesus Christ as Lord and Savior and declare with boldness, I AM SAFE!

God bless you!

Stop Worrying.

Some people worry themselves to sickness. You know what I am talking about. They worry it might rain tomorrow, or it may be too hot or too cold. They worry about their outfit or hairdo or their shoes not matching the clothes they have on. **NEWSFLASH**: no one really cares about that! Besides, it's your personality that makes you a lot more attractive than any outfit.

Worry over paying bills, buying food… Here's a new one: worry about buying gas for your car! Stop it! Please! If you are honest with yourself, you will confirm that sitting around worrying never solves anything! Jesus speaks about worrying in Matthew Chapter 6, Verses 31 through 33 when He says, "So don't worry about having enough food or drink or clothing. Why be like the pagans who are so deeply concerned about these things? Your heavenly Father already knows all your needs, and He will give you all you need from day to day if you live for him and make the Kingdom of God your primary concern." So rather than worry turn your fear into faith, do the will of our Lord, Jesus Christ and know for certain that He will make a way out of no way!

As the Australians say, "No worries, mate!"

God bless you!

Receive the Prize.

Have you ever felt as if you are running a marathon and the finish line is nowhere in sight?

We all have been there at some point in life. Some people stay there all their lives. Let's do everything possible to avoid that. The only proven way I know is to start running the race to Heaven. Christians can turn to the book of Revelation, and the Holy Spirit will very clearly show us our end! One of the great things about running the race to Heaven is that everyone who crosses the finish line will get a prize! The apostle Paul says in Philippians Chapter 3, Verse 14, "I strain to reach the end of the race and receive the prize for which God, through Christ Jesus, is calling us up to heaven."

Never take your eyes off Heaven because of situations weighing you down, or just because things aren't working the way you think they should. Keep on pressing on; rid yourself of any "junk" which may be holding you back. Fix your eyes on Jesus, and you will see the path to the finish line. I guarantee it! Stay on the path to receive your prize.

God bless you!

It's Alright.

Praise be to God, it's all right! Well; not really, you might say. After seeing the word separated you might change your mind and instead of saying it's all right, you might say it's partially right. Some may say it's all wrong, depending on what you are going through.

Well, listen to this: If you are a believer in the Lord Jesus Christ and you live for Him daily, you can truly say it's alright. The Bible teaches us in Romans Chapter 8, Verse 28 that, "… we know that God causes everything to work together for the good of those who love God and are called according to His purpose for them." No matter what the situation may look like, we can rest assured that God has a plan through it all. When it's cloudy, just praise God with a smile! When it's rainy, break out the umbrella and praise Him! If it's hot and sunny, put on your sunglasses and say hallelujah! Praise Him no matter what -- it will all work out for you! It's alright!

God bless you!

Reach for the Sky.

You've probably heard the phrase, "Reach for the Sky." It could mean many things. For instance, pursue whatever it is our hearts desire; strive to be the best in your field or aim for the moon and if you miss, you will fall among the stars. These goals are great however, for me, "reach for the sky" also has a spiritual meaning.

In Isaiah Chapter 45, Verse 22 God says, "Let all the world look to me for salvation! For I am God; there is no other..." You can clearly see that God wants us to reach for him first then we will have attained the highest position in the sky! Once our salvation is secure, God will open doors which take us higher and higher!

So in our daily pursuit to be "out of this world," call on Jesus Christ to direct your path. He is the best road map to get you out of this world into the sky and unto eternity with him!
Reach for Jesus — He will take you to the sky!

God bless you!

Disciple Or Disaster?

You've heard it before: "He's not a Christian; he's a hypocrite!" Because of something that Christian said or did, the onlookers came to that conclusion. It's one thing to be an obvious hypocrite, but what about the so called "disciples of God" who are outrageously sinful behind closed doors? Oh, you know the ones who sound Godly most of the time when they're not talking badly about people. They call on Jesus every Sunday and when they think no one's watching, they mimic the devil from Monday to Saturday. If the spirit of God is speaking to you or of someone you know, please take note of what Jesus says in Matthew Chapter 7, Verse 21. "Not all people who sound religious are really godly. They may refer to me as 'Lord,' but they still won't enter the Kingdom of Heaven. The decisive issue is whether they obey my Father in heaven."

Don't be a disaster. Become a disciple! Obey God and prove once and for all that you love Him. The world is watching to see what the Christian does. Let's give them something good to look at without hypocrisy. More importantly: Jesus is also watching!

God bless you!

Blessed Not Lucky.

Mary tells her best friend, Julie, that she is going to class to take a history test. Julie responds, "Good luck to you!"

Good luck. It is something people say without giving it much thought. However, luck is good one day and bad the next. It is "wishywashy," you could say. Therefore, luck is not of God because God is stable in all things, without changing or compromising His word. God cannot be associated with luck. In the Bible you will repeatedly find the word, "blessed" for doing God's will, and the word, "cursed" for not doing His will.

I love what the Bible says in James Chapter 1, Verse 25: "But if you keep looking steadily into God's perfect law – the law that sets you free – and if you do what it says and don't forget what you heard, then God will bless you for doing it." In order to live a life of blessings, obey the word of God. If you decide you can't be bothered, then you will embrace the luck of this world that Satan has to offer. Be mindful of what you say. Rid yourself of luck and begin to speak blessings! Try saying, "God bless you!" and/or "May God bless your endeavor!"

Until next time: God bless you!

Be Delivered.

Praise God who loves us so much that He sent His only begotten son, who loves us so much He gave His life to deliver us from eternal suffering.

This is not a big topic on the lips of people these days; not even for some Christians. It is really scary when you think of the many "so called Christians" who are not delivered. They lie, steal and curse just as people in the world do. Deliverance is vital in order to change the way we walk with the Lord. Jesus' disciples asked Him how to pray, and in Matthew Chapter 6, Verse 13, His model for prayer He said, "…And don't let us yield to temptation, but deliver us from the evil one."

So you see we must pray for deliverance from whatever it is the evil one is using to cause us to sin. Sin will separate us from God. Separated, we end up in a downward spiral of spiritual and physical destruction. Surely we should do our very best to prevent that from happening. So, confess to Jesus all of your sin and be delivered by His spirit!

God bless you!

God's Representative.

Every time we honor the Lord Jesus Christ in what we say or do, we are honoring God, the Father. We also stand out in the eyes of people who see or hear us honoring God. That in turn puts us in a unique position — we can follow up, continuing to be a good representative of God, or we can fail by being a bad representative.

Let's speak words and do things the way Jesus would! As a matter of fact the Bible tells us in Colossians Chapter 3, Verse 17 that "... whatever you do or say, let it be as a representative of the Lord Jesus, all the while giving thanks through Him to God the Father." Wow! That is powerful! We can do it one day at a time by seeking God's will for our lives. Self will and other sinful acts will never result in becoming God's representative.

Analyze yourself. Pray and ask God to rid you of the struggles you face, and start walking and talking as Jesus would! We have the power of the Holy Spirit himself living in us so that we are able to do it. If He is not in you don't you think it's well past time He is? He is waiting for you!

God bless you!

Teamwork.

There is no "I" in the word, team. That means, it is not an individual effort. It is two or more people working together. Working together is the key. If a team is divided and everyone does their own thing, then nothing will get accomplished.

We, the church of Jesus Christ, are all part of God's team. We need to work hard during our daily lives for the kingdom and not just on Sunday. One of my favorite examples of teamwork is found in Proverbs Chapter 6, Verse 8 which says, "they labor hard all summer, gathering food for the winter." If you are not familiar with this area of scripture, it is talking about the ant. They have no king, however, they all work together for the greater good. Let's in our witnessing imitate the teamwork principle the ant practices. We can team up, visit the local grocery store and share the gospel. We can begin prayer chains, lifting up the unsaved for repentive hearts.

There is so much we can accomplish as a team. Let's be geared towards teamwork and make our team captain, Jesus Christ, proud!

God bless you!

Picture Day.

Picture day at school is a fun time! Everything's got to be "just right" as the young girls and boys want to look their best for friends and family! As much as we may have enjoyed those moments there is a "picture day" coming that is far more important, and we need to dress our best for it.

A man was in the back of a cab. It was lightning out. The man put his face up against the window and started to smile. The driver being puzzled asked what he was doing. The man said, "Don't you see God is taking my picture!"

Jesus says in Matthew Chapter 24, Verse 27, "For as the lightning lights up the entire sky, so it will be when the son of man comes." There will be no mistaking that day. It will be a picture perfect day. Make sure you are properly dressed for the occasion! You need to put on Jesus Christ. He will always have the most modern digital camera! Throw away Satan who uses the 1980's disposable. You will either smile or cry on that picture day. Let's choose to smile!

God bless you!

Jemimah.

When people hear the name Jemimah, they instantly associate it with "Aunt Jemima." You know, "Aunt Jemima" pancake syrups. People will associate things with food in a heartbeat; I know I do!

So where did this name originate from? Well, as a part of Job's blessing for his faithfulness to God, seven more sons and three more daughters were granted to him. The Bible tells us in Job Chapter 42, Verses 14 and 15, "He named his first daughter Jemimah, the second Keziah, and the third Kerenhappuch. In all the land there were no other women as lovely as the daughters of Job…" So in other words, Jemimah and her sisters were lovely blessings to their father.

Are you a lovely blessing to your heavenly father? He pays close attention to the hearts of all people. Does He see a lovely heart free from corruption, pride, hate, anger, selfishness, greed, lust, idolatry, sexual immorality and the like? If He does not, you have some work to do! Rid yourself of them so God will see you as lovely as Jemimah. Shine the light of Christ and your beauty will never fade!

God bless you!

Which Way To Go?

Life is full of signs. While walking or driving down the street we see many signs. We see stop signs, turn to the left signs, turn to the right signs, warning signs, etc. We tend to pay attention to these signs and obey them.

Ironically it is not always so when it comes to signs in the Bible. Many refuse to follow them. Please keep it fresh in your mind – Jesus is the way! In John Chapter 14, Verse 6 Jesus tells us, "I am the way, the truth and the life. No one can come to the Father except through me."

You may be wondering which way you should go today. Life may be weighing you down emotionally, physically, financially. Turn to Jesus! He is not only the way to Heaven, but He is also the way to solve all of life's problems! He does things in His way and in His timing. Don't take the wrong road and fall over a cliff! Pay attention to the signs of the time! Choose Jesus Christ and His will for your life! Make Him your best friend. He is the way to go even after this life ends!

God bless you!

Wedding Invitation.

People get married all the time. Weddings are very popular. The sad thing is many who say "I do" shortly say, "I won't;" and then head for the divorce attorney. Much more important than any wedding invitation from us is the invitation we get from Jesus to be a part of His bride (which is the church). When we accept that invitation – WOW!! Words cannot express how we should rejoice! The Bible says in Revelation Chapter 19, Verses 7 and 8, "Let us be glad and rejoice and honor Him. For the time has come for the wedding feast of the Lamb, and His bride has prepared herself. She is permitted to wear the finest white linen." (Fine linen represents the good deeds done by the people of God.)

Are your garments white as snow? Are you a part of the bride of Christ? If you answer no to these questions, why not make a change today by accepting the wedding invitation. Just say, "Yes Lord, I want you in my life to lead and guide me, to be my savior and best friend. Thank you for dying on the cross for me. I receive you, Jesus.

Welcome to the wedding! All the believers and Host of Heaven rejoice with you!

God bless you!

Our Hidden Protection.

When someone mentions protection to a Christian, they may instantly tell you about the many angels they have. This is true. Angels do watch over us, but what are we doing to protect ourselves? Stop thinking about that alarm system on your home; that isn't what I'm talking about. How do we protect ourselves from getting a bad name?

Integrity is often overlooked, but if it's not exercised our witnessing won't be effective! I love what David says in Psalm Chapter 25, Verse 21: "May integrity and honesty protect me, for I put my hope in you." We need to be protected by these hidden attributes. When things are going great for the Christian many will not notice, however should a Christian fall by stealing or lying, look for it on the six o'clock news!

I encourage you today – trust in the Lord Jesus Christ each day for strength and protect your good name! The Bible says a good name is better than great riches! In life we will be tested, but through Christ let us stay protected!

God bless you!

Where Do You Call Home?

It's five o'clock PM on a Friday afternoon. You've just finished working hard all week, and now you start heading to your – hotel? No; I'm kidding. Well, sort of. You start heading – home; or so you think! Your earthly residence is a temporary lodging. You may as well call it a hotel – a private hotel. The Bible says in Hebrews Chapter 13, Verse 14, "This world is not our home; we are looking forward to our city in Heaven, which is yet to come." So you see, we are just passing through this world! Have you ever wondered why God allowed you to occupy this space at this time? Well, the answer is this: He knows you have the potential to do great things for the kingdom of Heaven! Consider all the great things you've done for God as confirmation to your heavenly home. On the flip side, if you are not doing anything great for God it's confirmation that you don't have a heavenly home.

So here is the question: Where do you call home? Jesus suffered and died so we could have access to our heavenly home. Seek His will for your life. Don't invest all your time building "an earthly hotel" for someone else to destroy in the future. Our heavenly home is forever and ever. Do your best to make it home!

God bless you!

What's Your Mission?

While some look at life as "mission impossible", I believe life is "mission possible" – if Christ Jesus is in your life!

People run into trouble when their focus is on self will and the will of God is not on their agenda. That must change in our lives because God truly has a mission for each and every one of us! Isaiah spoke about Jesus when he wrote in Isaiah Chapter 49, Verse 5, "And now the Lord speaks – he who formed me in my mother's womb to be his servant, who commissioned me to bring his people of Israel back to him. The Lord has honored me, and my God has given me strength."

In the middle of the word "commissioned" you find the word "mission". Let's pray and ask God, what is our mission. For if we fail to accomplish our mission, we have missed the mark. If we miss the mark, it's a sin and we know that sin cannot enter into the presence of God.

Let's put self will on the sideline and focus on God's will for us. Embrace, attack and accomplish your mission for Christ!

God bless you!

Who Should You Honor?

People well known for their deeds and honorary mentions usually receive a title. For example, they may be announced something like this: "The Right, Honorable Marcus Garvey" or "Grammy Award Winner, Yolanda Adams".

Far too many times people who also deserve to be honored, often go unnoticed. One example – our moms and dads. Do you really honor your parents? Jesus had to straighten out some of His fellow Jews in Matthew Chapter 15, Verses 3 and 4 which read, Jesus replied, "And why do you, by your traditions, violate the direct commandments of God? For instance, God says, 'Honor your father and mother,' and 'Anyone who speaks evil of father or mother must be put to death.' Can you imagine if everyone were governed by the laws of God like they should, instead of the law of "anything goes"? For fear of your life you would honor your parents! Let me say this: God's word never changes. If you are dishonoring your parents you are dying spiritually while inviting demonic spirits to lead your life! Please consider what Jesus said; start honoring your parents regardless of how they treat you. God will reward or punish each one of us individually. Just do your part by honoring them.

God bless you!

In The Belly Of The Fish.

Do you feel consumed by your problems? Maybe it's an emotional hurt, physical sickness beyond a doctor's ability to heal or financial troubles. Whatever the case, these things can easily consume or "swallow up" an individual.

If you or someone you know fall in this category, I have great news for you! The prophet Jonah was consumed by a great problem. His problem was in the form of a big fish which swallowed him. Jonah had no flashlight, diving gear or food! Talk about a situation! So what did Jonah do? The Bible tells us in Jonah Chapter 2, Verses 1, 2 and 10, Then Jonah prayed to the Lord his God from inside the fish. He said, "I cried out to the Lord in my great trouble, and He answered me. Then the Lord ordered the fish to spit up Jonah on the beach, and it did. (NLT)

Are you kidding me? God heard Jonah's prayer from inside the fish? Yes He did, and He will hear your prayer in whatever circumstance may consume you. By faith in the Lord Jesus Christ our Savior, He will save us and order our "big fish" to spit us out. Take it to the Lord. He is just a prayer away!

God bless you!

Prepare For Your Land.

God loves to give us nice things. Any father that truly loves his children will always keep a look out for gifts he could give them. Our father in Heaven gives us some guidelines in order to prepare for the land that He is giving us. Deuteronomy Chapter 18, Verse 9 says, "When you arrive in the land the Lord your God is giving you, be very careful not to imitate the detestable customs of the nations living there." (NLT)

We are living in very serious times. Perversion is no longer frowned upon. Nudity and homosexuality are the norm. The list goes on. However, anyone who trusts in the Lord Jesus Christ need to abstain from detestable things. God will then grant us our land! Your land could be a successful business; a great family; peace; joy or just overall favor from God. Then in the near future, the rapture of the church when we will go and be with Jesus in a land that human words cannot adequately describe! So please prepare yourself! Be mindful of what you entertain, and do all things in Jesus' name! Remember: if it cannot be done in Jesus' name, please refrain!

God bless you!

Email From God.

What a blessing to hear from our maker! God speaks to us from His written word. Another awesome way God speaks to us is in a still small voice. Talk about an instant message! That is what I call getting and email from God. Our heavenly father has always been in the wireless business, getting a message to us at just the right time.

King Hezekiah was about to die, and he cried out to God. God heard his prayer, and the Bible tells us in II Kings Chapter 20, Verses 4 and 5, "But before Isaiah had left the middle courtyard, this message came to him from the Lord: Go back to Hezekiah, the leader of my people. Tell him, 'This is what the Lord, the God of your ancestor David, says: I have heard your prayer and seen your tears. I will heal you, and three days from now you will get out of bed and go to the Temple of the Lord…' Isaiah was on his way home when he received an instant message, and he returned to the king with the news!

Are you getting emails and instant messages from God? If not, it may be because you haven't sent any messages to him in prayer. Why not get started!

God bless you!

Call Upon Your Angels.

For lack of knowledge, people really do perish. Sometimes, we take on a lot more than we can handle. Many Christians try to do everything they can to save a family member, friend or coworker. While this is commendable, that person needs a more constant influence than we can render.

This is where our angels come into play. We can dispatch them to work on our behalf to the glory of God! Hebrews Chapter 1, Verse 14 says, "But angels are only servants. They are spirits sent from God to care for those who will receive salvation." (NLT) Servants. Wow! Imagine that! We have angels serving us; so we should serve each other! No matter what the situation may be: marital, financial... our angels are willing and able to help us sort things out. It is time now for the church to understand this information and start using it, in Jesus' name! Do not accept the foolishness Satan throws at you! Fight back with God's mighty angels who are at your disposal! Just pray, "Heavenly Father in the mighty name of Jesus, please dispatch your angels to come to my aid; to touch the heart of a family member for salvation, or, to bring about peace in my home. You can now see the picture well. So, dispatch your angels!

God bless you!

Sweet Tooth.

Many people have a sweet tooth. Myself included, I might add. I often desire something sweet; a piece of cake or some kind of pastry. There is nothing wrong with having a sweet tooth, but be certain to follow the rules! What rules, you might ask? Well, one rule is to brush your teeth after eating sweets! Failure to do so will result in cavities.

A spiritual sweet tooth is what God desires for us to have – a craving for His word. Psalm Chapter 119, Verse 103 says, "How sweet are your words to my taste; they are sweeter than honey." Can you imagine going a day, a week or a month without something sweet? There is nothing sweeter than the word of God, so don't ignore it! Read it; bask in the glory of it, and tell someone about it! Fall in love with Jesus; don't just say you love Him. Prove to yourself and to others that you are in love with Him by digging deep into His sweet word.

Eat up His word daily. It is sweet without cavities!

God bless you!

Healing From Distress.

Many people are in distress. What does the word mean anyway? Webster's Dictionary defines it as, "Great pain, anxiety or sorrow; acute physical or mental suffering; affliction; trouble." Distress is not good. Often times we try to deal with distress on our own, which may not end in a satisfying way. But there IS a way that will bring about the perfect result – maybe not exactly the way we envision it – but the perfect result. That way is to take it to the Lord in prayer.

Let's learn from the children of Israel. Psalm Chapter 107, Verses 19 and 20 say, "Lord, help!" they cried in their trouble, and He saved them from their distress. He spoke, and they were healed – snatched from the door of death." (NLT) The God we serve today is the same God the children of Israel prayed to. He delivered them, and He will deliver us. We all need some form of healing. It may be financial, emotional, physical or mental. Whatever your need, allow Jesus to be your representative. He will take it to the Father who'll get it resolved!

From your heart pray; your healing is on the way!

God bless you!

Be One With Christ Jesus.

"Everyone wants to go to Heaven, but no one wants to die." Have you ever heard that saying? Well, you may not have to die. By the look of things I am quite confident that Jesus Christ will rapture "His church" in this generation. Take notice of what has been said: Christ will rapture "His church", not every church. This is truly profound when you thing about it.

So what qualifies an individual to be a part of the rapture? He or she needs to surrender it all to Jesus and start living to please him. In other words, be one with Him. The Bible tells us in Ephesians Chapter 2, Verses 5 and 6 that, "...(It is only by God's special favor that you have been saved!) For He raised us from the dead along with Christ, and we are seated with Him in the heavenly realms – all because we are one with Christ Jesus."(NLT) Let Jesus Christ through the power of His Holy Spirit flow freely in and through you. Accept Him today! Let His will be done today and always! Your navigation system cannot take you to Heaven – only Jesus knows the way! To be a part of the rapture, that Heavenly departure, be one with our savior!

God bless you!

Hot Air Balloon.

Some people talk a lot. Most times about nonsense. They make promises to God without thinking it through. Such people are like hot air balloons that deflate over a period of time. They have no real substance. Ecclesiastes Chapter 5, Verses 2 and 3 tell us, "And don't make rash promises to God, for He is in heaven, and you are only here on earth. So let your words be few. Just as being too busy gives you nightmares, being a fool makes you a blabbermouth."(NLT)

Never argue with a blabbermouth. Such people need attention to feel good about themselves. Pray for them and all the other hot air balloons you know. Remember to be forgiving, patient and loving.

At times, we may slip and become the hot air balloon. If you are guilty, ask the Lord to burst your bubble – literally! It is better to never speak again than to speak nonsense! Our Lord and Savior Jesus Christ will return soon. Pop your hot air balloon, and start speaking the word of God from noon until noon!

God bless you!

Busy, Busy, Busy!

Have you ever felt so busy that you wished there were two of you to complete all of your tasks? I know the feeling very well. We need to better plan our days; sometimes, we overbook ourselves. God often gets put on our "back burner", and yet another day goes by without accomplishing His will.

What is it that keeps us so busy? More than likely work and other means for obtaining wealth is the number one culprit. However, don't allow your "quest for success" to prevent you from being blessed. There must be a balance in how you spend your time. David says in Psalm Chapter 39, Verse 6, "We are merely moving shadows, and all our busy rushing ends in nothing. We heap up wealth for someone else to spend."(NLT)

Let's accumulate wealth in Heaven that moths cannot destroy nor thieves can rob us. Don't become so busy focusing on earthly wealth. Satan is very crafty. He will distract anyone he can with the cares of this world, making them extremely busy, ending in failure to work for the world to come. Use your time wisely and share the good news about Jesus Christ! Great will be your reward, both on Earth and in Paradise!

God bless you!

Welcome Home.

Imagine… a dad works hard all day, then arrives at home to hear his wife and children ask, "Why are you here? Don't you have a night job or something you can do somewhere else?" That wouldn't be much of a home, now would it? Sad to say, many people live in this way. Unless you feel the love and welcome a home gives, a place to lay your head surely isn't a home. If you are single, your angels should welcome you back home.

Single or not, we can make the Lord our home! Moses said in Psalm Chapter 90, Verse 1, "Lord, through all the generations you have been our home!" The children of Israel had no abiding city, however, they felt at home with the Lord. What does that mean to us? The feeling of a heartfelt welcome home depends on your accepting the Lord Jesus Christ as your savior. Further, in order to keep that peace and joy you need to maintain your walk and do the Lord's will daily. It's just as you would clean and maintain your house. The difference is your walk with the Lord is far more important than your earthly home! Let's start walking and remember to maintain our walk! Soon we will hear, "Well done, my good and faithful servant!" Now that's a welcome home!

God bless you!

Sing To The Lord!

Many people don't sing; for various reasons. Some don't believe they have a good voice, while others are simply not interested in singing. Unless, of course, it's in the shower!

Have no fear. No matter how good or bad you think your singing voice is, it will sound glorious once you're singing to the Lord! In fact, God encourages us to sing in His word. Psalm Chapter 96, Verses 1 and 2 say, "Sing a new song to the Lord! Let the whole earth sing to the Lord! Sing to the Lord; bless His name. Each day proclaim the good news that He saves." *(NLT)*

So there you have it. Start singing! In the shower – Sing! In the car – Sing! Praise and worship time in church – Sing! Singing does the body good; I'm convinced it is better for you than an apple! If you are singing ungodly songs, however, that is a whole different story so be careful of what you sing!

Lift your voice to the Lord! He loves to hear from you, and He gives the greatest applause!

God bless you!

The Gate.

People walk through gates daily. Some lead to work, school, home, travel or play. We need to make sure, however, that we enter through the most important gate of all. Jesus says in John Chapter 10, Verse 9, "Yes, I am the gate. Those who come in through me will be saved. They will come and go freely and will find good pastures."(NLT)

Salvation may not be popular among rebellious people who choose to ignore God but to us who live for God, there is nothing more important. At the end of life salvation is all we are concerned about, and Jesus said He is the gate in order to be saved. Many people try to get to God the Father without God, the Son. If this is you, stop wasting your time! We are all sinners; our sin disqualifies us from approaching a perfect, holy, sinfree God (the Father). The story doesn't stop there. Praise God, Jesus died on the cross for the sins of the world and now we have access to God, the Father. The blood of Jesus was perfect enough to pay the price for us all. Accept Him today! Don't delay! If someone should die without first entering through this gate, for them it's too late.

God bless you!

Who Will Be There? Can You Say, I Will?

Back in the day when a party or major secular event was scheduled my response was, "I'll be there!" You know what I mean! We always wanted to attend the main event! Well, just to remind and encourage you, we have a few major events coming up in the very near future! One, being the rapture of the true church! Another is the New Jerusalem coming down to Earth!

The Bible says this in Revelation Chapter 21, Verse 7: "All who are victorious will inherit all these blessings, and I will be their God, and they will be my children." This pertains to everyone partaking of the New Jerusalem. So I ask, "Who will be there? Can you say, 'I will?'" This is an event you don't want to miss, my friends! However, it's only available to those who are victorious over sin! Satan is the master of distractions, setting up God's people to fall! Stay focused on God and our Lord, Jesus Christ, and He will guide you into all righteousness! Once you stay on the straight and narrow path you can say with confidence, "I will be there!" If right now you are reading this without the confidence of salvation, cry out to God now! Repent of all your sins, and invite Jesus into your heart! Only Jesus can grant you access to the New Jerusalem! I know I will be there! Hope to see you there!

God bless you!

Life Is Short; Keep It Clean!

Ever visited a home so clean you felt the need to compliment the homeowner? As nice as that may be, the cleaning of one's heart and lifestyle are far more important! When we realize and then analyze how short our lives really are, it should prompt us to keep it clean!

David wrote this in Psalm Chapter 39, Verses 4 and 5: "Lord, remind me how brief my time on earth will be. Remind me that my days are numbered – how fleeting my life is. You have made my life no longer than the width of my hand. My entire lifetime is just a moment to you; at best, each of us is but a breath."

Jesus Christ, the bridegroom, will be coming soon for his bride – a church without a spot or a wrinkle! We only become spotless when we confess and repent of our sins and ask Jesus to enter into our hearts! To stay clean, we should wash daily – which means repent daily and sincerely ask Him to rid us of all sinful activity. If we stay on this path and allow the Holy Spirit to lead us daily, then we'll stay clean. Everything else is insignificant! Life is short; Keep it clean! The bridegroom won't accept a dirty bride!

God bless you!

The Great Examination!

Students from elementary to university are constantly being examined. The examinations show the teacher that a student understands what is being taught and also that a student is ready for promotion to the next level. The same is true spiritually, my friends! God is always examining His people to see where we are! David wrote in Psalm Chapter 139, Verses 1 and 2: "O Lord, you have examined my heart and know everything about me. You know when I sit down or stand up. You know my thoughts even when I am far away."

It's scary to think that God knows everything about us including our thoughts! How filthy are your thoughts? Well, you may want to clean them up because they're part of your examination! In school, there are final examinations; the same is true for each individual, spiritually! We will all stand before the judgment seat of Christ as stated in Revelation Chapter 20, Verse 12. What we need to remember is this: Passing the small examinations we endure throughout our lifetime will lead to our passing The Great Examination! Continue to pass your exams so you may spend forever with the Great I Am! Study to show yourself approved, or, don't study and lose!

God bless you!

Keep Your Spirit Lifted!

The enemy of our soul is constantly trying to bring us down; to have our spirit crushed and ultimately turn our backs on God. I've seen many fall away from God because of this. Satan may start by attacking one's body and then the mind and spirit. The body heals faster than a crushed spirit ever will!

Solomon wrote this in Proverbs Chapter 18, Verse 14: The human spirit can endure a sick body, but who can bear a crushed spirit?" My favorite Bible example comes from the man of God, Job. Satan took his family and everything he owned away from him in hopes he'd sell out his faith.

Perhaps your spirit has been crushed. The Holy Spirit is the best way to keep your spirit lifted! Take note however that the enemy, Satan, has placed many secret weapons in the pulpits. Be careful how you hear! Don't allow anyone to bring down your spirit and then crush you! Please listen to wise counsel; flee from any person, place or situation that has crushed your spirit! Reach out to God! He will grant you peace like a river and joy overflowing! A crushed spirit leads to death if not healed; a revived spirit leads to life everlasting!

God bless you!

My Rock, My Shield, My Savior, Jesus.

"Oh, so you are Jack of All Trades!" said the lady to the handyman who had experience in plumbing, electrical and carpentry. What she may not know is that there are different levels of experience that are yet to be mastered. It is not impossible for an individual to master all those trades, but it is highly unlikely. Jesus, on the other hand, wears many hats that fit perfectly! The Bible says this in Psalm Chapter 18, Verse 2: The Lord is my rock, my fortress, and my savior; my God is my rock, in whom I find protection. He is my shield, the power that saves me, and my place of safety. It is comforting to know that in spite of life's many challenges, we have a source for strength that we can always turn to! Friends may desire to facilitate for our inadequacies, but fail due to their own. However, Jesus, our rock, shield and savior never fails!

It's time to establish a right relationship with Him so you'll come to know just how awesome He is! If you are restless for whatever reason, the Prince of Peace will help you to achieve the peace you desire. Whatever the need, He will supply according to His riches in glory! Don't delay any longer! Come to Him now! If you have strayed, come back home to The Rock! The Rock of Ages will either help you succeed or allow you to fail. Think about it, and choose well.

God bless you!

Not Fear Factor, but Facts When We Fear God.

While impossible to remember every TV show, one in particular came to mind. It was called Fear Factor. It led me to think about fear with regard to who or what. After searching the scriptures, I concluded that I only fear God! When we have a respectful fear for God as Creator, Master, Sustainer, Leader and King, He is well pleased with us! I'd like to share with you this fact with regard to fear of God: The Bible says this in Psalm Chapter 34, Verse 9: "Fear the Lord, you His Godly people, for those who fear Him will have all they need."

I like the sound of that! My next thought? Because God's word is true anyone whose needs are not being met, chances are, they do not fear the Lord! While they pray, they lack faith! They witness sparingly to friends and coworkers, but without enthusiasm.

What is it that keeps you stuck on Fear Factor? Don't fear what man may say or do! Fear God who will reward or reject your soul!

God bless you!

Paradise In The Making.

I've often heard Caribbean Islands advertise themselves as "Paradise" in an effort to attract more tourists. Well, okay; but I can't help but envision the believer's Paradise in the making! We should always long for the "real" paradise, the Kingdom of Heaven, and work diligently so that we're able to enjoy it!

Jesus says this in John Chapter 14, Verses 2 and 3: There is more than enough room in my Father's home. If this were not so, would I have told you that I am going to prepare a place for you? When everything is ready, I will come and get you, so that you will always be with me where I am.

We are still on Earth; the rapture hasn't occurred yet so Christ continues to prepare our Paradise! We need to make sure we maintain our salvation; not merely church affiliation, study the scriptures daily, fast, pray and ask God to show us anything in our lives that might cause us to stumble. Don't take your Christian walk simple! Jesus will return for a church without a spot or wrinkle! Let's wash ourselves clean, iron out some things so we'll know without a doubt that we are Paradise bound! Can't wait to see you there!

God bless you!

Death Is On The Hunt, So Beware!

We try to avoid thinking about some things in life. For example, people dying. However, it's a proven fact that ten out of ten people die; or get raptured! We don't have to look for death actually; death is always on the hunt for us! The Bible tells us this in Proverbs Chapter 27, Verse 20: Just as Death and Destruction are never satisfied, so human desire is never satisfied."

While humans are busy trying to get more, Death and Destruction are doing the same. My friendly advice: Seek life the way God ordains it through Jesus Christ! This should be everyone's number one priority! If not, you need a priority change! Please be aware of who and what you choose to put ahead of God! The devil doesn't play fair! His main purpose is to kill us, but Jesus' main purpose is to give us life more abundantly! (John Chapter 10, Verse 10).

Why am I saying all this? To scare you? Absolutely not! It's to aware you and prepare you for the future! We choose to spend eternity with God or eternity with the devil. When we look at things in that perspective, we'll monitor our lives! Choose to be wise! The spiritually dead is deceived and will be hell received. Choose real life in Christ!

God bless you!

The Great Home Run!

The greatest play in baseball games is when a player hits a home run. If the bases are loaded, it also frees up other players so they, too, can make it home. It's often the same principle for us believers; once we receive Christ, others tend to follow! Spiritually speaking, what does a great home run look like? Jesus puts it this way in Revelation Chapter 3, Verses 2021: "Look! I stand at the door and knock. If you hear my voice and open the door, I will come in, and we will share a meal together as friends. Those who are victorious will sit with me on my throne, just as I was victorious and sat with my Father on his throne."

Once we're home with Jesus, we'll have made the Great Home Run! Making millions of dollars and forfeiting heaven is not profitable. It's time to play the game of life with Heaven in sight! Repent of your sins now while Jesus is still knocking on your heart! Warning: Failure to soften one's heart and accept Jesus as Lord may lead to a permanent hardening of the heart and a permanent home in hell. To end up there would be worse than a foul ball; it's a fall with no hopes of getting up again! It's so much better to be a friend of Jesus! Be a part of The Great Home Run! End the game of life well; don't let it end you!

God bless you!

Don't Just Take A Look At The Best Book.

We love to "take a look at" things. We attend movies and plays on a small scale, and on a larger scale we travel to scenic places such as the Grand Canyon… just to take a look! The thing is when we take a look we may or may not share with others what we saw. Let's not treat the Bible that way! Don't just take a look at the best book; live it and share it! The Bible says this in Psalm Chapter 119, Verses 1 and 2: "Joyful are people of integrity, who follow the instructions of the Lord. Joyful are those who obey His laws and search for Him with all their hearts.

There IS a remedy for joy, my friends! Search the best book with your whole heart and follow the instructions you receive! Unfortunately with all the gadgets and social media out there, we don't read the Bible as often as we should! Let's change that! Let's dig deep into God's word, and share the blessing with others! The Bible contains stories that are far better than any movie! I know we have all spoken about a good movie; now let's start talking about a good move of God from His written word! You can choose to remain silent, but don't get angry when your blessings are marked absent! Share the Bible!

God bless you!

Be On Your Guard, Stand Firm, Be Courageous, Be Strong!

Don't think for a moment that this topic has anything to do with a gentle reminder. These are encouraging words for battle! If you don't believe there is a war going on, you have already been defeated! Satan, the enemy of our souls, wants us to believe that "all is well" so he can trick us to Hell! That is the fate of all whom refuse to fight the enemy.

The Bible says this in 1 Corinthians Chapter 16, Verse 13: "Be on guard. Stand firm in the faith. Be courageous. Be strong."

Small and/or large battles will come our way when least expected! Win, lose or draw we must fight – in Jesus' name, always showing love to mankind. Here is good news: When true Christians get to Heaven we will have won the war, so don't worry about failed battles! No one will be tempted by Satan in Heaven! In the presence of Jesus is where it's at! To call out His name and see Him face to face will be the greatest feeling one could ever have! So – Be on your guard from the enemy, Satan. Stand firm in your faith as a follower and soldier of Jesus Christ. Be courageous, because God didn't give us a spirit of fear! Be strong in the Lord and in the power of His might. Fight!

God bless you!

Don't Hang Yourself, Cut The Ropes.

Many have used rope to hang themselves by way of suicide. Others were hung by way of the judicial system. How about the persons not living for God and all wrapped up in sin? You will be surprised at what the Bible has to say on the subject. Proverbs Chapter 5, Verses 22 and 23 say this: "An evil man is held captive by his own sins; they are ropes that catch and hold him. He will die for lack of self control; he will be lost because of his great foolishness."

Often I hear people say, "I'm not wicked. I have never robbed or killed anyone." They fail to understand that a wicked person is one who refuses to live for God. It doesn't matter how good you think you are; we all have sinned and fallen short of God's glory. If we are not born again, we are hanging in ropes.

Please don't hang yourself, my friend; cut the ropes! Accept Jesus now before you are pronounced dead! There is no repentance in the grave! Resurrect from your spiritually dead state and really start living! This way, you'll be free to help others cut their ropes!

God bless you!

In Whom Do You Really Trust?

A red flag is raised within me whenever someone I just met says, "Trust me!" I've also heard the popular phrase, "In God We Trust – all others pay cash! Now, I know there are trustworthy individuals out there, as well as those that we can't trust as far as we can throw them so how do we make the distinction? It starts by trusting in the One who will never leave us nor disappoint us! The Bible tells us this in Proverbs Chapter 3, Verses 5 and 6: Trust in the Lord with all your heart; do not depend on your own understanding. Seek His will in all you do, and He will show you which path to take." Everyone trusts someone in this life; if you're an employee, you trust that your employer will provide a paycheck for your labor. Let's take it a step further. We trust the tire manufacturers for our cars, which is why we do not worry when driving 30 miles per hour or more! Since we're already trusting, why not trust the Lord? Don't do life without Him! While sin may seem like fun – drinking, fornicating, lying and cursing – sin comes with a price. The unrepentant sinner that dies in sin will spend eternity regretting the decision to not trust God entirely! A better alternative to the Lake of Fire? The New Jerusalem! To get there, start trusting Jesus today! He already paid the price for the sins of all!

God bless you!

Do You Hear What The Church Hears?

"Do you hear what I hear?" is a line from a famous Christmas carol. We hear many things on a daily basis, and often times we may turn a deaf ear. There is One, however, who hears His people when we call Him for help – He is our Lord and Savior, Jesus Christ! The Bible says this in Psalm Chapter 34, Verse 17: "The Lord hears his people when they call to him for help. He rescues them from all their troubles."

This is very comforting to know because when troubles come, we need not worry about the outcome! Family members and friends are not always available to hear us, but God is always available! You don't need Internet or a cell phone to reach Him; just seek Him! Matthew Chapter 6, Verse 33 says we should seek FIRST… The Kingdom of God and all His righteousness and everything else will be added! Here's how it works: God hears us at all times. But when we truly seek Him, we also hear Him! That makes for a much better conversation! It's frustrating when there's a bad connection on the phone, and we cannot hear. How is your connection to God? Better yet – Do YOU hear from God? During our prayer, a still small voice whispers. Do you hear?

God bless you!

While The Gods Are Watching.

In everything, we should give thanks. God appreciates when we're aware that we didn't accomplish great things on our own! What about the distractions in life? You know, the lower case "gods" that try and zap our thought process from God. They are the people, places and things that take our focus away from the true God. Be sure not to praise these gods above the true God! I love what David says in Psalm Chapter 138, Verse 1: "I give you thanks, O Lord, with all my heart; I will sing your praises before the gods."

While false gods try to steal our devotion, let us sing praises to God even the more! Let our lives be full of praise and thanksgiving in the way we treat others. Pass all compliments on to God! Simply say, "To God be the Glory!" These practices will keep us in line and away from serving false gods. We cannot stop them from watching; so why not give them something good to look at? Keep in mind that the true God is also watching! Don't deny Him! If you're more reserved due to social status, don't be! I urge you – let your praises to God ring out, and watch your blessings come forth! May they see us keeping our eyes on Jesus!

God bless you!

Talk Is Cheap; Get To Work!

There is a time and a place for everything. Sometimes we need to talk about what needs to get done; other times we need to just do it! Far too many times I've noticed that talk alone produces no fruit. We must caution ourselves when engaged in conversation without action.

The Bible says this in Proverbs Chapter 14, Verse 23: "Work brings profit, but mere talk leads to poverty!" If we show up to do a job but all we do is talk about it, we shouldn't get paid! The same is true for church attendees that talk about the gospel in church, make plans to go out and evangelize but then do nothing! We can rest assured that the reward we'll receive from representing the Lord far outweighs our pay check!

Want to generate real profit? Walk in the ways of a prophet! The blessings from the Lord will open your eyes to finally see that the harvest is plentiful but the workers are few! Pray to the Lord of the Harvest to send more workers and few talkers! In conclusion: Talk is cheap; Get to work!

God bless you!

Getting What We deserve Can Get On Our Nerves!

People often complain about deserving better than what they've received. Spiritually speaking, this is a tricky place to be! Most people believe they are good; but when measured up to God's standard they are bad, and God will reward accordingly! As a matter of fact, this is what the Word of God says in Jeremiah Chapter 17, Verse 10: "But I, the Lord, search all hearts and examine secret motives. I give all people their due rewards, according to what their actions deserve."

Here is how it works: Sin releases a curse over our lives! If we don't stop the sin, one curse leads to another, then to another! The bad news: A person not being blessed (in the way they could), cannot see that they are under a curse! All they do is complain because getting what they deserve gets on their nerves! We can change that by repenting of sin and allowing God to release His blessings.

How much longer are you willing to hold on to the curse? A wise person rids themselves of what is bad and clings to what is good! Here's good news: When we do good in the eyes of God, our rewards will be good! Chew on that thought for just a moment, and I pray you taste the sweet flavor and hunger for more!

God bless you!

Stop The Foolishness!

We're challenged with Wisdom vs. Foolishness on a daily basis. For some, wisdom is not for them! They are stuck in their old way, and you can't tell them anything at all! For others, however, they are wisdom seekers! They're reading the Bible daily, praying and crying out to God for direction and favor. All you have to do to recognize ones level of wisdom is stop for a minute and let them speak. I guarantee: You will hear wisdom or foolishness.

The Bible says this in Proverbs Chapter 15, Verse 2: The tongue of the wise makes knowledge appealing, but the mouth of a fool belches out foolishness.

The question now is this: What are your conversations about? Perhaps you need to stop the foolishness, read more of God's word so you can speak more of God's word. Rather than appear cool in the eyes of mankind and foolish in the eyes of God, change your mindset! Be cool in the eyes of God! If friends can't handle your holy speech, pray for them and keep it moving! Remember: friendship with the world makes you an enemy to God! Although we are IN the world, we should not be OF the world... especially in our conversations and actions! Let's win the battle!

God bless you!

Passport Check.

On a recent trip to Jamaica while waiting to board the aircraft, I heard an announcement; a few names were called to report to the gate for a passport check. This made me think about the very near future. One trip we want to make sure our passport is in order for is Heaven! The Bible says this in Revelation Chapter 20, Verse 15: "And anyone whose name was not found recorded in the Book of Life was thrown into the lake of fire." This is very serious! Many people don't check their spiritual passport to make sure it's current and says, Citizen of Heaven! It all comes down to priorities.

When travelling to another country we check the physical passport, don't we? Food for thought: We are travelling to Heaven, and each day brings us closer to our passport check point! Let's prioritize Heaven while we can. There is no repentance in the grave; now is the time to seek God while He may yet be found! Call upon Him! Cry out to Him! If your passport to Heaven has expired, renew it! Don't be denied entrance to Heaven because you chose to deny yourself a right relationship with Jesus! To enter Heaven your passport can't say, "Know of Jesus"; it must say, "Know Jesus"!

God bless you!

Don't Refrain From Him, Remain In Him!

Recently I heard Military Chaplains are forbidden to pray in Jesus' name. This is a very alarming situation! You see, the name of Jesus packs power that will seal the deal and release the blessing! So if we're not talking about Him, training our military, our children and ignoring Him in our homes, we'll be powerless to the enemy! Look at what Jesus says in John Chapter 15, Verse 7: "But if you remain in me and my words remain in you, you may ask for anything you want, and it will be granted!"

Often times I hear people complain that God's not giving them a husband, a wife, a job, a healing... My question is this: Do you refrain from Jesus or do you remain in Him? True faith will be evident when one is in Christ Jesus! Not true fear! If we are truly in Christ, we would call His name everywhere without shame! I am all for observing the laws of the land but if they contradict the Word of God, I have to stand with God and not the law!

We are living in the last days! Things are all twisted. However, we should not allow Satan to twist us out of a right relationship with Jesus! Remain in Him, and His words will flow freely from you! If you refrain from Him now and die that way, you refrain from Him forever.

God bless you!

Are You Approved?

It's a wonderful feeling to apply for a car or home loan, and you're approved! Even a department store credit card brings joy at approval and disappointment at denial. We can do all sorts of things to rebuild credit and eventually be trusted again with money. However when this life is over we can't rebuild, only accept the inevitable. In Matthew Chapter 25 beginning at Verse 14, Jesus tells a story of three servants receiving money to accomplish great things and to produce fruit. Two of the servants did well and received approval from the master. Matthew Chapter 25, Verse 23 reads: "The master said, 'Well done, my good and faithful servant. You have been faithful in handling this small amount, so now I will give you many more responsibilities. Let's celebrate together.'" The third servant was cast into the Lake of Fire where there will be weeping and gnashing of teeth (Verse 30).

Big question: Are you approved? 1 John 5, Verse 13 says these things were written that we may know we have eternal life. We can be denied by a credit card provider, boyfriend, girlfriend, wife or husband and bounce back from that. However when the time comes for Jesus to judge you, there is no recovery from His denial! Solution: Get approved now before it's too late!

God bless you!

Let The Sin Be Gone; Put Down The Sin Detector.

You're at the beach lying on the sand and you realize you've lost an expensive earring in the sand! Chances are you will look for it. One might even acquire the use of a metal detector to assist in finding the earring. Once the metal detector locates the ring, a good time will be had by all!

How does this relate to us spiritually? When God forgives us of our sins, this is what happens. Psalm Chapter 103, Verse 12 says: "He has removed our sins as far from us as the east is from the west."

Because the sins are gone, please put down the sin detector! If you don't, I guarantee a good time WON'T be had by all! Romans Chapter 6, Verse 23 says: "For the wages of sin is death..." That, my friend, is one salary you don't need! Death, by way of separation from God – so you don't read the Bible or pray like you use to; you don't desire church fellowship, prayer meetings or Bible study. These are signs that your sin detector is on point in locating areas in which for you to sin.

Put down the sin detector before it puts you down! Search for God with all your heart. Now that's smart!

God bless you!

Jesus Christ, Our Lawyer.

It's good to know the right attorney if you are being prosecuted on a matter. You wouldn't hire a divorce attorney for a criminal case, or a real estate attorney for a child custody case. Certain things seem like a no brainer until it gets spiritual, then skepticism gets the best of folks. People tend to forget, or should I say "ignore" the fact that there is an enemy to our souls and his name is Satan. He convinces us to sin so we can separate ourselves from God and His blessings. However, I have some good news! When we feel our lives are on trial (which they are) we have Jesus Christ as our lawyer. The Bible says this in 1 John Chapter 2, Verse 1: "My dear children, I am writing this to you so that you will not sin. But if anyone does sin, we have an advocate who pleads our case before the Father. He is Jesus Christ, the one who is truly righteous."

You heard right; Jesus pleads our case! So, just in case you didn't know you have a lawyer – now you know! Satan is busy trying to get us the electric chair but with Jesus as our lawyer, we will not go there! When we repent of our sins, we hire Jesus as our representative! So, what are you waiting for my friend?! Keep in mind that without Jesus, your sentence is Hell and then the Lake of Fire. Avoid those now; hire Jesus! He won't cost you a dime!

God bless you!

Can You Handle Some Treasure?

If you knew you had millions in your bank account, you wouldn't live impoverished. If you did, you belong in a mental institution! Why suffer when you can make a withdrawal and pay your bills? I often wonder the same thing when it comes to the house of the Lord. People are not as aggressive to partake of the treasure like they did for the California gold rush.

This is what the Bible says in Proverbs Chapter 15, Verse 6: "There is treasure in the house of the godly, but the earnings of the wicked bring trouble." Can you handle some treasure? If you can, start by going to church on the regular to hear a word then share a word daily! When you begin to do these two simple exercises, treasure will make its way to your house! God's Word is true, and the Godly will have treasure in their house! Treasure will come in different ways – not merely financial. By way of genuine love within the family, peace, good health, salvation of entire family; not just one or two members! Start a treasure hunt! God will see to it that you're successful. Just remember – if you don't seek, you won't find! Don't make excuses; instead make the right choice and find your treasure! A Bible teaching church is a great hunting ground! See you around!

God bless you!

If You Can't Show Mercy, You Are Spiritually Sick.

Some past hurts are quite severe, I know. People cut us with words or deeds, and it is not easily forgotten. However, sometimes in life those very same people who caused us hurt will resurface as a test from God. So; what's the test? To see if we extend mercy, grace and forgiveness, or do we accept failure and disappoint God. The Pharisees did the same with regard to Matthew. Here's how it went down in Matthew Chapter 9, Verses 10 through 13: Later, Matthew invited Jesus and his disciples to his home as dinner guests, along with many tax collectors and other disreputable sinners. But when the Pharisees saw this, they asked his disciples, "Why does your teacher eat with such scum?" When Jesus heard this, he said, "Healthy people don't need a doctor – sick people do." Then he added, "Now go and learn the meaning of this Scripture: 'I want you to show mercy, not offer sacrifices.' For I have come to call not those who think they are righteous, but those who know they are sinners." When we show mercy, it proves we are walking right in the eyes of the Lord and we can expect mercy from Him! The opposite is also true; if we don't show mercy, we won't receive mercy! That can be catastrophic! Mercy, Grace and Forgiveness are antidotes to spiritual sickness.

God bless you!

We Are All Soldiers, But Whose Army Are You Fighting For?

God has a way of revealing things to us that sometimes cause us to stop and really look into it. For instance, "We are all soldiers, but whose army are you fighting for?" If we dig deep, we'll discover the validity of that statement. Anyone honoring Satan by living a lifestyle of lying, stealing, hatred, unforgiveness, fornication, murder and the like are in Satan's army. They then refuse to suffer even the slightest personal injustice.

A true soldier looks like this: 2 Timothy Chapter 2, Verses 3 and 4 say: "Endure suffering along with me, as a good soldier of Christ Jesus. And as Christ's soldier, do not let yourself become tied up in the affairs of this life, for then you cannot satisfy the one who has enlisted you in his army."

My friend: the writing is on the wall. Decide this day which army you'll serve! All it takes to enlist in Christ's army is a willing and repentant heart. Read the Bible each day and get closer to Jesus! As a warrior, the battle will rage but in the end the Christians still stand on the front page! Enlist today!

God bless you!

Here Is A Thought, What If You Lose The Beating Of Your Heart?

The thought of dying and existing in another world is not on the list of priorities for individuals. However it should be a priority and here are a couple of reasons why. (1)Ten out of ten people die. (2)If death wasn't so common there wouldn't be so many funeral homes and cemeteries. Since any heart can stop beating at any given time, the wise person would diligently prepare for that day. The Bible says this in Luke 16:22-23 "Finally, the poor man died and was carried by the Angels to be with Abraham. The rich man also died and was buried, and his soul went to the place of the dead. There in torment he saw Abraham with Lazarus by his side." If you read Luke 16 starting at verse 19-31 you will see that the rich man was a good person. None the less when our hearts stop beating only the true followers of Jesus Christ will be by Abrahams' side.

So be wise and think about it daily so you can get saved and walk the straight and narrow path. Don't take these instructions for granted thinking you will follow later. True Salvation is the key to eternal life with God.

Think about it, when your name is written in Heaven, and your heart stops beating on Earth, you automatically go to Heaven.

God bless you!

We All Make Mistakes; Correct Them!

One common excuse known to man for doing wrong is the statement, "We all make mistakes." The problem is this: not everyone is quick to correct the mistakes they make. Instead, they keep on making them. I love what the second greatest preacher, the apostle Paul, did when he realized he made a mistake. The Bible tells us in Acts Chapter 23, Verses 4 and 5: Those standing near Paul said to him, "Do you dare to insult God's high priest?" "I'm sorry, brothers. I didn't realize he was the high priest," Paul replied, "for the scriptures say, 'You must not speak evil of any of your rulers.'"

It takes a spiritually mature person to admit they are wrong, apologize and keep it moving.

Maybe there is someone in our own circle whom we have offended, and God is holding on to our blessing until we make things right. Pride comes before a fall, so don't allow pride to stop you! Correct your mistakes, forgive, show love and shine! This is far better than keeping your distance to hold onto wrongdoing. No one is perfect, I agree, but we are made perfect by our love for mankind through the righteousness of Christ! Jesus is perfect; the more we become like Him, the less mistakes we will make! Admit and correct your mistakes today!

God bless you!

Don't Get Attached To Your Demons; Set Sail Without Them!

We are often unaware of the many demons surrounding us. They are everywhere – from the grocery store, to the bank, from the church, inside the schools – you name it! I've heard people say, "Demons are not in church," which leads to my question: Whom do you think keeps the lost in their seats once an alter call has been given? The answer: The demons do!

In Mark Chapter 7, there was a woman battling for her daughter's deliverance from demonic activity. Jesus denied her at first, but she was very persistent! Verses 29 and 30 say: "Good answer!" he said. "Now go home, for the demon has left your daughter." And when she arrived home, she found her little girl lying quietly in bed, and the demon was gone.

Don't get attached to your demon! So many have been evident right here during Jesus Team Ministries' ten year anniversary cruise! God has revealed to me that the only way to set sail without them is to repent of your sins allowing the Holy Spirit to kick the demons to the curb! Yes, a man or woman of God can cast out a demon, but if the individual doesn't live for God, those demons come back! Free yourself; attach to Jesus!

God bless you!

I Want The World To Know; Do You?

Go tell it on the mountain; over the hills and everywhere! Go tell it on the mountain, that Jesus Christ is born!

We sing this very famous hymn and personally speaking, I do want the world to know about my Jesus! How about you? The Bible says this in John Chapter 4, Verses 28 through 30, and I love the reaction of the Samaritan woman at the well: The woman left her water jar beside the well and ran back to the village, telling everyone, "Come and see a man who told me everything I ever did! Could he possibly be the Messiah?" So the people came streaming from the village to see him.

I wish the church would get back to that place of excitement about Jesus where we put our daily activities on pause in order to share Him with others. It only takes a few minutes to change someone's eternal destiny! If we say we want the world to know, then God will present the opportunity to make that happen! Don't just think about Him; talk about Him and see what happens! Your world is everyone you know and come in contact with! Start sharing Jesus in your world!

God bless you!

It's Only Things; Be Impressed With God!

If I had a penny for each time someone is impressed with a car, a house, a piece of jewelry or money... I would not be able to spend my riches! However, God being a jealous God wants us to enjoy all things but not glorify them. Some people say they "worship God, not money" yet, they spend more time thinking about money than they think about God!

The Bible says this is Psalm Chapter 89, Verse 7: "The highest angelic powers stand in awe of God. He is far more awesome than all who surround His throne."

When we think of our great God, nothing should compare! Some argue against God because their selfish requests are not granted in a timely manner. Please change your attitude before your time on Earth is cut short! Others are more interested in the "glitz and glamour" this world has to offer, so they ignore God entirely, ending up in a spiritual slammer!

Whatever the "thing" may be in your life that gets most of your devotion, prayerfully uproot it from its #1 spot and put God there! It's time to repent and start seeing God for whom He truly is: The creator and sustainer of us all! Now that's impressive!

God bless you!

Are You Still Thirsty?

There are many so-called thirst quenchers on the market today: Gatorade, Powerade… However, water is still the best thirst quencher in the natural and in the spiritual! Spiritually speaking when we drink the Living Water, who is the Holy Spirit Himself, we won't thirst anymore! Jesus says this in John Chapter 4, Verses 13 and 14: "Anyone who drinks this water will soon become thirsty again. But those who drink the water I give will never be thirsty again. It becomes a fresh, bubbling spring within them, giving them eternal life."

In essence, my friends, anyone who is not yet saved and hasn't received their guarantee of eternal life with our Lord Jesus Christ is still thirsty! Are you still thirsty? Here's what you need to do: Repent of your sins today and don't delay! Time is winding down toward your departure from this life! Drink the Living Water before you're zeroed out! It's annoying to be thirsty when we have access to a drink, but just think: being unable to quench our thirst will be more annoying!

Coming to Christ brings a twofold benefit; thirsty free on earth and thirsty free in Heaven! Separation from Christ will make you thirsty on earth and thirsty in Hell! Quench your thirst!

God bless you!

We Could Really Use The Messiah's Rewards Right Now!

Ever do something kind and your good deed is overlooked? Maybe you've opened and held a door for others to enter only to not receive a thank you. Not to worry though; every act of kindness is noticed by God, the Father, and Jesus, our Lord and Savior!

The same is true spiritually. We do good, walk uprightly and may feel unrewarded. Sometimes we might say to ourselves, "We could really use the Messiah's rewards right now!" If you feel that way, I have great news from Isaiah Chapter 62, Verse 11! It says, The Lord has sent this message to every land: "Tell the people of Israel, 'Look, your Savior is coming. See, he brings his reward with him as he comes.'"

Salvation can only be found in Jesus Christ! Do you believe this? If you believe that statement, share your faith with another! When we do good deeds and spread the gospel, yes, the enemy will apply more pressure on us! But keep the good fight going knowing this: a reward now would be great, but a reward later will be far greater!

God bless you!

I Don't Have To Go To Church! Or Do I?

"I don't have to go to church to be a Christian." We've all heard that phrase at some point or another. I agree to some degree. Let me explain. You can receive salvation on your couch! However, living a Holy lifestyle comes from training in the Word! I'll start with this: Jesus, even as a young boy, understood the importance of going to church, and He said this in Luke Chapter 2, Verse 49: "But why did you need to search?" he asked. "Didn't you know that I must be in my Father's house?"

Jesus' parents who had been looking for Him were not on the same wavelength! Same is true today; many adults don't feel the need for church – they may put up with it every once in a while, but that's it. Please take note of what the wisest man whom ever lived said: "Didn't you know that I must be in my Father's house!" The word "must" stands out to me, and knowing how I feel if I'm absent from church confirms what Jesus meant! We are strengthened in church and empowered to do great things! Make church attendance a priority, so you're able to hear what's required of you to better serve God!

The Lord will never force us to come into His house, but He rewards us abundantly when we do!

God bless you!

Church of God Or Church of Man?

There are many churches out there, as you know. There are some featuring quiet worship and others a more upbeat worship style. Unfortunately, there are also churches that make up their own doctrines that are contrary to the Word of God! Those churches are widespread and very deadly, so please be aware!

Jesus had this to say in Mark Chapter 7, Verses 6 and 7: Jesus replied, "You hypocrites! Isaiah was right when he prophesied about you, for he wrote, 'These people honor me with their lips, but their hearts are far from me. Their worship is a farce, for they teach manmade ideas as commands from God."

Have you ever heard something in church or seen some way the service was conducted and wonder, "Where is that in the Bible?" Exactly! Where? Maybe nowhere in the Bible, because it is made up by man! Test the spirit by the spirit! If it does not look like Jesus, chances are Jesus is not in it! Be a part of the church of God! The true church! The church of man may tickle your ears or have become your comfort zone but without the leading of the Holy Spirit, you will be eternally miserable! Which church will you choose?

God bless you!

A Strange Reason To Rejoice.

It's common sense we'd all rather rejoice than sit around feeling sad. However, there are many reasons to rejoice even some that may not be too popular among believers. For instance, would you rejoice after being fired from your job for saying, "Praise the Lord"? Would you rejoice when your closest friends stop calling because you talk about Jesus too much? These are just a few scenarios in which a Christian may come face to face with.

Let's take a look at what the Bible says in Matthew Chapter 5, Verses 11 through 12: God blesses you when people mock you and persecute you and lie about you and say all sorts of evil things against you because you are my followers. Be happy about it! Be very glad! For a great reward awaits you in Heaven. And remember, the ancient prophets were persecuted in the same way.

A great reward awaits you in Heaven my Christian friend, so be encouraged! Soon we will be going home, and that's the ultimate reason to rejoice! If you are reading this and don't have true salvation, turn to Jesus before it's too late! Repent of your sins, and begin living for the King of kings! Then your true rejoicing will begin!

God bless you!

Miraculous Signs of the Times.

Through the years many miraculous signs have occurred. Some great and some small. For example, a baby falls from a seven story building and isn't harmed, or, a major earthquake leaving no casualties. Let's look at Biblical days. The prophet, Isaiah, said this in Isaiah Chapter 7, Verse 14: "…Look! The virgin will conceive a child! She will give birth to a son and will call him Immanuel (which means God is with us)." As we know, the Prophet's word came to pass when the virgin Mary gave birth to Jesus! That was a miraculous sign, and later, Jesus rose from the dead to give us hope! The hope we have in the resurrection of the dead keeps us focused on Heaven! This, too, is a miracle in itself because most of us use to focus only on ourselves!

God shows us miraculous signs every day! We need to pay attention! Keep close to Jesus! Watch, stay awake and ready for the next miraculous sign of the time, the rapture! Don't be like the foolish who hear this Good News and do nothing with the information! Turn from the wrong path while the turning is good! Look at the world we are living in and realize that Jesus is soon coming! Be a part of the next major miraculous sign! Don't get left behind!

God bless you!

We Are Encouraged To Filter, Just Don't Filter The Word!

We filter many things in life: relationships, TV programming, radio... while those are actually encouraged, I have a problem when people filter the Bible. The filtering process allows people to believe and live some parts of the Bible while ignoring other parts.

Jesus had this to say to the Pharisees in Mark Chapter 7, Verses 9 through 11: Then he said, "You skillfully sidestep God's law in order to hold on to your own tradition. For instance, Moses gave you this law from God: 'Honor your father and mother,' and 'Anyone who speaks disrespectfully of father or mother must be put to death.' But you say it is all right for people to say to their parents, 'Sorry, I can't help you. For I have vowed to give to God what I would have given to you.'"

Priorities are important to set and follow. Make it priority to live God's word entirely and the very best way you can! This world is full of things filtered, but don't filter yourself from the King! Don't follow the advice of fools trying to keep you from God's Word! Some of the Word will convict us to change, but listen to this: It is better to be convicted to change than evicted from Heaven! Don't filter the Word: Live it!

God bless you!

Don't Break Your Eggs Outside The Pan!

The things we choose to engage in life will either be good or bad. It can be likened to the usage of eggs. Ever have an egg fall out of your hand and break on the stove or the floor? No one in their right mind drops an egg on the floor just for fun; sometimes accidents happen… To engage in wickedness "just for fun," of course, is worse than breaking an egg on purpose.

The Bible says this in Proverbs Chapter 12, Verse 2: The Lord approves of those who are good, but he condemns those who plan wickedness.

Break your egg over a frying pan, now that's beneficial! The same is true when we plan on doing good and walk in God's plan. Be mindful of your hopes and dreams; don't allow them to be washed downstream because you want to be mean! Use your time wisely; trust in the Lord and do good! Wickedness will lead to a mess that may never get cleaned up!

Repent of everything that breaks your eggs outside the pan! Be productive in life; live to honor Jesus Christ! To break an egg on the floor is a waste; but to not break your wicked plans is a whole lot worse! Be good!

God bless you!

When Will You Listen To Your Voicemail?

It can be frustrating at times to call someone only to get voicemail. Even more frustrating to hear, "This voicemail box is full." You may get the feeling that your message is not important. I get the feeling this is how God feels. He's left us countless voicemail and to some their mailbox is full with unheard voicemail.

The Bible says this in Luke Chapter 16, Verse 31: "But Abraham said, 'If they won't listen to Moses and the prophets, they won't listen even if someone rises from the dead." In this parable, the rich man is in Hell speaking to Abraham who's in Heaven. He's pleading with Abraham to warn his five brothers not to end up in Hell where he is! The same voicemail has been left for you who play with life, not realizing that you, too, can end up in Hell at a young age!

When will you listen to your voicemail, and act on it? Be aware of this: When your spiritual voice mailbox is full your heart is hardened and the Word of God is not received well. That is the pathway to Hell! Listen to your voicemail! Make the necessary changes to ensure the right walk with Jesus Christ, our Lord! To live your best life starting with each passing day, listen and obey Jesus who is the way!

God bless you!

He Is Who He Is!

Titles are very important when addressing dignitaries. In the Navy you must call a lieutenant, "Lieutenant," a commander, "Commander" and a captain, "Captain." The President of the United States is called, "Mr. President." While all these titles given to men are temporary, there is a title that will remain intact for all eternity! Exodus Chapter 3, Verses 13 and 14 reads: But Moses protested, "If I go to the people of Israel and tell them, 'The God of your ancestors has sent me to you,' they will ask me, 'What is his name?' Then what should I tell them?" God replied to Moses, "I Am Who I Am. Say this to the people of Israel: I Am has sent me to you"

He is who He is; the God who give us the title, "Christian." This truth ordains us to tell others about the Gospel. By following His lead, we recognize Him as head of our lives. To become a better servant, a better follower of Christ, embrace who He is! Don't put His work on the back burner, because you may just get burned! If an employer asks you to perform a task, you probably do it speedily to keep your job! Keep in mind that God asks us to do a job also – to get the gospel out! I implore you to get to it speedily, so that you can keep your life! Jesus says anyone trying to keep their life, will lose it! He Is Who He Is, but are YOU who you are supposed to be?

God bless you!

Talk About A Blessing!

There is nothing quite like the blessing of the Lord! Satan will curse an individual in the form of a blessing, but it's not the same! I'll explain. Ever hear someone say, "I'm too busy for church because of work," or, "I have to clean the house" or "I have to mow the lawn?" Satan is good at tricking people into worshipping the "blessing" and not the "Bless-or," and so the blessing becomes a curse! However, when we allow nothing and no one ahead of God, then this blessing will stand!

The Bible says this in Psalm Chapter 115, Verses 12 through 15: The Lord remembers us and will bless us. He will bless the people of Israel and bless the priests, the descendents of Aaron. He will bless those who fear the Lord, both great and lowly. May the Lord richly bless both you and your children. May you be blessed by the Lord who made heaven and earth. Talk about a blessing! I am excited about that! Are you? Prove it! Live life the way Jesus asks us to in Mathew Chapter 6, Verse 33: Seek first the Kingdom of God and ALL His righteousness and everything else will fall into place! There are no shortcuts to true worship; true worship can be seen by the way we live! Don't get it twisted or confused; the blessing has been released for true worshippers! Repent, then begin a worship lifestyle to God today!

God bless you!

Let's Talk About The Temple.

I love to hear people say with enthusiasm that they go to church every Sunday – that's a good start! However, when some are asked about their temple - the responses get a little weak. Studies show that many Christians are failing in the area of sexual sin.

So – let's talk about the temple… The Bible says this in 1 Corinthians Chapter 6, Verses 18 through 20: Run from sexual sin! No other sin so clearly affects the body as this one does. For sexual immorality is a sin against your own body. Don't you realize that your body is the temple of the Holy Spirit, who lives in you and was given to you by God? You do not belong to yourself, for God bought you with a high price. So you must honor God with your body.

Our price tags are way more expensive than any car or house! We are priceless! Let's start behaving that way! The way we treat our temple – our bodies – will reflect our understanding of our worth. The spirit of God should feel welcome in our temple! If He does not, we will not be welcome in Heaven! Let's make some changes in our daily lives for holiness! Going to the temple is good, but keeping our temple holy is great!

God bless you!

It's Bad To Fool Others, But Worse To Fool Yourself.

Some people love fooling around; you know – playing jokes, being the life of the party... there's a time for everything and while that may be okay, what is NOT okay is ignoring the Word of God and His standard of living, while giving the impression that you are in right standing with God! You may be fooling others, but get this – you are also fooling yourself by staying in that reprobate mindset!

The Bible says this in Psalm Chapter 119, Verse 118: "But you have rejected all who stray from your decrees. They are only fooling themselves." The fact of the matter is this: God cannot be fooled! He knows us better than we know ourselves! What's the antidote? Be truthful! Let me elaborate on this being truthful... Pretending to be holy just for show or status is the same as lying! Repenting of our sins and climbing off our high horse is much better than falling off it! The choice is ours to make. Stop fooling others and ourselves, or keep on fooling, which makes us fools. Should we keep on the path of playing the fool, keep in mind: all of our actions lead to a blessing or a curse! Doing the Lord's will is the way to go, my friend! Should you lose a few friends in the process, don't worry! You have a friend in Jesus! Don't be a phony and get ridden like a pony! Be real with man and God, then forever be glad!

God bless you!

Nothing Can Compare.

We need to really know the God whom we serve! Often times we may feel down in the dumps, broken hearted or abandoned. This does not mean we should turn our backs on God and begin hanging out with the devil! No, my friend! Whatever we go through should make us stronger and cling to God more than ever! Friends and family may try to assist, but fall short. But God never fails, and He shows up right on time!

Psalm Chapter 113, Verses 5 through 7 say this: "Who can be compared with the Lord our God, who is enthroned on high? He stoops to look down on Heaven and on Earth. He lifts the poor from the dust and the needy from the garbage dump."

Are you in need today? We serve a God who is able to supply all our needs according to His riches in glory! Get out of the dumps; clean yourself up! Trust in God to whom none can compare! Eyes have not seen all that He has in store for you! The prerequisite is to repent of your sins and your doubts and invite Jesus into your life! A relationship with the devil does not compare to a right relationship with God! So – where are you?!

God bless you!

In Case Of Emergency, Use The Stairs.

"In Case Of Emergency, Use The Stairs." We see these signs posted all around buildings having multiple floors, warning us to use the stairs in case of an emergency. This is good advice! The Holy Spirit desires that we apply the same principle in life! John Chapter 1, Verses 49 through 51 say this: Then Nathaniel exclaimed, "Rabbi, you are the Son of God – the King of Israel!" Jesus asked him, "Do you believe this just because I told you I had seen you under the fig tree? You will see greater things than this." Then he said, "I tell you the truth, you will all see Heaven open and the angels of God going up and down on the Son of Man, the one who is the stairway between Heaven and earth." My question? Do you call on Jesus in an emergency? You are doing well if you do! Do remember this: Preventative maintenance is always better than repair! In Jude Verse 24 the Holy Spirit tells us God is able to keep us from falling! So, climb the stairs of Jesus Christ one step at a time! Don't rush, and don't stop before arriving at your destination – Heaven! You can use the stairs in case there is an emergency, and your world is burning. Keep in mind that Jesus is the fire marshal. He will put out the fire and prevent you from burning! Surrender to Him today! If you already have, remain on the stairs!

God bless you!

Prepaid Card Or Preplanned Sin?

Why would one commit a deliberate sin? There are many reasons why, for fun, for spite, out of anger, revenge, rebellious to God etc. Rebellion, now there is a thought, if you know something you do causes you to sin against God yet you keep on doing it, you are just simply rebellious. Many use prepaid credit cards and phone cards on a daily basis, the cards were first loaded so they can be used. On the flip side, humans who plan their sinful acts and carry them out have been loaded with Satan's spirit to become his puppet. The reality show on TV is not as real as this, "Deliberate preplanned sins makes us a foul for Satan." David prayed about this in Psalm 19:13 "Keep your servant from deliberate sins! Don't let them control me, then I will be free of guilt and innocent of great sin." Don't treat your sinful lifestyles or as you do your prepaid cards by reloading them. Get connected to Jesus, repent of your sins while you still have a chance to. You will feel great, better than frosted flakes. Just remember that this wonderful place we call heaven, no sin can enter in. Instead of preplanned sins, preplan your righteous living.

God bless you!

CPSIA information can be obtained
at www.ICGtesting.com
Printed in the USA
LVHW022028070423
743801LV00009B/130

9 781684 863914